Toward a Psychology of Persons

Toward a Psychology of Persons

Edited by

William E. Smythe
University of Regina

Routledge
Taylor & Francis Group

LONDON AND NEW YORK

First published 1998 by
Lawrence Erlbaum Associates, Inc., Publishers

Published 2014 by Routledge
2 Park Square, Milton Park, Abingdon, Oxfordshire
OX14 4RN
711 Third Avenue, New York, NY 10017

Routledge is an imprint of the Taylor and Francis Group, an informa business

Cover design by Kathryn Houghtaling Lacey

Library of Congress Cataloging-in-Publication Data

Toward a psychology of persons / William E. Smythe, editor.
        p. cm.
Includes bibliographical references and indexes.
ISBN 978-0-8058-2718-7 (alk. paper)
1. Psychology. I. Smythe, William E.
BF121.T67   1998
155.2—dc21

                                                                97-33510
                                                                      CIP

ISBN 978-0-8058-2718-7 (hbk)
ISBN 978-1-138-00289-0 (pbk)

Contents

Preface

This volume, like a previous work—Tolman's *Positivism in Psychology: Historical and Contemporary Problems* (1992)[1]—emerged from the deliberations of the Western Canadian Theoretical Psychologists (WCTP). The WCTP comprises a group of scholars primarily from western Canadian universities with shared interests in the history and theory of psychology, many of whom are among the founding members of the International Society for Theoretical Psychology (ISTP) and Section 25 (history and philosophy of psychology) of the Canadian Psychological Association (CPA). From its founding in Edmonton in the Fall of 1989 to the present, the WCTP has been actively engaged in promoting and contributing to the development of theoretical psychology. We have all greatly benefited (over the past half dozen years) from the close collaboration and collegial support that participation in the WCTP makes possible. Our annual meetings provide an opportunity for us to catch up on each other's work and also to pool our expertise to work on topics of shared interest. Our first systematic undertaking was an exploration of the legacy of positivism in contemporary psychology. This led to a sym-

---

[1] Tolman, C. W. (1992). *Positivism in psychology: Historical and contemporary problems*. New York: Springer-Verlag.

posium presented at the annual meeting of the CPA in Ottawa in 1990 and then to the book edited by Charles Tolman (1992).

For the past 3 years, our principal topic has been the nature of persons and the problem of depersonalization in contemporary psychology. Once we had gotten past our philosophy of science preoccupations in dealing with the positivism issue, we felt the need to move on to a more psychologically substantive theme, and the topic of *person* seemed to capture much of what was perceived to be central in our own work and also what seemed to be most lacking in contemporary psychology in general. Many of us were of the opinion that modern psychology had, to a substantial degree, "lost the person" and were intrigued by the kind of restoration project that a renewed psychology of persons presented. We were by no means able to reach consensus on what a psychology of persons actually entailed or even on what the problem of depersonalization in psychology amounted to, but we nonetheless found our discussions of these issues sufficiently illuminating—to be worth sharing with the interested reader. What we offer in this volume is nothing so ambitious as a general framework for a psychology of persons, but rather an attempt to re-open a form of discourse that has been absent from mainstream psychology for some time.

We are fortunate to have John Shotter as a contributor to the present volume. Professor Shotter was an invited guest at our annual meetings in Banff in 1993 and 1994 and has maintained close ties with the WCTP ever since. The psychology of persons is a theme that is clearly of fundamental importance to his work and so he contributed an integrative chapter to conclude this volume.

We acknowledge, with appreciation, the advice and encouragement of our colleagues, especially those in Section 25 of the CPA and in the ISTP, and the support and facilities provided by our respective institutions, especially the University of Regina. I also extend a special note of thanks to Maxine Stroshein for her help in reviewing and correcting the original manuscript and to Susan Smythe for checking the camera-ready copy.

— William E. Smythe
University of Regina
Regina, Saskatchewan

About the Contributors

John B. Conway, Department of Psychology, University of Saskatchewan, Saskatoon, Saskatchewan.

D. Vaden House, Philosophy of Science and Technology Program, Institute for Christian Studies, Toronto, Ontario.

Don Kuiken, Department of Psychology, University of Alberta, Edmonton, Alberta.

Marvin J. McDonald, Counseling Psychology Program, Trinity Western University, Langley, British Columbia.

Leendert P. Mos, Department of Psychology, University of Alberta, Edmonton, Alberta.

Anand C. Paranjpe, Department of Psychology, Simon Fraser University, Burnaby, British Columbia.

Tim B. Rogers, Department of Psychology, University of Calgary, Calgary, Alberta.

John Shotter, Department of Communication, University of New Hampshire, Durham, New Hampshire.

William E. Smythe, Department of Psychology, University of Regina, Regina, Saskatchewan.

Henderikus J. Stam, Department of Psychology, University of Calgary, Calgary, Alberta.

Charles W. Tolman, Department of Psychology, University of Victoria, Victoria, British Columbia.

Introduction

William E. Smythe
University of Regina
Regina, Saskatchewan

When we use the term *person* in everyday speech, it is usually with clear intuitions as to its meaning. A *person* is an individual human being, a bearer of rights and responsibilities, a participant in a social order, a being capable of certain kinds of life experiences and the capacity to interpret, reflect, and act on those experiences. The notion of *person* clearly occupies a central place in our commonsense-intuitive psychology, which perhaps explains the common preconception among beginning psychology students that studying psychology helps to enrich their understanding of themselves as persons.

The concept of person has never received much sustained systematic treatment by psychologists, however, and is becoming increasingly problematic in contemporary psychology, with its steady advance toward depersonalized views of its subject matter—toward what Rogers (chap. 7, this volume) called the "personless view of persons." The current threat of depersonalization in psychology comes from a number of different directions. It is evident, for instance, in the hegemony of subpersonal modes of explanation in the cognitive and neurosciences, which attempt to reduce human functioning to the blindly mechanistic terms of biological or computational processes. It is evident, in a different way, in some of the more radical versions of social constructionism and cultural psychology, with the view of the person as an entirely situated entity—a faceless node in a network of social and cultural relations and practices— or with attempts to deconstruct the notion of person altogether. The middle ground that once seemed to secure psychology's autonomy and define its distinctiveness from cognate disciplines in the biological and social sciences is rapidly being evacuated on both sides. Intertwined with these developments is the complex and much conflicted legacy of positivism and Cartesianism in modern psychology. From positivism comes the tendency to objectify our subject matter, to view persons as *objects* rather than *subjects*, whereas the Cartesian legacy is evident in our tendency to speak of persons in terms of *inner selves* rather than as actual flesh-and-blood human beings.

The chapters in this volume seek to explore the roots of depersonalization in contemporary psychology and suggest some alternative perspectives aimed at restoring persons to center stage in the discipline. The authors of the various chapters in this volume are united in their dissatisfaction with the status quo of depersonalized psychology, but propose different diagnoses of the underlying problems and different approaches to dealing with them. Our aim in this volume is not to present a unified view of the psychology of persons, but to open up discussion of the topic to a discipline that, for too long, has been depersonalized. The volume is divided into three parts. Part I includes chapters 1 through 4 and undertakes conceptual, discursive, and historical analyses of the concept of person in psychology; Part II comprises chapters 5 through 7 and examines some aesthetic and nonlinguistic dimensions of personhood, with a particular focus on the visual arts; Part III includes chapters 8 through 10 and offers some critical perspectives on the issues raised in Parts I and II.

Part I of the volume begins with Tolman's frontal assault on the Cartesian ontology of self in chapter 1. As Tolman points out, the term *self* continues to have much more currency among psychologists than the term *person*, and one of the main difficulties the discipline has had in coming to grips with real flesh-and-blood people is that it still clings to an obsolete Cartesian notion of self. Tolman begins with a vivid illustration of just how how deeply entrenched the Cartesian notion of an inner, incorporeal self has become in popular culture. He then shows how this same basic picture of self underlies virtually all modern forms of psychological theorizing on the topics of self and personality, from traditions as diverse as behaviorism, humanistic psychology, and cognitive psychology. Even some of the more significant debates among the different traditions occurred largely within the Cartesian framework; the framework itself has rarely been challenged. Tolman concludes that what contemporary psychology calls a "scientific" concept of self is "not really a scientific concept of self at all...but a scientized version of a popular ideological concept of self" (p. 7). The alternative view that Tolman proposes involves shifting the locus of self from intraindividual to interindividual space (i.e., a self is no longer a ghostly sort of entity in the head, but something constituted by an individual's relations to the world, especially to the social world).

This does not, however, constitute a denial of the subjectivity of individual conscious experience, but provides the basis for its proper understanding. The view is nicely encapsulated in Tolman's anti-Cartesian slogan: *sumus ergo sum*—"We are, therefore I am." Tolman traces support for this anti-Cartesian conception of self from the philosophies of Hegel and Wittgenstein, to the objective semiotics of Volosinov, to more modern developments in discursive psychology and German critical psychology. He concludes:

> An individual does not become a person in a private space, but only in a public one....In order to understand people, we must understand the social–historical relations from which they emerge. Only knowledge of these relations can truly inform us about what it means to be a person or to be depersonalized. (p. 22)

Chapter 2 approaches the concept of person through an examination of the theory and language of folk psychology. Folk psychology encompasses the kind of practical, commonsense psychology that we use to describe and account for human behavior in terms of *intentional idioms*, with reference to such mentalistic notions as belief, intention, desire, purpose, and so forth. Two general types of theoretical approaches to folk psychology are identified, and their implications for an understanding of person are considered. The first type of approach includes cognitive science perspectives, which are generally committed to a naturalistic conception of scientific explanation and tend to focus on the analysis of causal mechanisms and internal processes. Three such perspectives are identified, none of which can provide a satisfactory conception of person, given their explicit denial of *agency*—one of the key criteria of personhood.

The second type of theoretical approach to folk psychology includes human science perspectives, which emphasize interpretive methodologies and tend to focus on social and cultural (rather than internal) determinants of psychological phenomena. Although these approaches offer a more satisfactory treatment of agency, they ultimately fail to provide a unified conception of person. Finally, the language of the intentional idiom itself is examined in an attempt to unearth the implicit concept of person that underlies the actual discursive practices of folk psychology. It is shown that there is a basic asymmetrical relation in folk psychological discourse between person and folk psychological attitude and between person and self. This demonstrates that *person* is the more inclusive term than *self* and posits *personal unity* and *agency* as being among the more criterial attributes of personhood in commonsense psychology.

In chapter 3, Paranjpe traces the decline of the concept of person in psychology to factors leading to the rise of modern personality theory. When the term *person* is used in contemporary psychology, it tends to be in connection with theories of personality; however, as Paranjpe points out, *person* and *personality* are fundamentally different concepts:

> Person is an ethicolegal concept that views human beings as inexorably social beings in a community governed by an ethos....In contrast, the term *personality* has generally designated individuality marked by the externally observable stylistic features that distinguish one person from another. (p. 49)

Our modern Western notion of person is a product of the sociopolitical history of Europe and is reflected in the writings of some of the more influential Enlightenment philosophers. Moreover, in Enlightenment philosophy, the ethicolegal concept of person developed side by side with the *trilogy of mind* —the psychological conception of a person as a being who thinks, feels, and acts. This trilogy of *cognition*, *affect*, and *volition* finds expression in the writings of such continental rationalists as Leibniz and Kant, is promoted by Scottish commonsense psychology, and receives its last systematic treatment in the hands of British psychologist William MacDougall. The final abandonment of the trilogy of mind, and of the traditional concept of person in psychology, coincides with the beginnings of modern personality theory, initiated by Gordon Allport's (1937) landmark book on the subject.[1]

This decline in the psychology of persons was accelerated by the naturalistic scientific zeitgeist that swept through psychology in the first half of the 20th century and continues to assert itself today. It is marked by an emphasis on mechanistic, nomothetic, analytical, empiricist, and value-neutral modes of inquiry; although these features played an essential role in the development of the natural sciences, they had a generally negative impact on the psychology of persons. Although Paranjpe does not wholly reject the application of natural science methods in psychology, he maintains that "the term *person*, by definition, designates those aspects of a human being whereby he or she is *not* a thing or an animal. The domain of personhood begins where that of physics and biology ends" (p. 67). Moreover, he proposes that it is possible to have a psychology of persons without excessively encumbering the discipline with ethical and moral issues. Paranjpe writes:

> It simply means that we recognize humans as beings with rights and responsibilities capable of comprehending, creating, revising, following, as well as breaking norms of right and wrong....We should be able to find a place in our discipline for the study of those psychological processes that are involved in becoming and remaining part of a social ethos. (p. 67)

Mos, in chapter 4, takes a broadly hermeneutic approach to articulating a constitutive understanding of persons. Rejecting both the objectivist perspectives of naturalism and the deconstructionist initiatives of poststructuralism, Mos seeks an understanding of persons that flows from a human science conception of the psychological. The point of departure for the discussion is the phenomenon of self-deception which, Mos says, "presupposes an understanding of human nature that shares nothing with the false consciousness that emanates from an objectivist view of per-

---

[1] Allport, G. (1937). *Personality: A psychological interpretation.* New York: Holt, Rinehart & Winston.

sons or a poststructuralist dissolution of our inwardness that would repudiate history in a never-ending quest of self-making" (p. 74). From the
standpoint of traditional epistemologies, self-deception presents something of a paradox in that the self-deceived individual is both deceiver
and deceived.

This paradox can, however, be dissolved according to an analysis of
self-deception by Fingarette, which is considered in some detail. According to Fingarette's analysis, self-deception represents a subversion
of personal agency and moral integrity. This is evident in the discrepancy between an individual's engagements in the world and what he
says about his engagements to himself and others. In this way, self-deception opens up some deep issues of personal identity in that it is the
capacity for spelling out one's engagements that is basic to becoming a
person with a distinct identity. Personhood, in this sense, is an achievement and not merely something that is given.

This naturally leads to the kind of constitutive understanding of persons that Mos then proceeds to flesh out, drawing from the works of
Taylor, Hegel, and most importantly, Dilthey. For Dilthey, the process of
becoming a person is grounded in the dialectical relationship between
our reflexive, immediately intuitive understanding of our lived experience and our reflectively discursive understandings of its expressions in
language. These expressions are among the objectifications of mind that
make personal life essentially continuous with its social–cultural and
historical context. Mos concludes, "It is from within this standpoint of
life (this standpoint of the historical world) that we bring to consciousness our understanding, including our self-understanding as persons" (p.
95). This, in turn, informs our understanding of what it means to be self-
deceived, for "the possibility of our being deceived, does not solely belong to our capacities as agents...but becoming a person belongs to those
articulatory practices wherein we come to a conscious understanding of
ourselves as a moral expression of social–cultural, historical life" (p.
95).

As necessary and as useful as it may be to attempt to clarify the concept of person in terms of the conceptual and discursive analyses of the
authors in Part I, this still does not get to the heart of the problem of
depersonalization, according to the authors of Part II of this volume. As
Kuiken states, in chapter 5, "the pragmatics of interpersonal affairs—

and neither epistemology nor ontology—constitute the most formidable obstacle to psychologists' inquiry" (p. 102). These pragmatic constraints serve to prevent psychologists from seriously and concretely exploring the depths of human experience, a mode of inquiry that must be opened up by addressing the aesthetic dimension of experience.

Indeed, it is Kuiken's contention that "*depersonalization* in psychological research *is* the failure to locate and understand expressions of the depth of human experience," expressions that reflect "the experiential fullness and complexity of life events" (p. 102). The principal aim of Kuiken's chapter is to explicate the depth metaphor that underlies this view of depersonalization and, ultimately, of persons. His particular focus is on the role that the depth metaphor plays in aesthetic experience, as the aesthetic is a mode of experience that inherently invites depth. With reference to some vivid autobiographical examples, Kuiken articulates and illustrates some of the characteristic features of depth in aesthetic experience. It first involves a change in the locus of experience— or a boundary crossing—from experiencing the world containing a work of art to experiencing a possible world constituted by the work of art. Next, it involves an accentuation of felt meanings within that world, both personal feelings and the felt presence of objects and events therein. Then, there is a transformation of these felt meanings to suggest something beyond the banal and familiar. Finally, this transformed aesthetic present is brought together in an intimate way with an implicitly and explicitly remembered past. This kind of process often leads to a powerfully transformed sense of one's identity as a person; as Kuiken states, "the person is effectively saying: 'These transformed meanings are my personal experience, present and past. I now realize that the felt meaning of who I am is as I am experiencing it within this aesthetic moment'" (p. 115). Kuiken's chapter ends with an appeal for a new kind of depth psychology, one that would seek to probe the depths of human experience as revealed in the more profound moments of human life.

For some further examples of this kind of depth psychology, one should turn to chapter 6. Conway's chapter explores some ways of enriching, enlivening, and humanizing representations of persons through the medium of fine-art photography. The discussion is directed at a number of examples of fine-art photographs of people by artists such as Helen Levitt, Walker Evans, Dorothea Lange, Diane Arbus, Nicholas Nixon, and Cindy

Sherman. Many of the issues that are raised in regard to these artistic photographic portraits of people resonate, to a surprising degree, with basic issues in the psychology of persons. Familiar tensions in psychology between objective and subjective epistemologies, between knowledge of universals and knowledge of particulars, and between individualistic and socially constructed views of persons all have their analogues in different approaches to photography. Moreover, photographs of people, like the psychological study of persons, inevitably invite paradox, ambivalence, and multiple interpretations. Conway's main claim is that fine-art photography, at its best, is evocative and true to lived experience—in terms of Kuiken's metaphor, it invites depth—and that a psychology of persons could constructively aim toward a similar objective. As Conway states:

> To be evocative, believable, and compelling, psychological understandings of persons must ring true to lived experience—must be grounded in important emotional truths in the lives of humans. Ambivalence and paradox are inescapably a part of human experience and should be accepted as such. Our quest for order and formal integrity in psychological renderings of persons can be life-affirming and can bring meaning to life in a way that is similar to how formal beauty in a work of art can affirm life. (p. 141)

However, although visual imagery has the potential to reveal the depths of personhood in the ways that Kuiken and Conway illustrate, it may also be used to promote and reinforce depersonalization in psychology, as Rogers shows in chapter 7. Rogers presents an analysis of visual rhetoric in recent textbook cover art in psychology. This is a significant domain for rhetorical inquiry for, as Rogers points out, "here, we find one of the few places where the discipline attempts to crystallize its basic beliefs into a single visual image" (p. 149). Such images are among the institutional resources that the discipline relies on to promote and sustain the *personless view of persons*—the view of a person as a locus of variables rather than as a unique individual, a view that was ushered into psychology with the rise of the mental testing movement. Rogers' examination of recent trends in textbook cover art reveals an abstract–modernist genre that seems especially characteristic of the person-related subdisciplines of psychology, such as personality, psychological testing, and social psychology. In modern personality texts, this genre takes two different forms: One uses purely abstract visual forms with no attempt to represent people at all; the other uses highly abstract nonrealist depictions of people.

The relative absence of realistic depictions of people is striking in a field dominated by a realist epistemology that purports to offer an understanding of actual people. Drawing on the methods and perspectives of semiotic–rhetorical analysis, Rogers identifies the rhetorical function that this abstract–modernist genre serves for the different communities involved in the textbook marketing process. For professors, use of the genre helps to forge an association between the disciplinary matrix of contemporary depersonalized psychology and a socially accepted, valuable, and elite form of art, which conveys a sense of legitimacy, social approval, and elite knowledge. From the students' perspective, abstract–modernist imagery suggests a novel and unexpected view of persons that seems to promise a mode of self-understanding superior to common sense. In general, the genre serves to reinforce, for all parties concerned, the personless view of persons—"the abstract, featureless, contextless approach to the person" that has become the norm in the person-related subdisciplines of psychology (p.168).

Moreover, as these rhetorical messages are largely implicit and are supported by a substantial commercial enterprise, it has become exceedingly difficult to challenge them. As Rogers points out, the manner in which the personless view of persons is now marketed to everyone involved in the process tends to "conspire against making even the slightest dint in the depersonalized view" (p. 170).

The chapters in Part III of this volume offer some critical perspectives on themes raised by the previous chapters. One clearly emergent theme from earlier chapters is the propriety of human science versus natural science perspectives on discourse about persons and personhood. The term *person* seems to belong to a hermeneutic, moral mode of discourse that is utterly alien to the causal, deterministic framework of natural science. However, as House and McDonald argue in chapter 8, to frame issues of personhood in terms of such black-and-white contrasts as hermeneutic versus naturalistic approaches is to oversimplify and even distort them; although there are fundamental differences between these approaches, there are some noteworthy points of convergence as well. In their words, "there is no single issue that unites or divides the contemporary landscape in theoretical psychology," and "the question of a science of persons or the choice between science and persons is a tangled web of overlapping issues" (pp. 182–183). House and McDonald attempt to bring these issues into focus by first presenting a detailed critique of some of Shotter's proposals for a moral science of persons. Shotter's antirealism and conversational essentialism are contrasted with Harré's less radical and more inclusive version of social constructionism. Second, they illustrate how multiple discursive contexts, from the naturalistic to the humanistic, can mutually inform and reinforce each other by considering in detail the case of Jonathan I., a visual artist who suffered a cerebral loss of color vision. The case of Jonathan I. dramatically demonstrates the value of treating the natural sciences as part of the conversation about human beings.

Contrary to the traditional stereotype of the natural sciences as wholly objective and morally neutral forms of inquiry, House and McDonald argue that our knowledge of the natural world, like any form of knowledge, is inevitably interpretive and cannot help but generate moral consequences. Moreover, they argue against any form of essentialism in regard to human beings: "In our view humans are not essentially anything;" humans must be understood from multiple perspectives in terms of mechanisms and in terms of meanings (p. 202). These different kinds of accounts are neither reducible nor fully independent of each other, and there is no unified science of the person that can incorporate all of them. Nonetheless, we can realistically seek a "nonreductive coordination of...multiple accounts" that will enrich our understanding of what it is to be a person (p. 213).

In chapter 9, Stam raises some doubts about the entire project of recovering the person in psychology. Might this not be, he suggests, only a kind of misplaced nostalgia? Persons are, for Stam, "abstractions in the world of opinions" and, like all abstract notions, the concept of person fails to capture embodied life and thought as "it lives in the very gestures of life" (p. 240). Drawing on Deleuze and Guattari's poststructuralist philosophy, Stam reflects on the possibilities and limitations of thought in psychology, especially as it concerns a psychology of persons. These issues largely derive from the peculiar way in which psychology is situated with respect to both philosophy and science. According to Deleuze and Guattari (1994), philosophy is the creation of concepts against the background of a "plane of immanence," whereas science is not at all concerned with concepts in the philosophical sense, but with functions formalized as propositions in discursive systems (p. 41).[2] In Stam's view, "psychology, however, is the history of the attempt to make scientific the philosophical concept," and the problem with this is that the attempt to transform a philosophical concept into scientific propositions ultimately destroys the concept (p. 231). Hence, the prospects for a reconstituted scientific psychology of the person are bleak. He concludes:

> Depersonalization in psychology is now merely the obvious result of a failure of nerve. Modern psychology could not exist other than in its thoroughly functional orientation....A reconstituted notion of the person in psychology would suffer the same fate...as most other concepts have; they are reducible to abstract, functional entities. Our concepts have to be other, recovered, or both (p. 241).

Chapter 10 by John Shotter is an attempt to bring together the various strands from the previous chapters and to place them in the context of the "broad movement...currently afoot...to overcome the lifelessness of the humane and social disciplines" (p. 246). Modern psychology, Shotter argues, is to be criticized not only for its excessively individualistic orientation, but also for its commitment to a disembodied, solely theoretical stance toward its subject matter. The proper study of persons, however, must be grounded in the everyday, concrete social activity of persons in relation to one another. This means taking the practical and the dialogical as primary, rather than the theoretical and monological. It is an institutional demand that requires we conduct our academic inquiries in psychology in a depersonalizing fashion; this, in turn, blinds us to the embodied, relational activity between people that is the basis for our life as persons. Drawing together various emergent themes from the other chapters of this volume, Shotter articulates a view of psychology located in the field of the personal, the relational, and the dialogical.

The contributors of this volume are unanimous in their assessment of

---

[2] Deleuze, G., & Guattari, F. (1994). *What is philosophy.* New York: Columbia University Press.

depersonalized psychology being a dead end. However, there remain many tensions among their views of what a fully enriched psychology of persons would actually look like and the extent to which such a psychology is possible: There is the tension between human science and natural science approaches to the person, between discursive and non-discursive aesthetic/rhetorical modes of inquiry, between the depths of individual personal experience and the breadth of inter-personal social relatedness, between a constructive versus deconstructive orientation toward a psychology of persons, and many more.

Clearly, a unified psychology of persons remains a distant objective, if it is an achievable one. Nonetheless, some of the essential requirements for a psychology of persons have clearly been identified by these chapters. We first need a richer, more developed ontology of persons. The subtle ontological distinctions among *self, person, individual, character*, and *personality* need to be articulated and need to become a standard part of psychological discourse as they are of literary discourse. We need to understand persons as socially and historically constituted beings rather than as autonomous selves. We need to understand how persons articulate their self-identity through language, and the depths of personhood that go beyond language. It will take some time to comprehend these requirements fully, let alone to fulfill them. In this volume, we hope to have made a start.

PART I

THE CONCEPT OF PERSON

CHAPTER 1

Sumus Ergo Sum: The Ontology of Self and How Descartes Got it Wrong

Charles W. Tolman
University of Victoria
Victoria, British Columbia

Sie reden immer von Selbstverwirklichung. Ich finde das schwierig. Ich habe noch nie daran gedacht, mich selbst zu verwirklichen, offen gestanden. Weil ich gar nicht wüßte, was ich selbst bin. Ich werde doch durch das Leben gebildet, durch das, was ich tun muß, und durch die Menschen, mit denen ich zusammen bin.[1]
—Marion Gräfin von Dönhoff (*Die Zeit*, 1994, p. 5)

self. 1. An obsolescent technical term for a person, but a person thought of as incorporeal and essentially conscious. Sometimes the self is simply identified with Plato's concept of soul. But Descartes, arguing in the **Discourse** *that the "I" of his "I think, therefore I am" is essentially a thinking substance, presents a substance theory of the self....Most contemporary philosophers would bypass the whole issue, urging that experiences can only be identified as the experiences of flesh-and-blood people.*
—Flew (1979, p. 322)

---

[1] Translation: You are always talking of self-realization. I have difficulty with that. To be honest, I've never thought of realizing myself. I wouldn't know what my self is. I have been shaped by my life, by what I have to do, and by the people around me (Marion Gräfin von Dönhoff in conversation with three young, self-styled punks).

It may be obsolescent in philosophy, but psychologists still prefer to speak of self rather than of person, and, as I attempt to show, they also still lean toward incorporeal substances of the Platonic or Cartesian variety, while having great difficulty in coming to grips with flesh-and-blood people, all of which, I think, significantly contributes to the problem of depersonalization.

When speaking of the self, it is important to inquire about the nature of the object to which one is referring. One needs to ask what kind of self it is that he or she has in mind or that is necessarily implied by his or her usage. Three treatments of the concept of self in recent academic and popular psychology are examined.

THE SELF INSIDE

Where is the self? Traditionally, it has been spoken of as deep inside the person where it may be equated with the mind or soul, or treated more abstractly as a concept or set of beliefs in the mind. Katherine Mansfield provides us with a literary, biographical example. She died of tuberculosis at 35 years of age in 1923. A year earlier, she wrote the following entry in her journal:

> A bad day...horrible pains and so on, and weakness. I could do nothing. The weakness was not only physical. I *must heal my Self* before I will be well...This must be done alone and at once. It is at the root of my not getting better. My mind is not *controlled*. (cited in Sontag, 1979, p. 46)

Her husband and collaborator, John Middleton Murry, later wrote that Mansfield :

> had come to the conviction that her bodily health depended upon her spiritual condition. Her mind was henceforth preoccupied with discovering some way to "cure her soul;" and she eventually resolved, to my regret, to abandon her treatment and to live as though her grave physical illness were incidental, and even, so far as she could, as though it were nonexistent. (cited in Sontag, 1979, p. 46)

The references here to soul, spirit, mind, and self (which Mansfield wrote with a capital S) treat it as distinct from and in control of the body. The self's mind is the controller of the body. When the self loses control (i.e., becomes sick), the body goes out of control, becoming weak and physically ill. Moreover, strengthening the self is its own lonely responsibility. It can only turn to itself to make itself well and strong again. If one were to inquire as to the location of this self, one would unquestionably be referred to a space internal to the body. Self appears to be the spiritual center of which the body is merely a physical, outer, surrounding manifestation.

For two distinctly more academic examples, we can consider Weiten's (1992) introductory textbook, *Psychology: Themes and variations*. Its second edition was published recently and is generally considered to be authoritative, or at least representative.[2] There was no entry in the index for *self* alone, but there were 23 hyphenated entries ranging from *self-actualization* to *self-stimulation*. I did not expect anything from entries like *self-help groups*, *self-modification*, and *self-report inventories*. One on *self-control* looked interesting, but proved to be concerned with the application of behavior modification techniques for oneself (which I will ignore for now, although it is interesting for, among other things, the way in which it enlists the individual in his or her own control over others). Most of the remaining entries were concentrated in the chapter on personality. Indeed, they were entirely identified with three theories.

The first was Bandura's social learning theory. Here, there was a discussion of *self-efficacy*, defined as "one's belief about one's ability to perform behaviors that should lead to expected outcomes" (Weiten, 1992, p. 438). Such beliefs influence the challenges we tackle and how well we perform, but nothing was said of how such beliefs are formed.

Bandura's theory is classified as a *behavioral perspective*. It is distinguished from the *humanistic perspective*, which is represented here by Rogers' person-centered theory. Readers are told:

> Rogers viewed personality structure in terms of just one construct. He called this construct the *self*, although it's more widely known today as the *self-concept*. A *self-concept* is a collection of beliefs about one's own

---

[2] It is specifically Weiten's portrayals of these theories and views that I am concerned with here, not their accuracy.

nature, unique qualities, and typical behavior. Your self-concept is your own picture of yourself. (Weiten, 1992, p. 441)

It is mentioned that unconditional parental affection encourages a strong self-concept and conditional affection has the opposite effect. Our self-concept is important because we tend to behave in ways that are consistent with it; that is, it bears a causal and explanatory relation to our behavior.

The second humanistic theory was Maslow's theory of self-actualization. One reads that "Maslow's key contribution to personality theory was his description of the *self-actualizing person* as an example of the healthy personality" (Weiten, 1992, p. 442). Moreover, people are driven by a need for self-actualization: "What a man can be, he must be" (Maslow, 1970, p. 46). Self-actualizing people, we are told, are those who have "exceptionally healthy personalities, marked by continued personal growth" (Weiten, 1992, p. 443).

The chapter on personality also spoke of the "person–situation" controversy, focusing on the role of Walter Mischel. The debate was sparked over the issue of where the most important determinants of behavior lie. Behind this controversy was a long history in American psychology of theories of personality as a collection of traits. These were challenged by the view that it was not the person or trait variables that best predicted (and thus, explained) the behavior of individuals, but the environmental situations in which they found themselves. Of course, to insist exclusively on one or the other—person or situation—soon proved too abstract and a compromise, eclectic position emerged called *interactionism*. The point that is important for our present ontological concern is that all participants in this debate were in agreement on the definition of a trait as something situated *within* the person; at issue was its relative importance in the prediction and control of behavior.

In the *Penguin Dictionary of Psychology*, Reber (1985) offered the following definition of *trait* (with which, in most details, Weiten and Mischel would surely agree):

Generally, [a trait is] any enduring characteristic of a person that can serve an explanatory role in accounting for the observed regularities and consistencies in behavior. This is the proper use of the term; it is incorrect and misleading to use it for the regularities themselves. The point is that a trait is a theoretical entity, a hypothesized, underlying component of the individual that is used to explain that person's behavioral consistencies and the differences between the behavioral consistencies of different persons. (p. 782)

Of course it is known that many trait theorists have in fact preferred the "regularities themselves" and leaned heavily on an operational definition as a way of avoiding what they thought to be metaphysical understandings of personality. Yet, the "underlying component of the individual" is always implied, even when not admitted, and it is always "used to explain."

The debate itself emphasizes this "underlying component" of traits. It is a manifestation of the traditional tension between internal and external causes. As mentioned, by assuming such a dualism, proponents of trait theory, as well as their opponents, the situationists, were eventually forced into an interactionism. This label is, in my view, not ontologically insignificant.

At least two observations can be made about these accounts of self and personality. First, the theories cited, however they are classified, are very much alike. The self or its equivalent is treated as a *middle term*, an internal something that mediates between external input and behavior. It appears as a set of beliefs, a concept, a source of need, and not infrequently as something incorporeal. It is something that, from inside us, determines and explains (usually causally) our actions and our physical and social relations. It is characterized by its strength and health and, as is perhaps most clear in Maslow's version—the self is often thought of as being responsible for its own health, especially when facing difficult times.

Second, this scientific concept of self is virtually identical to that of Katherine Mansfield. It is not really a scientific concept of self at all—that is, a concept deriving from scientific investigation and reflection—but a scientized version of a popular ideological concept of self. It is the ontology of this self that needs to be examined.[3]

---

[3]The ideologized version of this self can be traced to the classical liberalism that took shape in the 16th and 17th centuries (see Hunt, 1978).

CARTESIANISM

The ontology of self that has dominated both popular thinking, such as Katherine Mansfield's, and most official psychologies, such as those described by Weiten, for the last four centuries found its clearest articulation in the works of René Descartes. The entry on Descartes in Flew (1979) made a significant observation:

> "Cartesian dualism," as Descartes' conception has come to be known, has exerted a profound an influence on the philosophy of mind as has his method of doubt on the theory of knowledge. A great deal of work in our own century has been devoted to trying to avoid Descartes' absolute division between the mental and the physical. But unless and until the phenomenon of consciousness and its relation to physics is better understood, the Cartesian picture is unlikely entirely to lose its hold on the imagination. (p. 92)

Of course, psychology has contributed precious little in this century to a general understanding of "consciousness and its relation to physics," which is perhaps better expressed as the conscious person in relation to the physical, embodied, flesh-and-blood person in the world.

Let me specify the Cartesian view a little more closely. For Descartes, the *self* (the ego, the essential person) was not the body, but something with a location inside the body. It was the stuff, a substance, that is different from the body's matter: It was *res cogitans*—unextended and free, thinking substance—as opposed to *res extensa*—extended and determined substance. From its position within the physical body, it was related to the world by causal relations.[4] These three characteristics—location, distinct substance, and mechanical causality—define the general Cartesian ontology of the self.

---

[4] It seems problematic from the start that something in which the principal, defining characteristic is a lack of extension could have any location at all, but this is exactly what Descartes asserts. For example:

> It is however easily proved that the soul feels those things that affect the body not in so far as it is in each member of the body, but only in so far as it is in the brain, where the nerves by their movements convey to it the diverse actions of the external body which touch the parts of the body [in which they are inserted] (Descartes, 1644/1927, p. 305).

Psychology in this century, particularly North American, mainstream psychology, has, through all its apparent transformations, effectively preserved this ontology, as we might already suspect from the examples found in Weiten's textbook. John B. Watson provided us with a stunning example of how easily the ontology persists even in systems that pretend explicitly to reject it. Watson was obviously troubled by metaphysical dualism and thought he could do away with it by throwing out questions about mind and consciousness altogether and by insisting on the restriction of scientific attention to publicly observable stimulus inputs and response outputs.

Yet even with this insistence on observability, he could not avoid assuming a middle term as a vaguely formed, neutral transmitter of stimulus energy. It was just this neutrality of the transmitter that led him to the extreme environmentalism expressed in his much quoted claim:

> Give me a dozen healthy infants, well-formed, and my own specified world to bring them up in and I'll guarantee to take any one at random and train him to become any type of specialist I might select—doctor, lawyer, artist, merchant-chief and, yes, even beggar-man and thief, regardless of his talents, penchants, tendencies, abilities, vocations, and race of his ancestors. (Watson, 1930, p. 104)

The persistence of Cartesianism in Watson's behaviorism was clearly identified by Edna Heidbreder (1933):

> There is still another difficulty, and a more serious one, that grows out of the behaviorists' attitude toward the mind–body problem: the inability to state precisely what is meant by the rejection of consciousness. Sometimes behaviorism seems to deny flatly that conscious events occur, to assert that anyone who believes in them is the victim of an illusion. But sometimes it seems to say that the question of whether or not conscious events occur is beside the main issue—that they may or may not exist, but that if they do, they are essentially unamenable to scientific investigation, and that they can, therefore, have no place in a scientific psychology. By adopting the second alternative, the behaviorist can keep his science wholly free of consciousness; but in doing so he commits himself to a dualism and an indeterminism that run counter to the basic principles of his thinking. If he admits that there is something in the human make-up that is essentially—not merely temporarily and in the absence

of technique—inaccessible to scientific inquiry he asserts a duality in human nature by saying that human activity is of two different sorts, one of which is subject to scientific investigation and one of which is beyond the reach of scientific inquiry. But this admission is all that the most ardent advocate of freewill needs. With a component, however minute, of the human make-up that science can never know, he has at his disposal something not subject to the laws of science, something which the scientist cannot predict and control. And this is an outcome which the behaviorist obviously did not intend. (p. 280)

Heidbreder (1933) went on to point out that if Watson takes the path of denying consciousness outright, then:

He finds it extremely difficult to explain what he means by some of his terms. When he says that thinking is merely a matter of language mechanisms, or emotion an affair of visceral and glandular responses, he is at a loss to tell where he gets the terms "thinking" and "emotion." He cannot get them from his own awareness of his own inner speech or disturbed heart-beat, for, by hypothesis, such awareness is impossible. (p. 281)

In short, despite his protests to the contrary, Watson was himself stuck with *res cogitans* or something suspiciously like it—that is, a *de facto* substance or property dualism.[5]

Virtually all mainstream psychologies that came after Watson's behaviorism (and many that preceded it) could be shown to have exactly the same problem. If the middle term is filled with psychodynamics, engrams, cell assemblies, or information-processing models, all that is produced is abstractions that deceive psychologists into thinking they have given up Cartesian *res cogitans*, whereas they are really only softening or blurring the distinctiveness of the substance by making it look or sound like the stuff that is of concern to physics, physiology, or computer science. In modeling the middle term, that which is being modeled

---

[5] The parallels between Descartes and Watson are actually quite striking. Watson adopted a radical phenomenalism (not a materialism as usually supposed) in which only that which he sensed could be the object of scientific concern. The source of certainty about this was therefore necessarily internal, although, unlike Descartes, Watson refused to speculate on the nature of the sensing agent (Tolman, 1992).

is left in much the same mysterious state as was found in Watson or Descartes. This is particularly obvious in trait theories in which the traits are operationally defined in terms of scores on personality scales. To insist on operational definition is a frank admission of the mysterious and inaccessible nature of the trait in itself, which must be presumed (in the end) to provide the actual explanation of the behaviors or other traits to which their measures are correlated.

The third feature of the Cartesian ontology of self, its mechanical causality, also remains characteristic of thinking about the self. To my knowledge, there is no mainstream psychology that denies a causal, and usually explanatory, role to the middle term. Indeed, it is precisely the causality of the middle term that Skinner used against its usual role in explanation. If S causes M, and M causes R, then S can be said to cause R without the need to deal with M, the mediating middle term (Flanagan, 1984, p. 94). As in the theory of Descartes, this causality often proves to be problematic, like a faulty light switch that works only part of the time. The modern solution is provided by probability theory and error variance.

The Cartesian location is also universally duplicated by these theories. It is always in the middle, between input and output, inside the acting body itself, usually in the brain. One consequence of this kind of move for Descartes was a radical individualism. This is also repeated in the mainstream psychologies of our current century (Tolman, 1995).

It is this hegemonic commitment to the Cartesian ontology of self, in all its significant aspects, that creates the state of affairs in which no mainstream psychology appears to be different from any other except in petty details. Cognitive psychology, the result of the so-called cognitive revolution of the 1960s and 1970s, for example, turns out to be no more than a complexified and rementalized version of behavioral psychology. This, I submit, stems from the fact that psychological debates and innovations have, certainly in the mainstream, taken place within the Cartesian framework that characterizes the discipline. The framework itself has hardly ever been challenged.

CHALLENGING CARTESIANISM: HEGEL AND OTHERS

What would it mean to challenge this framework? What would an alternative ontology of the self look like? The key to breaking the Cartesian ontological grip lies, I suggest, not (at least, immediately) in challenging its substance or its causality, but in its location. The clue can be taken from Hegel. His conception of mind, person, or self is largely motivated by a concern for morality. Hegel (1807/1967a) speaks very little of Descartes, but when he does, he draws anything but support from him. On the contrary, and particularly with respect to the self and morality (which Descartes made an in-house issue of the relationship between the soul and its passions), he finds that those who follow Descartes "have not arrived at the thought that being, pure being, is not a concrete actual reality, but pure abstraction" (p. 594).

According to Flew (1979), the main point of Hegel's own psychology as expressed in the *Enzyklopädie* (1830/1975) was that "an adequate account of moral virtue cannot be given if the individual is divorced from society" (p. 142). This was the same psychology that T. M. Knox, translator of Hegel's *Philosophy of Right*, described as a repudiation of "desert island morality" (Hegel, 1821/1967b, p. 337). The emphasis of this psychology is on the concrete nature of the objective mind, which is mind in society. Hegel spoke, for example, of the "external subjectivity which is thus identical with me [as] the will of the other," and maintained that "the achievement of my aim...implies this identity of my will with the will of others" (p. 77). This was but one expression of a general principle that pervaded his thought, namely that the particular becomes individual only in the other.

Wood (1993) wrote in *The Cambridge Companion to Hegel*:

> Hegel sees the conceptions of person and subject as applying universally to all human beings....Both conceptions, however, are abstractions, which cannot be actualized directly....Personhood and subjectivity can be actualized only by being given concrete embodiment in the roles of a harmonious social system or ethical life. (p. 218)

That the moral self or personality becomes such only in civil society is at the center of Gräfin von Dönhoff's reply to the punks that she interviewed for *Die Zeit*. They had maintained that the self could only be actualized outside society. She responded that she knew of no self that needed actualizing other than the one that she found in her relations to the world, to its demands, and to the people around her. This is the customary continental view that can be traced back to Hegel.

Taking this view seriously has radical implications. Among these is the shifting of the location of the concrete self from intraindividual to interindividual space. This is the crucial move that then achieves the actual sublation of the Cartesian ontology of self.

The idea can be further traced back from Hegel to the ancients, Aristotle in particular, and it is inevitably linked to a concern with morality. The individual is nothing without the πολιζ, and to preserve and promote the latter is to preserve and promote the former. To act is to make a choice, and choice cannot escape the question of value—that is, of what is the societally right or moral choice.

In this century, the anti-Cartesian move was represented in Wittgenstein's rejection of the picture (representational) theory of meaning that he had elaborated on in his *Tractatus Logico-Philosophicus* in 1922. In the later *Philosophical Investigations* (1953), he rejected this theory in favor of one based on word use in social practice, which he called *language games*. Like all games, language games are governed by rules. Wittgenstein argued that these rules could only be conventions among people, and therefore, there could be no such thing as a private language. The result was a fundamental shift from a representational self in the mind to a self constituted by language in an objective, social space. For example, in his customary "notes-to-myself" style, Wittgenstein (1980) wrote:

> The expression "Who knows what is going on inside him!" The interpretation of outer events as consequences of unknown, or merely surmised, inner ones. The interest that is focused on the Inner, as if on the chemical structure from which behaviour issues. For one needs only to ask "What do I care about inner events, whatever they are?!" to see that a different attitude is conceivable.—"But surely everyone will always be interested in his *own* inner life!" Nonsense. Would I know that pain, etc., etc., was something Inner if I weren't told so? (p. 110)

The notion of an essentially social self has not been confined, however, to philosophy. In forms that are usually less explicitly ethical in nature, it is found in the work of Volosinov, Vygotsky, Leontyev, Lewin, and G. H. Mead, among others. It is also adumbrated, although in a foreshortened (and totally anethical) fashion, in Gibson's ecological theory of perception, in which the essentials of the process are moved from representations in the head to the pickup of information about affordances in the external world. If the work of these psychologists failed to have the revolutionary impact on our discipline that it ought to have had, it is largely because their followers did not recognize the profound paradigmatic shift that it represented. They then all too often succeeded in translating the substantive claims of those they esteemed into terms compatible with mainstream methodology, thus, necessarily, although inadvertently, forfeiting their revolutionary force.

A more fundamental grasp of the ontological requirements is, however, becoming increasingly apparent at the margins of our discipline. I could refer to recent work that follows Vygotsky more faithfully, work in activity theory, situated learning, collective memory, and distributed cognition, but especially work that is shifting the attention of psychologists to discourse. It is becoming increasingly clear to many that the models that have recently been shaped by cognitive psychologists, for instance, are not, as they were intended to do, modeling internal psychological or brain processes; in the events that they have succeeded at all, they appear in fact to be modeling the grammar that governs discursive contexts.

These recent peripheral psychologies are familiar to most of us. I cite an earlier example, before returning to a recent instance, in order to illustrate the link between the ontological move that I have described and the current discursive trend in psychology. Then, I move on to show how German critical psychology has proceeded from the same ontological move to establish an important link to social theory as well.

OBJECTIVE SEMIOTICS

The earlier example to which I referred is that of the Russian Marxist linguist Volosinov (1929/1973). He began his analysis by defining an objective, interpersonal space he called *ideology*. This included, but was not exhausted by, scientific knowledge, literature, religion, and ethics.[6] As a part of reality, ideology possessed meaning, that is, it was or entailed *signs*. "Without signs," Volosinov wrote, "there is no ideology"

---

[6] Volosinov's concept of ideology was idiosyncratic. It came closest to what Marx generally referred to as *superstructure*.

(p. 9). Ideology's place in human existence "is in the special, social material of signs created by man. Its specificity consists precisely in its being located between organized individuals, in its being the medium of their communication....Signs can arise only in *interindividual territory*" (p. 12). Yet, it is precisely in this territory that consciousness is shaped:

> Consciousness takes shape and being in the material of signs created by an organized group in the process of its social intercourse. The individual consciousness is nurtured on signs; it derives its growth from them; it reflects their logic and laws. The logic of consciousness is the logic of ideological communication, of the semiotic interaction of a social group. If we deprive consciousness of its semiotic, ideological content, it would have absolutely nothing left. (p. 13)

This does not imply or require the denial of a private, inner life of consciousness. On the contrary, it provides the basis for understanding its existence:

> Although the reality of the word, as is true of any sign, resides between individuals, a word, at the same time, is produced by the individual organism's own means without recourse to any equipment of any other kind of extracorporeal material. This has determined the word as the *semiotic material of inner life—of consciousness* (inner speech). Indeed, the consciousness could have developed only by having at its disposal material that was pliable and expressible by bodily means. And the word was exactly that kind of material. The word is available as the sign for, so to speak, inner employment. (p. 14)

An important implication of this ontological move for Volosinov was a distinction between *individual* and *person*. He spoke of the former as a "natural specimen." The person, on the other hand, "has the status of an ideological-semiotic superstructure over the natural individual and which, therefore, is a social concept" (p. 34).

To complete the picture of an anti-Cartesian psychology as developed by Volosinov (1929/1973), we found him urging that "individual consciousness not only cannot be used to explain anything, but, on the contrary, is itself in need of explanation from the vantage point of the social, ideological medium" (p. 12), and the explanation cannot be causal, "as if [experiences] were analogous to physical or physiological processes" (p. 16). Volosinov agreed, to this extent, with Dilthey that psychology "must pursue the task of understanding, describing, segmenting, and interpreting psychic life, just as if it were a document under philological analysis" (p. 26). Volosinov thus completes the ontological shift: he most emphatically moved that which makes us conscious persons to an interpersonal location; this automatically resolves the question of metaphysical stuff; he concluded by recognizing the need to reject the implication of mechanical causation in experience, favoring a hermeneutic description instead.

DISCURSIVE PSYCHOLOGY

My example of current discursive psychology is that of the recent book by Harré and Gillett, *The Discursive Mind* (1994). They began early in their book to identify the culprit:

> Traditional, experimental psychology—the Old Paradigm, as we have sketched it—was based not only on an outdated philosophical theory of science but also on a much criticized metaphysical thesis regarding human beings. It assumed mind–body dualism, sometimes called Cartesianism....Although the idea that there were two distinct kinds of "stuff" quickly lost its appeal, the idea that the mental life was "inner," as distinct from behavior, which was "outer," lingered on. (p. 4)

These remarks suggest that the "stuff" of Cartesianism is not sufficient to identify it as such. The relatively greater importance of location is apparent from their summary of the main principles of what they call the second (that is, discursive) cognitive revolution:

1. Many psychological phenomena are to be interpreted as properties or features of discourse, and that discourse might be public or private....
2. Individual and private uses of symbolic systems, which in this view constitute thinking, are derived from interpersonal discursive processes....
3. The production of psychological phenomena, such as emotions, decisions, attitudes, personality displays, and so on, in discourse depends upon the skill of the actors, their relative moral standing in the

community, and the story lines that unfold. (Harré & Gillett, 1994, p. 27)

It is important that Harré and Gillett (1994) moved the site of action from between the ears to interpersonal space without—it must be stressed—denying the validity of private experience. It is the source of explanation that is shifted to the space—which they designated as "arrays of people"—in which emotions, decisions, attitudes, personality displays (not traits) are shaped and unfold. This space, as it was for Hegel, is not simply interpersonal space, but societal and moral: "The explanatory task of psychology is to be defined by trying to answer the question: What is it that makes something right or wrong, the appropriate thing to feel, say, do, think, or experience?" (p. 33).

How does all this bear on our understanding of self? It is significant that Harré and Gillett (1994) devoted two chapters (over 25% of the book's text) to the topic. In these chapters, the question of location was further elaborated on and the aspects of substance and causality were explicitly addressed. For example, they maintained that, "The mind is not a substance. The mentality of people comprises certain of their skills and abilities" (p. 100).

These skills are both manual and discursive, but the latter are by far, the more important. Harré and Gillett (1994) discussed, among other things, the role of mastering the indexical pronouns in the development of the sense of identity, which then led back to the question of location. To experience ourselves:

as having a location in a manifold of places and in relation to others is a necessary condition for being able to use and to understand indexical expressions....We do not believe that learning a language is what is responsible for our having the sense of physical location. It is the learning of perceptual and motor skills that is responsible for that. But it is expressed in the indexical grammar of "I." (p. 111)

A sense of self "in a manifold of places and in relation to others" is only the foundation for what may be more important—the sense of self as agency. The causation involved here is social causation, which the authors reminded us "is very different than ordinary (physical science/ billiard-ball) causation" (Harré & Gillett, 1994, p. 121). This difference includes a consideration of the role that subjects play in actively structuring the domains of their own activity. This, in turn, led the authors to a conception of freedom, in which the major emphasis was on the freedom that people have in structuring their domains, given the latter's inherent openness. They advised us to become "sensitive to the human experience of freedom and what impairs it" (p. 125). This does not mean, however, an abandonment of the freedom of action in the world. Discourse and intentional action are too closely linked for that:

> To act with freedom, the discursive possibilities that are potentially available to an individual must be affirmed, owned, and used in some practice. To be free of constricting situations and the intrinsically limited meanings that create them, the significations giving rise to them have to be resisted by the subject/agent. (p. 127)

That this may not be as easy as it sounds is indicated in the following passage:

> An agent cannot simply choose the context within which they are born and subsequently live. There is therefore an important productive effect on a person's activity of signification by the conditions and discourses in which they develop their psychological constitution. Ultimately there will be customary and widely endorsed practices that do, in fact, constrain someone in that he or she is an agent with a certain historical, cultural, and mental position; these will both form the person and influence what he or she can become. (p. 122)

If I have a criticism of this position, it is just that these "customary and widely endorsed practices" are never elaborated on. We have allusions to the broader discursive context called "society," but the authors did not provide us with a theory of society with which to understand the connection. Yet, it is precisely in the subject–agent's relationship to this context that the problems of depersonalization are both found and explained.

GERMAN CRITICAL PSYCHOLOGY

The approach of German critical psychology is different from that of the discursive psychologies. It represents the same ontological move and consequently, converges with them on many significant points, but it places a heavy emphasis on placing its psychological considerations in an explicit account of the broader societal context (see Holzkamp, 1983; Tolman, 1994; Tolman & Maiers, 1991).

It is essential to take into account that individual human beings, in contradistinction to other animals, live not in a natural world, but a societal one. A *societal world* is a world of meaning structures elaborated by specifically human practice. These structures create an epistemic distance between us as individuals and physical objects. This is what affords us a space in which to exercise choice over whether and how we act in natural or artificial situations. Meaning structures provide a kind of buffer between us and the physical world that can be characterized in terms of possibilities. Our relationship to objects and to others is governed not by immediate necessity, but by a possibility relation. The execution of an action, therefore, is not directly determined by the objects of our experience, but by our own grounds (or reasons) for action as made available by the meaning structures and the possibilities that these structures create relative to the objects of the world and our felt needs. One result of this is that our relation to natural necessity assumes a socially "on average" character. Food and shelter must be produced if we are to survive, but individual needs for these are not met by individual production of them. A division of labor that is part of and governed by the meaning structures assures that our natural needs are satisfied on average, even when most of us do not directly act to produce that which we need. Meaning structures and their associated action possibilities thus vary from society to society and from individual to individual in a society (depending on the individual's position). What is reasonable for a particular person to do in a particular situation, varies accordingly.

Some important implications of this can be seen in the example of hunger. The circumstances of human hunger in a particular societal situation represent a different phenomenon than that encountered by nonhuman animals. An animal has an immediate relationship with the natural environment. When it is hungry, it goes directly to the source of its satisfaction and deals with it according to its need. If this need is not satisfied, it is ordinarily because not enough food is available or the animal is physically hindered from getting it. The relation of humans to food is infinitely more complex. There is, for us, an enormous gap between the food itself and our consumption of it. This gap is filled with complex societal arrangements, customs, traditions, meanings, and rules. Thus, people in advanced capitalist societies can be starving when there is ample food available and there are no natural, physical obstacles to its procurement. Rather, the obstacles take the form of rules and conventions (as when the hungry person refuses to steal in order to survive). The resulting hunger represents a breakdown or distortion of the social arrangements that mediate our relation to food (like unemployment, being with or without welfare, or failures in the distribution system). Thus, the satisfaction of human hunger is never simply a matter of the immediate provision of food; it is never just a physiological state. It is always a matter of the individual's relation to—inclusion in, or exclusion from—the societal system through which such provision occurs. The need for food is subsumed under the more general need for meaningful participation in social production.

Holzkamp coined the term *Handlungsfähigkeit*—action potence—to describe the individual's relationship with the world through societal meaning structures. *Action potence* is basically the capacity of the individual to satisfy his or her needs as a participant in societal arrangements. Action potence is always a function of a person's position in society. In most societies (most of the time), people have action potence and are not totally reduced to the prehuman state of immediacy (though some institutional settings approximate such a state). No society could otherwise function for long.

Two broad forms of action potence, however, can be distinguished: generalized and restrictive. *Generalized action potence* is that which is governed by a commonality of societal and individual interests. It is necessary for societal survival that this be maintained to some functional degree. This type of action potence is exemplified by any unimpeded effort on the part of individuals working in a cooperative division of labor to satisfy their own needs and those of others (biological, social, spiritual, etc.). Labour is unalienated and, therefore, it is not only functional within existing constraints, but also has the effect over time of transcending constraints. It not only uses possibilities, it extends them. It is creative and inventive. Moves by one participant to improve his or her own state of affairs also improve that state for others. The interpersonal relations here are mutually supportive and generally experienced as subjectively satisfying.

Restrictive action potence is associated with circumstances of conflict between individual and societal interests (or the dominant interests in society). The individual attains to action potence here in a partial and restrictive way, such that certain needs of his or her own are satisfied, while suppressing others. Whatever is achieved is achieved through use of available possibilities, which often entail compromise with those whose interests are served by the restrictions and are thus contrary to his or her own interests. An extreme example would be the Third World peasant who joins the army to gain a more secure existence for himself. More common in our experience is the worker who crosses the picket line and accepts lower wages because he or she has a family to feed or the young person who out of necessity, but willingly, takes uncontested but underpaid employment (the so-called "McJob"). The actions here do not transcend constraint, but are, at best, only functional within their limits. The interpersonal relations with fellow peasants or fellow workers and employers cannot be mutually supportive; rather, they become necessarily instrumental, the person using others to gain personal advantage, almost always at the immediate cost of the others' satisfactions (Tolman, 1995). Yet, it is important to see here that the exercise of restrictive action potence is nonetheless reasonable (because functional) from the point of view of the subject. What is interesting are the circumstances and nature of the discursive and practical contexts that make it so.

Here, there is an implied theory of self-actualization (cf. Lethbridge, 1992) and of its opposite, depersonalization. Becoming a fully developed person or being hindered from such development is seen not as a matter of actualizing—in an abstractly normative or Cartesian fashion—what lies latent within the person, but of realizing the historically produced possibilities for individuals corresponding to the current stage of societal development. At one time, it was mooted that the increasing automatization of production in capitalist societies would reduce the hours of back-breaking toil for all and allow a new way of life, characterized by guaranteed security, leisure, and the expansion of individual capacities through learning. Although this is a real possibility created by the technological advances of this century, it has never been realized. Instead, those still working are doing so under the stresses of even greater demands on them, and the increasing numbers of people no longer working are permanently excluded from social production. Virtually all who are either working or are unemployed are having to face mounting insecurities about their own and their childrens' present and future standard of living and their capacities to satisfy personal needs. To the extent that such possibilities are suppressed, either consciously by others or through systematic political and economic distortions in the societal arrangements for social production, and to the extent that the subjects are forced by circumstances into restrictive action potence and instrumental relations with others, these people can be said to be less than, or not yet, the people they could possibly be or have been, and in this sense, they remain unactualized and depersonalized.

CONCLUSION

An individual does not become a person in a private space, but only in a public one. There is a sense in which it is correct to claim that *I am* my relations to the world, both of things and of other people, but always as mediated by others; although, it must be stressed, consciousness of self prevents an individual from being reduced to a passive manifestation of those relations. Those relations may facilitate or inhibit one's development. They can give him or her the power to satisfy needs, they can withhold it, or they can take it away. They govern the range of possibilities for action that are open to the individual. They can extend or restrict his or her effective agency. They set the limits of what appears to be subjectively functional.

In order to understand people, we must understand the social–historical relations from which they emerge. Only knowledge of these relations can truly inform us about what it means to be a person or to be depersonalized. The burden of psychological explanation, then, is born by features not of the intracranial, Cartesian space, but of interpersonal, historical, societal, moral space. Psychology is a social, cultural, historical, moral science.

Karl Marx, following Hegel, already had it right in 1857 (and even earlier):

> The human being is in the most literal sense a ζῷον πολιτικον not merely a gregarious animal, but an animal which can individuate itself only in the midst of society. Production by an isolated individual outside society

is as much of an absurdity as is the development of language without individuals living together and talking to each other. (1857/1973, p. 84)

This is precisely what psychologists must understand if their theories are ever to achieve an adequate comprehension of concrete persons in all their historical and social vicissitudes.

REFERENCES

Descartes, R. (1927). Principles of philosophy. In R. Eaton (Ed.), *Descartes selections* (pp. 267–311). New York: Scribner's. (Original work published 1644)

Dönhoff, M. Gräfin von. (1994, August 26). Gespräch mit drei Punks. *Die Zeit*, Nr. 34, p. 5.

Flanagan, O. J. (1984). *The science of the mind.* Cambridge, MA: The MIT Press.

Flew, A. (1979). *A dictionary of philosophy.* London: Pan Books.

Harré, R., & Gillett, G. (1994). *The discursive mind.* London: Sage.

Hegel, G. W. F. (1967a). *Phenomenology of mind* (J. B. Baille, Trans.). New York: Harper & Row. (Original work published 1807)

Hegel, G. W. F. (1967b). *Philosophy of right* (T. M. Knox, Trans.). Oxford, England: Oxford University Press. (Original work published 1821)

Hegel, G. W. F. (1975). *Enzyklopädie der philosophischen Wissenschaften* [Encyclopedia of the philosophical sciences] (3rd ed.). Hamburg: Felix Meiner Verlag. (Original work published 1830)

Heidbreder, E. (1933). *Seven psychologies.* New York: Appleton-Century-Crofts.

Holzkamp, K. (1983). *Grundlegung der Psychologie* [Groundwork for Psychology]. Frankfurt: Campus Verlag.

Hunt, E. K. (1978). *Property and prophets: The evolution of economic institutions and ideologies* (2nd rev. ed.). New York: Harper & Row.

Lethbridge, D. (1992). *Mind in the world.* Minneapolis: Marxist Educational Press.

Marx, K. (1973). *Grundrisse* [Sketches] (M. Nicolaus, Trans.). New York: Vintage Books. (Original work published 1857)

Maslow, A. (1970). *Motivation and personality* (2nd ed.). New York: Harper & Row.

Reber, A. S. (1985). *The Penguin dictionary of psychology.* London: Penguin Books.

Sontag, S. (1979). *Illness as metaphor.* New York: Vintage Books.

Tolman, C. W. (1992). Watson's positivism: Materialist or phenomenalist? In C. W. Tolman (Ed.), *Positivism in psychology* (pp. 67–82). New York: Springer-Verlag.

Tolman, C. W. (1994). *Psychology, society, and subjectivity.* London: Routledge.

Tolman, C. W. (1995). Toward a societal conception of the individual in social psychology. In I. Lubek, R. van Hezewijk, G. Pheterson, & C. Tolman (Eds.), *Trends and issues in theoretical psychology.* New York: Springer Publishing.

Tolman, C. W., & Maiers, W. (Eds.). (1991). *Critical psychology.* New York: Cambridge University Press.

Volosinov, V. N. (1973). *Marxism and the philosophy of language*. Cambridge, MA: Harvard University Press. (Original work published 1929)

Watson, J. B. (1930). *Behaviorism* (rev. ed.). New York: Norton.

Weiten, W. (1992). *Psychology: Themes and variations*. Pacific Grove, CA: Brooks/ Cole.

Wittgenstein, L. (1922). *Tractatus logico-philosophicus* (D. F. Pears & B. F. McGuinness, Trans.). London: Routledge & Kegan Paul.

Wittgenstein, L. (1953). *Philosophical investigations* (G. E. M. Anscombe, Trans.). Oxford, England: Blackwell.

Wittgenstein, L. (1980). *Remarks on the philosophy of psychology* (Vol. 2). Oxford, England: Blackwell.

Wood, A. W. (1993). Hegel's ethics. In F. C. Beiser (Ed.), *The Cambridge companion to Hegel* (pp. 211–234). Cambridge, England: Cambridge University Press.

CHAPTER 2

Folk Psychology and the Concept of Person

William E. Smythe
University of Regina
Regina, Saskatchewan

In the practical psychology that we live everyday of our lives, there can hardly be a more salient entity than the person. Persons are at the very hub of everyday psychological reality; their actions and interactions, their social commitments and engagements, and their discursive musings, both private and public, are the very stuff of which practical commonsense psychology is made. How surprising it is, then, that, in recent theoretical treatments of this domain by cognitivists (the domain now thematized by them as *folk psychology*) the term *person* is hardly ever mentioned. One searches for it in vain in the index sections of works by any of the prominent theorists in this area, such as Dennett, Fodor, Searle, and others. The current controversy in cognitive science about the prospects for vindicating folk psychology has nothing at all to do with vindicating persons; it rather concerns the ontological status of folk psychological attitudes such as beliefs, intentions, desires, and the like. That the possessors of folk psychological attitudes may be at least as worthy of vindication as the attitudes they possess has not evidently occurred to the majority of cognitivists.

An oversight of this magnitude can only be grounded on some form of deep-seated theoretical prejudice. We shall work toward an understanding of that prejudice through the course of this chapter. However, to start with, it may be instructive to see just what any of the existing treatments of folk psychology have to say about the psychology of persons, however allusively. This will take some digging in most instances, because what is said about persons tends to be by way of tacit implication rather than explicit statement. The most strident claims about folk psychology in recent years have generally come from practitioners of cognitive science; however, more recently, the debate has been joined by advocates of human science perspectives as well. Hence, the following discussion is organized around cognitive science and human science perspectives on persons.

COGNITIVE SCIENCE PERSPECTIVES

Let us begin with a consideration of some perspectives inspired by cognitive science. These include views consistent with classical cognitive science and also some views directly critical of it. There are plenty of tensions among the cognitivists and their critics, but there is also a widely shared allegiance to a strictly natural science conception of psychological explanation. This includes a commitment to some form of mechanistic, efficient-cause account of psychological processes and a focus on their internal (biological or computational) determinants. From this type of perspective, the key issue about folk psychology is the issue of *vindication*: Will the essential characteristics and generalizations of folk psychology be ultimately supported by a science of mind or will they be found to be incompatible with it? One such essential characteristic, of course, is the *intentionality* or "aboutness" of folk psychological attitudes—that feature by virtue of which a belief is invariably a belief *that* something is the case, a desire is a desire *for* something, a fear is *of* something, and so on. Hence, one way of framing the vindication issue is as a claim about the ontological status of intentionality: Is intentionality a real feature of the causal machinery of the mind/brain or not?

Intentional Realism

Intentional realism is the view that a proper science of mind should, to a substantial degree, vindicate the intentional idiom of folk psychology. This would imply that folk psychological attitudes, and the intentionality they exhibit, are genuinely part of the causal structure of nature that is realized in the material substrate of the brain and nervous system. Fodor (1990) expressed this view as follows:

> I propose to say that someone is a *Realist* about propositional attitudes if (a) he holds that there are mental states whose occurrences and interactions cause behavior and do so, moreover, in ways that respect (at least to an approximation) the generalizations of common sense belief/desire psychology; and (b) he holds that these same causally efficacious mental states are also semantically evaluable. (p. 5)

The two most sharply contrasting versions of intentional realism in the recent literature are the proposals of Fodor and Searle. Fodor's (1987) version is the now familiar *Computational/Representational Theory of Mind*, which makes the following fundamental claim about intentional attitudes: "For any organism O, and any attitude A toward the proposition P, there is a ('computational'/'functional') relation R and a mental representation MP such that MP means that P, and O has A iff O bears R to MP" (p. 17). In essence, then, intentional attitudes are implemented by computational relations that people bear to their internal mental representations. Moreover, these mental representations are systematically organized in a "language of thought" (Fodor, 1975).

Searle's (1983) version of intentional realism is expressed in his Intrinsic intentionality thesis—the claim that "mental states are both *caused by* the operations of the brain and *realized in* the structure of the brain (and the rest of the central nervous system)" (p. 265). The claim is that there is a direct supervenience of mental states and processes on physiological ones. Intentional attitudes, on Searle's account, supervene on neurobiological processes in somewhat the same way that the thermodynamic properties of physical systems supervene on molecular motion. For Searle, in contrast to Fodor, there is no intervening computational story to be told to account for the implementation of intentionality in the nervous system. Moreover, there is no need to postulate the existence of internal entities such as mental representations, separate from the intentional attitudes themselves; representation is a logical function of the attitudes, not an ontological category.

Our question is: "What do these proposals have to say about persons?" One initial observation is that, in both Fodor's and Searle's accounts,

persons are cast in essentially relational terms. In Fodor's Computational/
Representational Theory of Mind, a person is conceived of as an organism capable of standing in certain kinds of computational relations to a
system of internal mental representations comprising a language of
thought. It is not quite clear what these relations might be, but we at least
know that they cannot be modeled on the relations that people bear to
expressions in the public languages they speak, for the latter are already
characterized in the intentional idiom and it is intentionality that is to be
explained. Rather, the relations that people bear to their internal representations must be, as Loewer and Rey (1991) pointed out, "a result of
the causal organization of the brain, much in the way a computer can
obey rules by virtue of the causal organization of its hardware" (p. xvi).
Thus, a *person*, on Fodor's account, is an appropriately configured vehicle for the physical implementation of mental representations.

Searle, too, offers a relational conception of persons, but the relations
are now between persons and the intentional attitudes themselves. Searle
(1992) stated that it is an essential feature of the mental that "its ontology is essentially a first-person ontology. Beliefs, desires, etc., are always *somebody's* beliefs and desires, and they are always potentially
conscious, even in cases where they are actually unconscious" (p. 17).
Again, the way to understand this kind of relation, according to Searle, is
by an appeal to the causal structure of the brain and nervous system. The
subjective, first-person character of folk psychological attitudes is simply a fact about how we are put together as biological organisms; as
Searle stated, "the facts are that biological processes produce conscious
mental phenomena, and these are irreducibly subjective" (p. 98). Again,
a person is conceived of as a biological vehicle for intentional attitudes
and for consciousness and subjectivity as well.

On the realist proposals of Fodor and Searle, then, a person is essentially a passive entity, a mere vehicle for the realization of intentional
attitudes. In both accounts, it is the attitudes that do all the work of intentional causation and that bear the full burden of folk psychological explanation; it is the attitudes that have the appropriate causal powers, not
persons. According to this currently fashionable style of intentional explanation, for example, it is my intention to attend this year's WCTP
conference which, coupled with the relevant beliefs and desires, causes
my action of getting into my car and driving to Banff. It adds nothing to

the account to say that *I* intended to come to the conference, that *I* had various and sundry beliefs and desires concerning it, and so *I* got into my car and drove to Banff; for, according to standard realist doctrine, "*I*" can have no genuine causal powers in this regard, it is my beliefs, desires, intentions, and other intentional attitudes that do all the work in causing my behavior. What this amounts to is a denial of *agency* which, as we see later, is an important criterion on an adequate conception of persons.

This type of realist explanatory strategy is one that ultimately marginalizes persons. A person becomes little more than a locus for the attitudes and their interactions, a place for intentional phenomena to occur. Therefore this view is referred to here as the *locus conception of persons*.

Eliminativism

If intentional realism marginalizes persons, the alternative view—*eliminativism*—pushes persons beyond the margins altogether. *Eliminativism* is the view that folk psychology is a fundamentally mistaken system of psychological explanation that needs to be dispensed with altogether in order to clear the way for a proper scientific understanding of ourselves. Among the earliest advocates of this position are philosophers such as Feyerabend (1963) and Rorty (1965); yet, in the last decade and a half, Churchland (1981, 1988, 1989) has been its leading spokesman. Churchland's (1989) version of eliminativism is stated succinctly as follows:

> Eliminative materialism is the thesis that our common-sense conception
> of psychological phenomena constitutes a radically false theory, a theory
> so fundamentally defective that both the principles and the ontology of
> that theory will eventually be displaced, rather than smoothly reduced,
> by completed neuroscience. (p. 1)

As in the case of realism, there are two distinct versions of eliminativism, a *computational* version and a *neuroscience* version. Churchland's eliminative materialism, with its appeal to an ideally completed neuroscience, exemplifies the latter. A computational perspective on eliminativism may be found in Stich's (1983) Syntactic Theory of

Mind (STM). What STM proposes is that we continue to posit computational states and processes as the underpinnings of mental activity, but refrain from interpreting them semantically; that is, mental processes are to be identified, for the purposes of psychological explanation, solely in terms of the formal syntactic features of their underlying mechanisms. This strategy is supposed to lead to a tidier, more manageable, ontology than is possible with the semantically laden vocabulary of folk psychology.

Where does eliminativism leave persons? The short answer is nowhere. Persons are entities so tightly bound to the intentional idiom of folk psychological discourse that the two must stand or fall together. Our normal ways of conceiving ourselves as moral agents with certain rights, responsibilities, and autobiographical histories are simply not available to us once the folk psychological resources of the intentional idiom have been cast aside. Virtually all of the things we are inclined to say about ourselves, as persons, are couched inescapably in the intentional idiom. If we were to jettison that apparatus entirely, we would throw away the only means at our disposal to construct ourselves as persons; in fact, there would then be no such entities left to talk about. If one would be an eliminativist with regard to the intentional attitudes, then, one must be an eliminativist with respect to persons as well. From an eliminativist perspective, there can literally be no such thing as persons; there remain only bodies, brains, and nervous systems as vehicles for the embodiment of neurological or computational processes.

This particular consequence of eliminativism has not been widely discussed in recent literature, although eliminativist skepticism along these lines goes back, at least, to Hume. Recent advocates of eliminativism tend to argue that *we* can dispense with folk psychology in preference for an entirely new scientific understanding of ourselves, without ever raising the question of who is this *we*, who now operates with the new understanding, and how this *we* is to be constituted without the resources of folk psychology to fall back on. Strictly speaking, there could be no such *we*, nor is there any "understanding" (another eliminable intentional notion). This view is referred to here as the *null conception of persons*; from an eliminativist perspective, there literally can be no such thing.

Intentional Stance Theory

Intentional Stance theory is the product of Dennett's (1978, 1987, 1991) ongoing attempt to stake out an intermediate ground between intentional realism and eliminativism and to avoid the "gratuitously strong forms of materialism" entailed by both (1991, p. 51). Dennett's view has traditionally been termed *instrumentalism*; however, he explicitly disowned the term and came to characterize it instead as *mild realism*. The core of the theory is Dennett's notion of the *intentional stance*, a normative strategy for interpreting and predicting the behavior of complex systems by assigning to them rationally coherent sets of beliefs, desires, intentions, and actions. According to Intentional Stance theory, "folk psychology might best be viewed as a rationalistic calculus of interpretation and prediction—an idealizing, abstract, instrumentalistic interpretation method that has evolved because it works and works because we have evolved" (Dennett, 1987, pp. 48–49). Moreover, the predictive leverage of folk psychology is seen as fundamental to its use as an interpretive instrument; as Dennett (1991) claimed, "our power to *interpret* the actions of others depends on our power—seldom explicitly exercised—to predict them" (p. 29). However, interpretation from the intentional stance necessarily gives rise to nonunique outcomes. This is an essential feature of interpretation in general, as it is intrinsic to the very notion of interpretation that competing, incompatible interpretations are always possible, and intentional stance theory is no exception. As Dennett (1991) stated:

> I see that there could be two different systems of belief attribution to an individual which differed *substantially* in what they attributed—even yielding substantially different predictions of the individual's future behavior—and yet where no deeper fact of the matter could establish that one was a description of the individual's *real* beliefs and the other not. (p. 49)

Given that there is no determinate "fact of the matter" concerning which particular intentional attitudes a person has, the attitudes are to be regarded as useful abstractions for the purpose of folk psychological prediction rather than as concrete facts. They are "real" in the same sense that abstract objects, such as centers of gravity in classical physics, are real; they are *abstracta* rather than *concreta*. Moreover, the patterns of events interpreted according to the Intentional Stance theory are considered to be real patterns in nature, for as Dennett (1991) pointed out, "the success of folk-psychological prediction, like the success of any prediction, depends on there being some order or pattern in the world to exploit;" if these patterns are real, then so presumably are the *intentional systems* that generate them (p. 30).

An obvious point of departure for an intentional stance conception of persons, then, would be to consider persons as a species of intentional system, but, clearly, they would have to be intentional systems of a very special kind, for the intentional stance, as it stands, can apply to nearly anything. One initially appealing suggestion is that a person is a self-interpreting intentional system, that is, a system capable of assuming the intentional stance toward itself. This is essentially the view that Dennett (1992) articulated in *Consciousness Explained*, in which he suggested that one important difference between human and infrahuman intentional systems is that:

> We...are almost constantly engaged in presenting ourselves to others, and to ourselves, and hence *representing* ourselves—in language and gesture, external and internal....Our human environment contains not just food and shelter, enemies to fight or flee, and conspecifics with whom to mate, but words, words, words. These words are potent elements of our environment that we readily incorporate, ingesting and extruding them, weaving them like spiderwebs into self-protective strings of *narrative*. (p. 417)

He then went on to present a definition of *self* as "a *center of narrative gravity*" (Dennett, 1992, p. 417) again, a kind of abstract object that exists only relative to an interpretation. As Dennett stated: "These strings or streams of narrative issue forth *as if* from a single source—not just in the obvious physical sense of flowing from just one mouth, or one pencil or pen, but in a more subtle sense: their effect on any audience is to encourage them to (try to) posit a unified agent whose words they are, about whom they are" (p. 418).

Moreover, there is no genuine agency at work here, for: "Our tales are spun, but for the most part we don't spin them; they spin us. Our human consciousness, and our narrative selfhood, is their product, not their source" (p. 418). A self is a rather ephemeral sort of entity for Dennett, being mostly the hypothetical posit of a narrative told by no one.

As we see later, a *self* is a different entity from a *person*, so to approach a conception of person in terms of self is getting on the wrong track. However, the more fundamental problem with this proposal is its appeal to intentional self-interpretation, for it is precisely here that the logic of intentional stance interpretation seriously begins to break down. The problem is that the intentional stance is supposed to be a viewer-relative strategy of interpretation, but it cannot be viewer-relative when applied to ourselves. The intentional stance is not just an interpretive strategy for making sense of our own behavior, but an essential condition for interpreting ourselves in any way at all. Moreover, the attitude of assuming the intentional stance is, itself, something characterized in the intentional idiom; and so, according to the theory, it would only have a normative status relative to another invocation of the intentional stance, which would need to be characterized in terms of yet another, and so on. Dennett's argument is that this regress eventually terminates with the evolutionary grounding of the intentional stance in the basic biological contingencies of survival and differential reproduction. However, he ultimately failed to provide a coherent account of how the abstracta of intentionality evolve from the concreta of biological processes (House & McDonald, 1992).

The notion of *self* as a "center of narrative gravity" is similarly problematic when considered from a first-person point of view. This is, strictly speaking, a principle of *interpretive coherence* only. It refers to the ways in which a sense of self can be grasped by interpreting the patterns of thematic coherence underlying someone's discourse. Clearly, much of what we understand about other selves is obtained in this fashion; we first listen to what they have to say, and then form an impression of what they are like. Certain kinds of self-understanding follow the same pattern; we occasionally learn things about ourselves that we did not really know before by closely listening to what we say in conversation (in fact, the most common forms of psychotherapy are based on just this form of self-understanding). However, from a first-person perspective, one's sense of self cannot rest on interpretive coherence alone. It depends also on the *expressive coherence* of one's utterances—that form of coherence by virtue of which the utterances I make are *my* utterances, the product of *my* active and ongoing intention to express myself in words, and to invest my utterances with a coherent sense of self that expresses how I already understand myself, prior to saying anything at all. This is a precondition for my expressing myself intelligibly in the first place. Dennett's account of self, with its stout denial of agency, leaves little room for this kind of expressive coherence.

This particular view is here termed the *stance conception of persons.* Its principal defect, as is seen, is that it fails to make sense of how persons understand themselves.

HUMAN SCIENCE PERSPECTIVES

Human science perspectives on folk psychology and persons include a class of views at least as diverse and open-ended as the cognitive science perspectives. They have, at least, the following two features in common. First, as an alternative to the natural science emphasis on mechanistic causal explanation, human science approaches tend to emphasize an interpretive methodology and the analysis of meaning. Second, human science perspectives tend to focus on external social or cultural factors rather than internal factors as determinants of psychological phenomena. The general strategy of approach to folk psychology also radically differs from that of the cognitive science perspectives. For the cognitivist, folk psychology is seen as something that needs to be vindicated by science, whereas, from a human science perspective, folk psychology is seen as a form of practice that is fundamentally constitutive of the psychological. The constitutive position, briefly, is that folk psychology constitutes the essence of the psychological, rather than being merely a surface manifestation of some deeper reality; in short, there would be no psychology without folk psychology. Bruner (1990), reacting to the claims of the eliminativists, expressed the essence of the constitutive argument as follows:

> Antimentalistic fury about folk psychology simply misses the point. The idea of jettisoning it in the interest of getting rid of mental states in our everyday explanations of human behavior is tantamount to throwing away the very phenomena that psychology needs to explain. (p. 14)

Cultural Psychology

Bruner (1990) carried the constitutive argument a step further, into a proposal for cultural psychology, when he wrote: "It is man's participation *in* culture and the realization of his mental powers *through* culture that make it impossible to construct a human psychology on the basis of the individual alone" (p. 12). In the program of cultural psychology that Bruner envisioned, folk psychology is conceived of as a cultural instrument. Its primary purpose is to situate the thought and action of individuals within the collective life of a culture. It includes all of the publicly negotiated means by which we account, through language, for our own actions and those of others, in ways sanctioned by our culture. Moreover:

> Because it is a reflection of culture, it partakes in the culture's way of valuing as well as its way of knowing. In fact, it *must* do so, for the culture's normatively oriented institutions—its laws, its educational institutions, its family structures—serve to enforce folk psychology. Indeed, folk psychology in its turn serves to justify such enforcement. (p. 14)

As an instrument of culture, folk psychology is a profoundly *normative system*—it is concerned as much with enforcing what should be as with describing what is. Our own native folk psychology, for instance, stipulates that we have beliefs and desires concerning the world we live in, that we have plans and goals for how to satisfy our desires in light of our beliefs, that our actions are carried out with reference to our plans and goals, and that our beliefs, desires, intentions, and other intentional attitudes should cohere in certain obvious ways even to the point of ultimately converging on commitments to particular ways of life. Any significant violation of these basic canons of folk psychology invariably calls for an explanation, characteristically in *narrative* terms. That is, departures from the canonical system of expectations put in place by folk psychology motivates the spinning of narratives to reconcile the intentional attitudes of individuals with the canonical pattern of folk psychology. For this reason, the basic organizing principle of folk psychology is said to be narrative rather than logical or categorical.

This conception of folk psychology ought to have some clear implications for our notions of person and self; as Bruner (1990) stated, "at their core, all folk psychologies contain a surprisingly complex notion of an agentive Self" (p. 41). The notion that Bruner seemed to find most congenial is the "distributive conception of self" that recently surfaced in various quarters of the social sciences. In the distributive conception, our selves, like our folk psychological attitudes, are not located internally, but are distributed in the patterns of our collective life in our culture; as Bruner remarked, "Selves are not isolated nuclei of consciousness locked in the head, but are 'distributed' interpersonally" (p. 138). Selves are also distributed temporally, on Bruner's account, which explains his emphasis on autobiography as a tool for the articulating of selves. However, these ideas are not systematically developed by Bruner, and he does not make it clear how he sees *self* in relation to *person* or whether he distinguishes the two at all. We need to look to other human science perspectives for a more systematic account.

Discursive Psychology

One such account may be found in Harré and Gillett's (1994) recent formulation of *discursive psychology*. What they term the *discursive turn* in modern cognitive psychology is the view that cognitive phenomena, in particular, and psychological phenomena, in general, are features of discourse, that this discourse—whether carried out publicly or privately— is founded on interpersonal symbolic processes, and that the important characteristics of people as cognitive agents depend on the discursive contexts in which they are situated and the discursive practices in which they skilfully engage. Harré and Gillett did not address folk psychology explicitly, but it is obviously central to their program. In fact, they expressed the basic constitutive argument for folk psychology quite clearly in stressing:

> the priority that must be given to ordinary languages in defining what are the phenomena for a scientific psychology. We will endeavor as far as possible to present and understand cognition in terms of the ordinary languages through which we think, rather than looking for abstract representations of them. (pp. 27–28)

Harré and Gillett (1994) also laid out a basic Vygotskian ontology for discursive psychology. According to this ontology, "arrays of people" constitute the basic locative systems of the discursive universe; the reason, they stated, is that when something is said, it does not much matter where in physical space it is said, but "it does matter a great deal who says it" (p. 30). The most basic entities or "things" of the discursive universe, "the entities that occur at the people points" are speech acts (p. 31). The relations that connect the speech acts are rules and narrative conventions; as in Bruner's cultural psychology, the basic organizing principle of discursive psychology would seem to be a narrative one.

The concept of person that is built into discursive psychology has certain resonances with the locus conception of persons that was considered earlier. That is, a person is conceived primarily as a locus or place at which speech acts occur, in much the same way that realist theory conceives of person as a locus for intentional attitudes. Indeed, the entire explanatory framework of intentional realism seems here to be recapitulated in a public domain. In place of intentional attitudes connected by internal mental processes, we have public speech acts connected by narrative conventions. Moreover, the speech acts, like the attitudes, are the main active entities that actually make things happen; a person is primarily a place at which such entities do their work. This locative conception of persons is further reinforced by some statements that Harré and Gillett (1994) made early in their book, such as: "An individual person in discourse with others is a meeting point of many discourses and must, to some extent, integrate the multifaceted subjectivity that arises from this intersection of influences" (p. 25). Also, "There is a people-space constituted by the individuals who can be speakers or counterspeakers or listeners. People are things specified something like spatial points, defined in terms of interpersonal, social, and political frameworks" (p. 31).

The implication of passivity invoked by the locative conception is countered somewhat by what Harré and Gillett (1994) had to say, later in their book, about human agency. Discursive contexts, they pointed out, are governed by *social causation*, which operates in a fundamentally different way from the mechanistic causation of naturalistic explanation. Relations of signification here take the place of rigidly determinate cause-and-effect dependencies. One implication of this is that the basic generalizations of discursive psychology will inevitably have a stochastic character:

Social causation disposes the person to certain reactions and ways of acting but does not determine that they will act thus and so. This means that we will be able to make statistical predictions of behavior on the basis of social variables but we will not necessarily be able to make sense of the actions and reactions of an individual in a particular situation. (p. 142)

A more important consequence of social causation is that it leaves room for individuals to exercise a limited form of agency:

The individual, whose intentions are structured by and emerge from the positions taken up in a social context and the discourses that pervade and structure it, is able to choose the rule-governed techniques that they will use to organize their psychological responses. Thus their commitments or positionings within discourses that they adopt in making them become formative of their personality, which increasingly reflects certain discursive contexts and positions but no one is perhaps irrevocably bound by them. (p. 122)

Moreover, what freedom of action we have in discursive contexts depends greatly on our discursive skills, for example, our ability to articulate the discursive practices that we either accept or reject, our ability to locate ourselves in discourse through the appropriate use of indexical pronouns and to constitute a sense of self thereby, and so on. In any case, it becomes clear that *agency* is mainly a matter of choosing a discursive context in which to participate, but, once that choice is made, what happens seems more under the control of the discursive context than of the person. If Harré and Gillett believed that, in addition to choosing their discursive contexts, people can also negotiate them, shape them, even create them for themselves, they offered no systematic account of such abilities. The problem with the discursive conception of agency is that it is too constrained by the locative conception of persons. In fact, there is an essential tension between this locative conception and the concept of a person as agent; the more people function as agents, the less they function as locations and vice versa.

Self-Interpretation

A more robust notion of agency is to be found in Taylor's (1983/1985b) analysis of agency and the self. The most basic condition of agency, according to Taylor, is that agents are beings to whom things "matter," where "to say things matter to agents is to say that we can attribute purposes, desires, aversions to them in a strong, original sense" (p. 99). This implies that an agent is fundamentally a *subject of significance*, that is, a participant in a field of significance relations that structure the world for the agent and provide a unique point of view with respect to it. Thus, part of what is entailed by being a person is that: "A person must be a being with his own point of view on things. The life-plan, the choices, the sense of self must be attributable to him as in some sense their point of origin. A person is a being who can be addressed, and who can reply" (p. 97). Yet, as Taylor pointed out, this is still not sufficient to capture what is special about human agency, as nonhuman animals may also be subjects of significance in much the same sense. The difference is that there are matters of significance for human agents that are qualitatively distinct from those of nonlanguage-using animals. There are certain things we care about, generally matters of moral significance involving pride, shame, dignity, integrity, personal worth, and so on that greatly depend on our ability to formulate them in language. Moreover, their linguistic formulation is strongly constitutive of this class of concerns; it would not be possible to have these concerns independently of language.

What is special about human agents, in Taylor's (1977/1985a) analysis, is our capacity to reflexively interpret and thereby constitute our own significance relations. The human agent, then, is necessarily a self-interpreting subject of significance:

> To say that man is a self-interpreting animal is not just to say that he has some compulsive tendency to form reflexive views of himself, but rather that as he is, he is always partly constituted by self-interpretation, that is, by his understanding of the imports which impinge on him. (p. 72)

This notion of a self-interpreting subject of significance is superficially reminiscent of Dennett's notion of a self-interpreting intentional system. Of course, the important difference is that Talyor's self-interpreting subject is conceived of as an *agent*, a maker, not merely a bearer, of interpretations. To use the terminology introduced earlier, an agent is a center of expressive coherence not just of interpretive coherence. Self-inter-

preting agents actively express and constitute their own patterns of significance, these significance patterns are not something merely attributed to them after the fact, as in Dennett's intentional systems; they are,
in a word, self-attributed.

However, the concept of person as self-interpreting agent raises some
problems of its own. The self of the self-interpreting agent is an inherently duplicitous sort of entity; it is an entity that both interprets and is,
itself, interpreted. One must, in a sense, split a person into two distinct
selves—the *self-as-interpreter* and the *self-as-interpreted*. Taylor (1977/
1985a) vaguely alluded to the possibility of unifying the two when he
stated that "the self that is to be interpreted is essentially that of a being
who self-interprets" (p. 75). However, the very idea of self-interpretation would seem to require that the two selves cannot be wholly identical. For the notion of self-interpretation to have any leverage, the self-
as-interpreter and the self-as-interpreted must be less than fully transparent to each other. The interpreted self must present something of a mystery to the interpreting self, else there would be no conceivable motive
for self-interpretation in the first place; by the same token, the interpreting self must be capable of opening up possibilities not originally envisioned by the interpreted self, if interpretation is to be at all productive.
Again, we begin to sense something of the difference between the notions of *person* and *self*. The interpreting and the interpreted selves are,
at best, aspects or phases of a person, not the whole person. The underlying unity that integrates these two aspects into one person remains to be
addressed.

THE FOLK PSYCHOLOGICAL GRAMMAR OF PERSON

So far, we have looked at the folk psychological concept of person through
the distorting lens of theory. We have seen that radically different
construals of persons emerge, depending on the claims that a given theory
makes about the nature and explanatory status of folk psychology. If a
coherent concept of person required a completely worked out and generally accepted theory of folk psychology, our inquiry would be all but
hopeless, because the status of folk psychology rests on a set of issues
that are riddled with dispute and are likely to remain so for some time.

Fortunately, there is a more direct approach. We can ask what folk
psychology, itself, has to say about persons. The folk psychological idiom

embodies a rich, if tacit, set of conceptions of person that do not need to be filtered through a particular theory of folk psychology to be understood. All that is required is a close examination of the language of the folk psychological idiom itself. Because this language is culturally and historically conditioned, we do not expect to arrive at universally valid generalizations in this way. At best, we can find out what assumptions about persons lie buried in our own native form of commonsense psychology. Although this form of folk psychology is widely consensual in modern culture, it is in no way privileged; other folk psychologies have and will exist at other times and places. However, a limited analysis of this kind is the best we can hope to achieve, given that the concept of person is, itself, thoroughly culturally and historically conditioned (Taylor, 1989).

Person and Attitude

To begin at the beginning, there is a basic predicative relation between persons and the folk psychological attitudes they bear; that is, folk psychological attitudes are, in the first instance, something predicated of persons. There are two basic types of expression we use for the purpose. First, there is the *active form* of expression, in which the intentional modality is expressed as a verb, as in "John *believes* (or *hopes* or *wants* or *expects*, etc.) that interest rates will decline." The second type of predicative expression relating persons to the attitudes is the *possessive form*, in which the intentional modality is the object of a verb such as *have*, *entertain*, *possess*, *consider*, and so on, *have* being the most generic verb of this type, as in "John has a *belief* (or *hope* or *wish* or *expectation*, etc.) that interest rates will decline." The possessive form seems to be the more basic of the two, as any expression in the active form has a directly corresponding expression in the possessive form, but the converse is not always the case. The reason is that (in the English language at least) there is a richer intentional vocabulary of nouns than of verbs.

One obvious but nonetheless important feature of folk psychological language is a basic asymmetry between person and attitude. This is most clearly seen in the possessive mode, where a person may be said to "have" a belief, intention, expectation, and so forth, but the belief or intention is not normally said to "have" the person. That is, a person is normally the logical subject (rather than the object) of predications of attitudes. However, this asymmetry between person and attitude is not absolute. It is easy to come up with examples in which a person seems to be cast in the role of object rather than subject of intentional attribution, as in: "A sudden desire came over John," "A powerful belief held Susan in its grasp," "A brilliant idea occurred to Pat," and so on. To distinguish such cases from ordinary ascriptions of attitudes, we term them *emphatic folk psychological ascriptions*. Their purpose is not just to ascribe an attitude to a person, but to call attention to some striking feature of it, such as its suddenness, unexpectedness, power, or sheer brilliance. Often the emphatic mode carries with it a suggestion of irrationality—a person too much in the grip of a particular belief, for instance, cannot be thinking wholly rationally. However, this mode may also be used to suggest unusual brilliance or originality, as in the case of the person who is seized by a great idea. In general, the emphatic mode points to some imbalance or disturbance in the normal folk psychological status quo, that is, in the usual pattern of coherence among one's beliefs, thoughts, intentions, and so on. Where there is no suspicion of any such disturbance, we tend to use the ordinary mode of folk psychological attribution, in which a person is the logical subject rather than object of predication. This is, so to speak, the *unmarked* case (whereas the emphatic mode is the more *marked* case) of folk psychological attribution.

The pervasiveness of the ordinary mode of folk psychological attribution may help to explain a certain sense of awkwardness associated with the emphatic mode and our usual way of compensating for this by resorting to the passive voice, as in "John was overcome by a sudden desire." Expressions like this at least preserve the person as the surface grammatical subject of the expression and thus, bear a superficial resemblance to the ordinary mode. The very existence of the emphatic mode and the ways in which we deal with it only reinforce the normative status of the ordinary mode of folk psychological ascription.

Person and Self

There is also a basic asymmetry between person and self that parallels, in some respects, the asymmetrical relation between person and attitude. This is not immediately obvious because the terms *person* and *self* function similarly in many contexts and even the most credible theorists in this area tend to use the two terms interchangeably, as we have seen. It is indeed the case that many of the things that may be said about persons may also be said of selves. A self, like a person, may be a bearer of folk psychological attitudes, and these may be ascribed using either the active or possessive forms of expression; again, there is a basic asymmetry between self and attitude in that a self may be said to "have" an intentional attitude, but the attitude does not normally "have" the self.

However, in other important respects, the discursive ontologies of *person* and *self* are quite different. In particular, folk psychological discourse displays the same sort of asymmetrical relation between person and self as between person and attitude. That is, a person may be said to "have" a self—there is *my* self, *your* self,[1] John Smith's self, and so forth—but a self does not, in the same way, "have" a person. According to folk psychological discourse, a self is something one has, whereas a person is something one is.[2] The same applies to the various hyphenated self-entities that are the perennial favorites of popular psychology, such as *self-image, self-concept, self-esteem, self-efficacy*, and so on; again, these are things that we have, not what we are.

Of course, there are some noteworthy exceptions to this way of talking about the self, which again only reinforce its normative status. There is an emphatic mode of discourse for the self just as there is for the attitudes. Jung (1964), for example, speaks of the *Self* (with a capital S), or Big-I, as something more inclusive than, and transcendent of, the merely personal ego. This way of speaking of the self is amply supported by a venerable mystical tradition as well. *Self*, in this sense, is something that does, indeed, "have" a person; to use one of Jung's metaphors, it is a kind of center of gravity around which a person orbits.

---

[1] Of course, there is a purely reflexive use of terms such as *myself, yourself, himself*, and so forth that is simply a way of securing reference to a particular individual. It is only when we interpret the embedded *self* terms psychologically that the possessive form of expression becomes significant.

[2] The expression "my person," for example, is a colloquialism referring to the physical body and its attachments and has an entirely different meaning from "my self." The only way to bring *person* into a possessive form of expression is as a property or criterion, as when we say that an individual possesses "personhood." This way of speaking is familiar from certain forms of legal and philosophical discourse, but it generally has not caught on in the folk psychological vernacular.

However, the fact that this usage of the term needs to be marked linguistically (using capitalization or italics, for example) only shows that this is a departure from normal discursive practice. Again, the unmarked case is the one in which we say that a person has a self, and not vice versa.

Person as a Unity

One of the functions of the possessive form of expression, in intentional and nonintentional discourse alike, is to identify part/whole and aspectual relationships. So when we say that John has a self, one of the things we might mean is that John's self is, in a certain sense, a part or an aspect of John, but we do not use the term *person* in this way because the term refers, not to a feature of John, but to who John is. *Person*, then, is among the more inclusive terms in the language for capturing our human individuality;[3] it stands, not for part of what we are as human beings, but for a totality, an essential unity of being. It is a unity that ties together all our actions and experiences, that connects all the diverse parts of ourselves, and that gives meaning to the pronoun *I* as we use it in conversation.

This is not to say that one's identity as a person is something fixed and immutable, however. We are sometimes inclined to say, with a genuine sense of conviction, things like, "I am not the same person I was a year ago" or "I am not the same person at home that I am at work." However, note that when we talk this way, we are still speaking of the person we are, not of the self we have. Thus, there is an important, if subtle, difference between this way of speaking and corresponding instances of self-talk, as when we say, "My sense of myself is not the same as it was a year ago" or "not the same at home as it is at work." In self-talk cases, one is speaking of a feeling or an impression one has of oneself; in person-talk cases, one is referring to one's total integration as an individual. So, to say "I am not the same person I was a year ago"—if seriously intended (that is, if not merely an oblique expression of self-talk)—is to say that the way I functioned as an integrated unity has dramatically changed from that time to this. Such discontinuities of personal functioning are perhaps not uncommon under the conditions of

---

[3] The term *person* is, of course, not unique in this respect; terms such as *individual, human being, subject,* and *agent* have a similar logical grammar; on the other hand, terms such as *mind* and *ego* function more like *self.*

modern life. Even so, we are rarely inclined to take these discontinuities as absolute. To totally and finally repudiate the person one once was or the person one may become would be unthinkable, except in the most extreme circumstances, as this would undermine an overriding unity, intrinsic to our very notion of person, that seems to extend necessarily over an entire lifetime. As Taylor (1989) argued:

> We want our lives to have meaning, or weight, or substance, or to grow towards some fullness...But this means our *whole* lives...It seems clear from all this that there is something like an a priori unity of a human life through its whole extent...the supposition that I could be two temporally succeeding selves is either an overdramatized image, or quite false. It runs against the structural features of a self as a being who exists in a space of concerns. (pp. 50–51)

The holistic way of thinking that is entailed by the folk psychological conception of person as a unity is likely the source of much of the theoretical resistance to the notion that we find in contemporary approaches. Self has become the much more congenial notion as it better fits with our modern tendency to analyze things into parts. In particular, the Cartesian tendency to conceive the self as an inner part of a person, "the self inside" to use Tolman's (chap. 1, this volume) phrase, has proven remarkably persistent, especially in the cognitive and neurosciences; this gives rise to notions such as the self as a "computational mind" (Jackendoff, 1987) or "the self and its brain" (Eccles, 1994). Only relatively recently has the alternative view of self in relation to others been able to gain a foothold in psychology, with the growing popularity of the various human science conceptions, such as the socially and culturally situated self, the discursive self, and the interpretive self, that we looked at earlier.

However, the more fundamental barrier to understanding persons has less to do with the distinction between inner and outer than with the distinction between parts and wholes. The socially distributed self in relation to others, like the Cartesian self, is but a part or aspect of a person, not the whole person; discursive practices, social commitments and engagements, acts of self-interpretation, and so on, like computational processes in the brain, are something we have, not what we are. Somehow we need to find a way to put the whole person back together again from this legion of selves that modern theory has created. What is the nature of the unity that integrates the discursive self, the socially situated self, the interpretive self, the neurophysiologically embodied self, and so on, into one person? Contemporary theory generally lacks the resources even to bring the question clearly into focus, let alone to answer it; clearly, an essential first step is to expand the discussions relating these various conceptions, in the way that House and McDonald (see chap. 8, this volume) suggest.

CONCLUSION: AGENCY REVISITED

Another significant stumbling block for our understanding of persons has to do with the notion of agency that we touched on earlier. Not only does a person have various self-constitutive parts, such as brain processes, discursive practices, social commitments, and so on, these are also things that a person does—activities in which he or she meaningfully engages. The sense of agency that is implied here is basic and irreducible. Persons are the ultimate agents of their own actions, the final term in the regress of reasons to which one appeals in justifying one's actions to others. Social life as we know it would be inconceivable without agency in this sense, that is, without the notion of personal responsibility for one's own actions. This, in turn, explains why *person* is, among other things, a moral category.

For advocates of cognitive science and neuroscience perspectives, agency remains a deeply repugnant notion, as it threatens to undermine their entire efficient cause scheme of mechanistic explanation. Advocates of human science perspectives, on the other hand, have no such qualms about the notion of agency; yet, as we have seen, their own accounts of it tend to undermine the unity of persons. We need to find a mode of explanation that can do justice to both personal unity and agency. Only then can we truly be said to have brought persons back into psychology.

REFERENCES

Bruner, J. (1990). *Acts of meaning*. Cambridge, MA: Harvard University Press.

Churchland, P. M. (1981). Eliminative materialism and the propositional attitudes. *The Journal of Philosophy, 78*, 67–90.

Churchland, P. M. (1988). *Matter and consciousness* (rev. ed.). Cambridge, MA: MIT Press.

Churchland, P. M. (1989). *A neurocomputational perspective: The nature of mind and the structure of science.* Cambridge, MA: MIT Press.

Dennett, D. C. (1978). *Brainstorms.* Cambridge, MA: Bradford Books.

Dennett, D. C. (1987). *The intentional stance.* Cambridge, MA: MIT Press.

Dennett, D. C. (1991). Real patterns. *The Journal of Philosophy, 89,* 27–51.

Dennett, D. C. (1992). *Consciousness explained.* Boston: Little, Brown.

Eccles, J. C. (1994). *How the self controls its brain.* New York: Springer-Verlag.

Feyerabend, P. (1963). Materialism and the mind–body problem. *Review of Metaphysics, 17,* 49–66.

Fodor, J. A. (1975). *The language of thought.* New York: Crowell.

Fodor, J. A. (1987). *Psychosemantics: The problem of meaning in the philosophy of mind.* Cambridge, MA: MIT Press.

Fodor, J. A. (1990). *A theory of content and other essays.* Cambridge, MA: MIT Press.

Harré, R., & Gillett, G. (1994). *The discursive mind.* London: Sage.

House, D. V., & McDonald, M. J. (1992, October). *"You're a figment of your own imagination": The case of Daniel Dennett and the disappearing mind.* Paper presented at the annual meeting of the Western Canadian Psychologists, Saskatoon, Saskatchewan.

Jackendoff, R. S. (1987). *Consciousness and the computational mind.* Cambridge, MA: MIT Press.

Jung, C. G. (1964). *Man and his symbols.* New York: Doubleday.

Loewer, B., & Rey, G. (1991). Editor's Introduction. In B. Loewer & G. Rey (Eds.), *Meaning in mind: Fodor and his critics* (pp. xi–xxxvii). Oxford: Blackwell.

Rorty, R. (1965). Mind–body identity, privacy, and categories. *Review of Metaphysics, 19,* 24–54.

Searle, J. R. (1983). *Intentionality: An essay in the philosophy of mind.* Cambridge, England: Cambridge University Press.

Searle, J. R. (1992). *The rediscovery of the mind.* Cambridge, MA: MIT Press.

Stich, S. P. (1983). *From folk psychology to cognitive science: The case against belief.* Cambridge, MA: MIT Press.

Taylor, C. (1985a). Self-interpreting animals. In C. Taylor (Ed.), *Human agency and language. Philosophical papers, Volume 1.* (pp. 15–44). Cambridge, England: Cambridge University Press. (Original work published 1977)

Taylor, C. (1985b). The concept of a person. In C. Taylor (Ed.), Human agency and language. *Human agency and language. Philosophical papers, Volume 1* (pp. 97–114). Cambridge, England: Cambridge University Press. (Original work published 1983)

Taylor, C. (1989). *Sources of the self: The making of the modern identity.* Cambridge, MA: Harvard University Press.

CHAPTER 3

Style Over Substance: The Loss of Personhood in Theories of Personality

Anand C. Paranjpe
Simon Fraser University
Burnaby, British Columbia

In contemporary psychological discourse the terms *person* and *personality* are often used synonymously. However, in the long history of these two related terms, a distinction has often been made between them. The term *person* has long been used to designate humans as beings with rights and responsibilities, as opposed to things, animals, or humans without rights, such as slaves. Person is an ethicolegal concept that views human beings as inexorably social beings in a community governed by an ethos. Persons are therefore always open to be judged by the community's standards. In contrast, the term *personality* has generally designated individuality marked by the externally observable stylistic features that distinguish one person from another. It is my contention that most—but not all—contemporary theories of personality have focused on personality in this sense, while neglecting the ethicolegal conception of personhood. This devaluation of personhood is explainable in terms of certain central features of the scientific Zeitgeist of the 20th century—emphasis on mechanism versus teleology, nomothetic versus idiographic, analysis versus synopsis and empiricism and objectivity versus subjectivity, and value neutrality. Although all these features were highly useful for the development of natural science, their application to psychology has led to the depersonalization of its subject matter.

PERSON, PERSONALITY, AND THE TRILOGY OF MIND

Person and personality are two closely related concepts with a history traced back to ancient Greek and Roman civilizations. A few years prior to the founding of the pioneering laboratories of modern psychology, Trendelenburg (1870/1910) published a detailed, scholarly essay on the history of person, personality, and related terms through the millennial history of Western thought. Allport (1937) mentioned this essay in *Personality: A Psychological Interpretation*, a text often credited for founding personality as a distinct area within psychology. In this book, Allport listed 50 different meanings of *person*, *personality*, and related terms that were known up until that time. Of those different meanings, two are important for the present purpose. The first is the term *personality*, which has usually meant individuality as manifest in distinctive features that account for individual differences. This meaning is traced to the Greek root *persona*, meaning theatrical mask. Consistent with the metaphor of the mask, it refers to externally observable features that may hide rather than reveal the true or inner features of the person wearing it. The second term, *person*, often refers to a human being as opposed to an animal or a thing, and usually implies the rights and responsibilities of an individual as a free born citizen as distinguished from a slave. This usage dates back to Roman law, which awarded rights and responsibilities only to upper class men rather than to all human beings. It is in this sense that corporations were often considered persons, but women were not. As late as 1928, the Supreme Court of Canada ruled that women were not persons and were therefore ineligible to hold public office. This judgment was reversed by the Judicial Committee of the Privy Council saying that "the exclusion of women from all public offices is a relic of days more barbarous than ours," thereby clearing the way for the appointment to the Canadian Senate of its first woman nominee.[1]

The concept of person as a being with rights and responsibilities is clearly an inseparable part of a social ethos. *Ethos*, or social code of

---

[1] For the judgment of the Supreme Court, see *Dominion Law Reports*, 1928, Vol. 4, pp. 98–125; and for the ruling of the Judicial Committee of the Privy Council on Edwards vs. Attorney General of Canada, see *Western Weekly Reports*, 1929, Vol. 3, pp. 479–495.

values, is variable from place to place and is open to change from time to time. What specific rights and responsibilities are accorded to persons, and which categories of individuals (gender, age, class, race, caste, etc.) are considered eligible for personhood, is subject to variation in time and place. Contemporary Western concepts of personhood are products of the sociopolitical history of Europe and bear distinctive marks of several influential Enlightenment thinkers such as John Locke, Thomas Reid, and Immanuel Kant. Among these, Locke was, by far, the most influential. The direct influence of his ideas on the U.S. Constitution is well known (Jones, 1969, p. 279). Some of his ideas are crucial for our consideration and hence, may be briefly quoted here. According to Locke (1690/1959):

> Person...is...a *forensic* term appropriating actions and their merit; and so belongs only to intelligent agents, capable of law, and happiness, and misery. This personality extends itself beyond present existence to what is past, only by consciousness,—whereby it becomes concerned and accountable; owns and imputes to itself past actions...desiring that the self that is conscious should be happy. (p. 467, emphasis added)

In this excerpt, Locke suggested that a person is one who understands or knows ("intelligent"), feels ("happiness and misery") and acts ("agent"), thereby implying the basic psychological trilogy of cognition, affect, and volition. Locke, like many others of his time, often used the concepts of person and self as synonyms. Almost a century later, Reid (1785/1975) echoed Locke's idea in the following words: "Whatever this self may be, it is something which thinks, and deliberates, and resolves, and acts, and suffers....I am something that thinks, and acts, and suffers" (p. 109). Reid's words are part of the work of a long chain of prominent European thinkers who entrenched a close connection between the concept of personhood and the trilogy of mind.

Personhood and the Trilogy of Mind

There is a close historical and conceptual relation between the ethicolegal conception of personhood on the one hand, and the trilogy of cognition, affect, and volition on the other. This trilogy of mind is a necessary complement to the psychological make-up of persons as responsible members of a community governed by an ethos. In *Critique of Judgment*, Kant (1790/1987) clearly and emphatically stated that "We can reduce all the powers of the mind, without exception, to these three: the *cognitive power*, the *feeling of pleasure and displeasure*, and the *power of desire*" (p. 394). In the same work, he repeatedly referred to the three powers and explained in detail how moral as well as aesthetic judgments are only possible through the joint working of these powers.

To help understand the close relation between ethicolegal concept of personhood and trilogy of mind, it is important to remember that cognition, affect, and volition were commonly regarded as necessarily and always interconnected, and were united in the conscious awareness of the person as one and the same individual across time and space. In his words previously quoted, Locke indicated how persons become concerned and accountable for their actions only insofar as they remember their own actions in the past, can anticipate pleasurable or painful consequences of their actions, and understand the merits and demerits of their actions in terms of a social code.

It was clear to Locke that to be able to claim one's rights, it was necessary for a person to experience in his own mind, and establish in the eyes of concerned others, that he was one and the same man. In his parable of a prince and a cobbler, where a prince and a cobbler mysteriously switch their memories, Locke (1690/1959) suggested how the prince in the cobbler's body must establish his *identity*—that the person claiming the privileges of princehood is the same as the one that married the princess, for instance (p. 457). Today, as in the days of Locke, it must be established in a court of law that the person accused of a crime is the same person as was witnessed while committing the alleged offense, hence the importance of identification. Certainly, the external features of personality are important in the identification for the purpose of establishing legal privileges and moral accountability. However, there is more to personhood in the ethicolegal sense than externally observable features of personality. For instance, what makes an action culpable is not simply its physical consequences, but intentions that ostensively prompted it. Thus, in an automobile mishap in which a pedestrian is killed, the driver may be deemed innocent if it turns out to be a sheer accident on a slippery road or deemed guilty of negligence if he was drunk, but deemed guilty of murder if witnesses had heard the driver's intention to kill the victim. In fact, a person may be blamed for attempted murder even if no harm is done to anyone, but the motive to kill is established beyond doubt. If the driver were expected to turn back, according to a road sign announcing bad driving conditions, he would be considered guilty of negligence, but innocent if he could not understand what the sign said in a language foreign to him. If, on the other hand, the driver was enraged by the victim's overtures toward his wife, the judge might be lenient, considering his misdemeanor a crime of passion. Feelings, intentions, understanding, and the like that are crucial in determining guilt or innocence are embedded in a person's consciousness.

Consciousness is the first obvious precondition for someone being held responsible for his or her actions. Individuals in the state of coma can hardly be called on to account for their past actions, for during such a state, they are incapable of understanding as well as feeling. Rewards and punishments make sense only when they are respectively pleasurable and painful; watching television could be a reward for most children, but only punishment to many adults. It makes sense to reward or punish animals to the extent that they ostensibly feel pleasure when fed and pain when hurt. Yet, it makes no sense to reward or punish robots because, as far as we can tell, they can neither enjoy nor suffer. Although many of us believe in animal rights, we cannot hold animals accountable for their behavior, for accountability presupposes an *understanding* of what is considered proper and what is not—a capacity we do not attribute to animals. Moreover, only those who are able to freely choose among alternative courses of action can be held responsible for their behaviors. Persons under confinement cannot be blamed for not doing things they were restrained from doing, nor could one be blamed for hurting others when forced to do so at gun point. Liberty (or freedom) and will are preconditions of responsible behavior, as are consciousness, rational thinking and knowledge of rules, and capacity to act in anticipation of both desirable and undesirable consequences. Thus, an approach to psychology that includes thinking, feeling, and will is clearly a necessary counterpart of an ethicolegal view of personhood.

Although the ethicolegal concept of personhood is not considered very important in psychology today, it is crucial in civil life, at least in democratic societies in which most psychologists function. Its importance in today's world is clearly indicated by the fact that many of us have been trying to enshrine charters of individual rights in our national constitutions and wish to protect human rights in countries where they are frequently violated. We want the rights and responsibilities of men, women, and children clearly defined within all kinds of social institutions: familial, educational, commercial, and political. As teachers, researchers, and practitioners of psychology (i.e., qua psychologists), we are responsible for protecting the rights of our students, experimental subjects, and clients. Indeed, a civic society without individual rights and responsibilities is unthinkable. However, rights and responsibilities of human beings hardly constitute a popular topic in psychology today. With the notable exceptions of the existentialist and Eriksonian models, most theorists of personality deal with individuality rather than the ethicolegal conception of personhood.

The Parallel Decline of Personhood and the Trilogy of Mind

From the period of the European Enlightenment to the early decades of this century, the trilogy of cognition, affect, and volition was central to psychology. In his historical review of the trilogy of mind, Hilgard (1980) cautioned against the temptation to trace the origins of this trilogy to early Christian and Hebraic traditions. However, he had shown how deeply the trilogy had permeated through the work of major thinkers of 18th and 19th century Europe: several Continental rationalists from Leibniz (1646–1716) to Kant (1724–1804), Scottish commonsense psychologists from Reid (1710–1796) to Stewart (1788–1856), as well as their American followers, and British psychologists from Bain (1818–1903) to MacDougall (1871–1944), While concluding his historical survey Hilgard (1980) said that "with William MacDougall the history of the trilogy of mind appears to have ended, nearly two centuries after it began in Germany and Scotland" (p. 114).

It is interesting to note that, according to Hilgard, MacDougall's (1923) *Outline of Psychology*, published in 1923, marks the end of the trilogy of mind. It is after this that the study of personality as we know it came into existence. In his historical survey of psychology in America, Hilgard (1987) noted that "[a] landmark book by Gordon W. Allport, *Personality: A Psychological Interpretation* (1937) did much to introduce the study of personality as a standard topic in the psychology curriculum" (p. 493). In this book, Allport (1937) first surveyed some 50 different historical conceptions and came up with his own definition: "PERSONALITY IS THE DYNAMIC ORGANIZATION WITHIN THE INDIVIDUAL OF THOSE PSYCHOPHYSICAL SYSTEMS THAT DETERMINE THE UNIQUE ADJUSTMENTS TO HIS ENVIRONMENT" (p. 48). Although Allport mentioned ethicolegal definitions in his survey, he disregarded them. Instead, he focused on *uniqueness*, which implies individuality, and adjustment to environment, which is in keeping with the functional–biological perspective prevalent in his time. At this point, it is useful to note some twists and turns in the usage of terms.

As noted by Hilgard (1987), "personality was not a widely used term in the 19th century, and much that would be called personality in the next century was then covered by the term *character*" (p. 492). Hilgard also pointed out that William James used the term *personality* in his *Principles* only in relation to alteration of personality, thus implying that in his view, personality meant individuality rather than personhood, which he generally designated by the term *self* rather than *person*. Although James' text was highly popular for decades after its publication, psychologists showed little interest in the self despite attempts at the turn of the century by his student, Calkins (1900), to popularize it. By the 1920s, when psychologists had lost interest in the trilogy of mind, they had also lost interest in self and in stream of consciousness. The side-by-side decline of the trilogy of mind, consciousness, self, and personhood is not a mere coincidence, for the phenomena designated by these terms are meaningfully connected. In what way can we make sense of the decline of psychology's interest in personhood and the trilogy of mind?

As an answer to this question, I suggest that this set of concepts fell into disfavor due to the rise of an uncongenial Zeitgeist, which at the same time, favored the idea of personality as individuality. What was the Zeitgeist like, and how do we know it was in force during the 1930s, the period of the decline of the trilogy of mind and the rise of personality? Answers to these questions can be found in Allport's American Psychological Association (APA) presidential address of 1939. In his address, Allport (1940) presented a quantitative analysis of research trends of the first 5 decades (1888–1938) since the founding of the APA. A compilation of ratings of 50 psychology journals by 30 psychologists indicated the following trends: a decline in the number of publications on the higher mental processes as well as facultative treatment of mental functions, a loss of faith in the causal efficacy of the unconscious, a decreasing interest in the single case, diminution in historical surveys, an increase in the use of animal subjects, an increase in the use of *methodology*, and a rapid rise in mentions of operationism.

In addition to presenting quantitative data indicative of these trends, Allport mentioned, in his address, a set of criteria defining the scientific credo as identified by Arthur G. Bills. In a paper published during the previous year, Bills (1938) articulated the "criteria of psychology as a science that seem to form the framework of our current credo...that play an active part...in shaping the course of our current research." According to Bills, psychology as a science is empirical, mechanistic, quantitative, nomothetic, analytic, and uses operational concepts (p. 378). Allport (1940) agreed with Bills in his characterization of the scientific credo, adding that his survey of the literature indicates its increasing prevalence (p. 26). It is interesting to note that Bills (1938) was prompted to clarify and affirm the criteria of the scientific credo, because he was provoked by "some of the caustic criticisms from the pages of Gordon Allport's latest book [on personality]," which, he said, "have helped to shake my philosophical self-complacency" (p. 377). In response to this veiled charge of apostasy, Allport (1940) asked for indulgence: "Why not allow psychology as a science—for science is a broad and beneficent term—to be also *rational, teleological, qualitative, idiographic, synoptic*, and even *non-operational?*" (p. 26).

Indeed, Allport was not only sympathetic to a rationalist, teleological, and qualitative approach, but he also strongly advocated an idiographic position, adopted a broad, synoptic approach, and often criticized positivist and operationist psychology. It is his holistic perspective that helped him look at the individual as a whole and led to the founding of an area of studies called *personality*. Throughout his long and illustrious career, Allport made substantial humanistic contributions to psychology. As early as 1931, he co-authored a paper on values with P. E. Vernon, and later became well-known for the Allport-Vernon-Lindzey (1959) test of values. He insisted that the issue of normality and abnormality was fundamentally concerned with values (Allport, 1960a), and clarified the value implications of the problem of prejudice (Allport, 1960b). The recognition he earned for his ethical sensitivities and contributions to the study of values led to his appointment as the first Richard Clarke Cabot Professor of Social Ethics toward the end of his long career at Harvard. As I try to show in the remainder of this chapter, Allport often staunchly argued in support of the idiographic approach and other such views conducive to the study of personhood (against defenders of the scientific credo such as Hans Eysenck). It is ironic indeed, that while the supporters of the natural science perspective silently conspired to depersonalize psychology, Allport himself bypassed the ethicolegal view of personhood notwithstanding his sympathies for a position antithetical to positivist views of science. I shall try to make sense of this irony by suggesting that, under the overwhelming weight of the Zeitgeist, Allport became an inadvertent instrument in banishing personhood.

SCIENTIFIC CREDO AND THE BANISHING OF PERSONHOOD

The rise of science was an important aspect of the European Renaissance and Enlightenment. While Galileo, Copernicus, Boyle, Newton and several other luminaries contributed to the advancement of science in specific areas, Bacon, Hobbes, Locke, and Kant took it on themselves to promote and defend the world view of science in various ways. On the one hand, many of these Enlightenment thinkers shaped the Western conception of personhood, on the other hand, they also sowed the seeds of undermining it. The remainder of this chapter examines several features of the scientific credo identified by Bills, along with a few other well-known ones, and their implications for the concept of personhood, as it developed since the landmark publication of Allport's book on personality.

Mechanism Versus Teleology

No one can doubt today that the natural sciences could not have advanced without the rejection of teleological explanations in natural science. Bacon's criticism of Aristotle's teleological explanations of natural events was clearly an important step in the advancement of science. Consider, for instance, Aristotle's teleological explanations suggesting that drops of water must reach the ocean due to "final causes"—like intentions—built into them, or that the *purpose* of leaves is to protect fruit from shade. Quite conceivably, such ideas would have prevented, or at least retarded, the development of the concepts of gravity and the discovery of chlorophyll. If such speculation seems preposterous, think of the Aristotelians of Galileo's time who refused to look through his telescope since the new discoveries contradicted the "truths" proclaimed by their master. By strongly criticizing the notion of final cause in *nature* (but not in human beings), Bacon facilitated the development of new science. Later on, following Bacon's advice to read the "book of nature" instead of books like those of Aristotle, Darwin's theory of natural selection undermined divine purpose or deity teleology, thereby demystifying the origin of species. Another development in 19th century science that contributed to questioning teleology in humans was Helmholtz's demonstration that what travels across limbs of the body is electric current. This discovery laid to rest the Cartesian notion that animal spirits convey the soul's commands to the limbs via connecting tubes. In the 20th century, Loeb's concept of tropism laid animism to rest once and for all.

Given the history of ideas just mentioned, psychology in the 20th century was poised for a completely mechanistic approach to human behavior. Psychoanalysis and behaviorism, which dominated clinical and academic psychology, respectively, from the 1920s to the 1950s, disregarded the causal efficacy of conscious plans and intentions. Freud's emphasis on unconscious motivation downplayed the role of conscious thinking and will. The mechanistic implications of Freud's plumbing metaphor are too well-known to need comment. Watsonian behaviorism implicitly rejected volition by refusing to accept introspective evidence; intentions did not matter because they were not observable. In Skinner's (1969) perspective, which is anointed as a personality theory regardless of his explicit rejection of the concept of personality, the adherence to mechanistic explanations is reflected in many ways. He approvingly mentioned Loeb's concept of tropism, flatly denied human freedom in favor of strict determinism, and believed that the "environment somehow or other *forced* the organism to behave" (p. 3).

Explicit rejection of volition, such as Skinner's, is relatively rare in psychological literature; Kimble and Perlmuter's (1970) article in the *Psychological Review* stands out as an exceptional attempt to clearly reject volition and offer a mechanistic alternative. As noted by Gilbert (1970), "the topic of will virtually vanished from the psychological texts in the 1930s. This happened either silently, or will was declared to lie outside the province of psychology...mainly in the legal profession, needing justification for punishing criminal acts" (p. 52). It was the philosopher Ryle (1949) who was most vocal—sometimes deliberately abusive as he put it—in rejecting the Myth of Final Causes. He poked fun at the concept of will by calling acts of volition "occult thrusts," and by branding the concept of human agency a "ghost in the machine" (p. 17). Although direct influence of Ryle's work on psychology is not readily visible, it looks as if he effectively helped bury the ghost. The machine metaphor rules supreme; its reign is strengthened by the increasing promise of robotics and computer technology. Terms like *conation* and *volition* have now almost completely disappeared from psychological discourse. The question as to what prompts people to action has not been dissolved, however; the volition part of the trilogy of mind simply metamorphosed and appeared for a few decades under a new label called *motivation*. According to Hilgard (1987), despite the efforts of the famous Nebraska Symposium on Motivation to keep the issue alive, interest in motivation faded with the rise of cognitivism (pp. 378–379).

The issue of motivation is inextricably concerned with the search for causes, but modern psychologists have, by and large, avoided the problem of causality. Although Rychlak (1981), Winston (1985) and few others have recently tried to rekindle interest in causality, they have not attracted many followers. It is tempting to attribute the century of neglect of the causality issue to psychology's commitment to empiricism. Hume, we may recall, had pointed out that causes, like intentions, are not observable. Psychologists are not likely to seriously examine the issue of causality so long as they stay committed to Humean empiricism, which has become a part and parcel of the world view of science.

Be that as it may, as far as personality theorists are concerned, existentialists Allport and Erikson are exceptions to the general trend toward either rejecting or neglecting the issue of volition. For existential psychologists, being a freely choosing moral agent is the essence of being human. Allport often sided with the existentialists and relentlessly criticized the behaviorists for their reactive view of human beings, while asserting the need to emphasize the proactive aspects of human behavior. For Erikson, autonomy and initiative are crucial aspects of human development. Yet, Erikson, like the existentialists, was generally marginalized in North American psychology; the idea of volition implicit in his work remains at the fringe (at best).

Nomothetic Versus Idiographic

Science, we are told, is *nomothetic*; it seeks to formulate laws that hold everywhere at all times. It is this universalist vision that helped Newton formulate the laws of motion. Equipped with the knowledge of universal and timeless laws of nature, we can not only build bridges on earth, but also send robots to the moon and beyond. From the nomothetic point of view, there is no need to single out any specific individual as a special case; each and every one of us is equally subject to the same inexorable timeless laws. When Allport proposed that persons are necessarily unique and deserve to be understood in their own terms, critics like Bills were apparently incensed, for in their view, the unique had no place in science. In the 1950s, Eysenck (1952; 1954) asserted the nomothetic viewpoint by invoking a medieval scholastic dictum, *scientia non est individuorum*—science does not deal with individual cases. In his view, a particular individual is "simply the point of intersection of a number of quantitative variables" (Eysenck, 1952, p. 18). According to Eysenck, a psychologist equipped with the knowledge of universal and timeless laws of the interaction of relevant variables can deal with unique individuals as effectively as an engineer can deal with a particular bridge or building with the help of Newtonian physics. So, there was no need to understand a unique person in terms of her or his own unique perspective on the world.

In the 1960s the idiographic–nomothetic debate continued, this time in the context of the controversy over clinical versus statistical prediction. Holt (1962) asserted that laws of probability as understood and applied by actuaries are good enough for the psychologist's business of prediction of individual behavior. Holt ridiculed Allport's appeal for understanding unique individuals from their own vantage point by declaring that "understanding is a subjective effect aimed at by artists, not scientists" (p. 389). In response to this nomothetist claim, Allport argued that an actuarial prediction (such as the one that specifies the percentage of passengers that will die in traffic accidents in the upcoming holiday season) is of no use to John Doe, who is concerned about his own safety and survival, not about the accuracy of actuarial predictions.

Particularity of persons is important not simply in the sense that each person is unique and unmistakably identifiable by distinctive features like thumb impressions; it is important because each person exists in a particular social niche that matters to him or her. As the existentialist Heidegger noted, each person—or *dasein* in his terminology—is born in a particular place, within a particular historical and social context. What is most relevant to a given person is not cosmic space and eternal time, but only the sphere that he or she cares about and that over a time span, extends only to the memorable past and foreseeable future. For a socially alienated person like Camus's *Outsider*, it does not matter much if he kills a stranger on the beach or if he is thrown in jail. Such things as duty, guilt, or punishment matter only to those who think and feel about their relationships with others, not to hardened psychopaths who do not care. Also, rights and responsibilities, which is what personhood is about, belong to particular persons. Only particular persons who have paid membership dues can vote in a society's elections, not just anybody; only that person who was witnessed while committing a crime may be punished for that particular criminal act. Ethicolegal matters are unmistakably idiographic, unlike scientific laws, which are equally unmistakably nomothetic.

Analytic Versus Synoptic

An important advance in science was made when the pioneering chemist Robert Boyle (1627–1691) distinguished between a chemical element and a compound. Whereas analysis of matter into subatomic particles and forces has helped unleash atomic energy for destruction as well as construction, chemical synthesis has made innumerable synthetic materials available for daily use. Attempts to apply the strategy of molecularization to the study of humans started long before its technological benefits materialized. In Boyle's days, his friend Locke introduced the notion of *simple idea* as the basic element of the contents of mind and knowledge. His strategy was to explain the whole in terms of its parts, complex ideas in terms of simple ones. Prior to the founding of modern psychology, John Stuart Mill spoke of mental chemistry. Ironically, Locke and Mill, who stand out as important architects of Western liberal democracies that enshrine individual rights, also sowed the seeds of molecularism that undermined the essential wholeness of persons within the field of psychology.

Following Mills's notion of molecular chemistry, Wundt searched for the elements of consciousness.[2] Other well-known attempts at molecularization include Angell's idea of functions and the behaviorist conception of stimulus–response psychology. Although Titchener and Angell's molecularist theories have become relics of the past, the behaviorist variety of molecularist analysis continues to be popular today. In the field of personality, analysis is attempted in different ways: in factor analytical models of R. B. Cattell and others that look for clusters of covarying responses to test items and in a large variety of attempts to identify innumerable personality variables. We cannot deny the advantages following from the study of traits or variables, but the question is whether the various forms of molecular analysis can account for personhood that demands consideration as a whole—the answer is no. Indeed, rights and responsibilities, guilt or innocence, reward and punishment are necessarily issues about the person as a whole; it makes no sense to talk about them in connection with parts or elements conceived in any form or shape.

We need to consider analysis (i.e., the division of the whole into parts) as applied not only to specific entities studied at a time, but also to the subject matter of science—nature—as a whole. A highly successful strategy in the natural sciences is to divide nature into convenient segments and their successive subdivisions and assign them to separate disciplines, specialties, and subspecialties. This strategy to divide and conquer has led to increasingly narrower segments of the frontiers of knowledge in which small bands of specialists keep foraying deeper and deeper without being bothered by complexities of the "big picture." A counterpart of this strategy in the field of psychology is the separate treatment of cognition, affect, and motivation. Although the separation of areas has allowed for specialized treatment of these aspects of personhood, it has obscured the essential overlap between them. None of the three aspects occur without the other; it is only for the sake of analytic convenience that we may

---

[2] The direct connection between Mills's mental chemistry and Wundt's experimental psychology is debatable (Danziger, 1980). However, it is quite clear that in *Outlines of Psychology* Wundt (1897) explicitly spoke of psychical elements and compounds in a manner that makes the analogy of chemistry quite transparent (pp. 28–29).

now focus on one, then on another.

Yet, this integrative view of the trilogy of mind is almost completely lost in psychology today. As noted by Hilgard (1980), Piagetians tend to "forget that children's lives are affected by sibling rivalries as well as stages of cognitive growth" (p. 115). Similar other examples can be easily cited. The general tendency in contemporary psychology is to overemphasize a particular aspect to the neglect of others. Moreover, during the past several years the tendency to separate cognition and affect has led to sterile debates over which of the two comes first (Lazarus, 1982, 1984; Zajonc, 1980, 1984).

In theories of personality, overemphasis on particular aspects is common: on affect in psychodynamic theories, on cognition in Kelly's theory, on behavior in behaviorism, and so forth. When, for the sake of convenience of analysis, a particular aspect such as feeling or cognition is emphasized, it is natural that the other aspects are subordinated. Yet, such subordination must be temporary or else it makes the account forever incomplete.

Empiricism and Objectivity Versus Subjectivity

An important part of a standard history of psychology course is the story of Galileo, who challenged the Aristotelians of his time to come and observe Jupiter's satellites rather than deny their existence by authority of the books they read (Russell, 1961, p. 35). Although Galileo's empiricism is exemplary, the application of empiricism to psychology has had problems all along. When Hume set out to observe the inner world of the mind, he looked for the self and candidly reported that his search showed nothing that may be called the self. Implicit in Humean empiricism was the assumption that the self must be an object to be observed rather than a subject (i.e., an observing center of awareness that is not itself observable). In other words, in Humean empiricism, the subject was *objectified*. This tendency toward objectification of the subject matter has become an integral part of empiricist psychology until this day.

During the first decade of the 20th century, introspectionists like Titchener followed Hume in assuming that the mind contained elements that were observable like discrete little objects. Regardless of what else may have gone wrong with introspectionism, its objectification of subjectivity guaranteed its failure. It is the failure of the Titchenerian variety of introspectionism that prompted Watson to reject introspection in any form. This, in turn, led to the loss of respectability of studies of consciousness for decades to come. The so-called failure of introspection entrenched an *extraspective stance* that consolidated psychology's tendency toward objectification. Thus, subsequent to Watson's behaviorist manifesto, the empirical and objective study of persons came to mean observing persons as if they were mere objects, ignoring the fact that they are also experiencing subjects. While studying humans, psychologists talk about things that are externally or publicly observable by them in the world "out there." As a result, psychological discourse on persons gets restricted to *personality* meaning no more than the mask or persona. Thus, in *Behaviorism* Watson (1924/1970) defined personality as "the sum of activities that can be discovered by *actual observation* of behavior over a long enough time to give reliable information" (p. 274, emphasis added).

As Skinner came on the scene, not only the concepts of person and self, but also that of personality were declared redundant. In *About Behaviorism*, Skinner (1974) dismissed each of these concepts as a mere "vestige of animism" (p. 167). The denial of personhood may be traced not only to Bacon's rejection of the final causes, but also to some other aspects of the Baconian legacy. Early empirical studies in psychology, such as those of the Wundtians, were like Baconian *experimenta lucifera*, for they mainly sought illumination. Skinnerian studies, however, were more of *experimenta fructifera*—studies that bear fruit by allowing us to control nature. Bacon believed that humans had a mandate to control God's creation—the world of rivers, trees, animals, and birds—because God made man in His own image. The Skinnerians extend this mandate to control not only objects, rats, and pigeons, but also other human beings.

Empiricism now means that the scientists can rely on their own experience, but they can deny experience and subjectivity among others whom they observe—and wish to control. This is not because their introspective reports are unreliable, but because others are primarily objects to be controlled. As Bakan (1965) correctly pointed out, the mystery complex is a necessary counterpart of the mastery complex. Preserving a mystery about the intentions of the experimenter, as well as the subject, helps the objectification of the subject. Control of other human beings can be carried out with apparent impunity when their reactions are pushed out of sight. Just pretend that those whom you observe and manipulate are objects, not persons. Small wonder, then, that according to Skinner (1974), questions like *"who* will control and to what *end"* are not worth asking (p. 206).

Value Neutrality

An important characteristic of the scientific credo is value neutrality. As noted by Taylor (1980), from its very beginnings in the 17th century, the task of science was thought to be giving an account of the world independent of how it figures in experience, whether desirable or undesirable, valuable or worthless (p. 31). It is an important lesson of the history of science that commitment to values can distort the search for truth, for it is often tempting to see the world as we think it ought to be. This lesson was particularly important in the 1930s, a period in which the Russian agronomist T. D. Lysenko had adopted the Lamarckian principle of the heritability of acquired characteristics, because it was consistent with Marxist ideology. As is well known, Lysenko's politically correct but unscientific policies led Soviet agriculture to ruin. In his book on the notorious Lysenko affair, Joravsky gave long lists of geneticists who were arrested during the 1936 through 1938 period for their politically incorrect views of science. Although it is not possible to make a direct connection between the Lysenko affair in Russian science and the view of science among American psychologists, it may be noted that the relation between knowledge and ideology was a live issue of the 1930s. Note, for instance, that Mannheim's famous book *Ideology and Utopia: An Introduction to the Sociology of Knowledge* was published in 1929 in German and its English translation appeared in 1936. At any rate, it should be hardly surprising if we assume that most psychologists of the late 1930s took it for granted that science must be value free. It makes sense, therefore, that when Bills specified the scientific credo to point out Allport's apparent departure from it, they quibbled over a long list of criteria, but not over the importance of value neutrality.

Allport (1937) made his value-free stance abundantly clear in his pioneering book on personality. In the very chapter in which he discussed the definition of the term *personality*, he strongly advocated the need to keep psychology separate from ethics. For instance, he sounded an alarm against the "mental hygienists" of his time for telling their clients what they "should" or "ought" to do. "Such 'guidance,' " he said, "is not psychology at all; it is pure ethics" (p. 52). Maintaining a sharp division between psychology and ethics, Allport assigned the study of character to ethics, and demanded that psychologists stick strictly to personality. "*Character*" he wrote, "is *personality evaluated*, and *personality* is *character devalued*. Since character is an unnecessary concept for psychology, the term will not appear in this volume" (p. 52). It should now be clear why Allport rejected all the ethicolegal definitions of personhood from his exhaustive historical survey, and focused instead on "definitions that refer to *style of life*, to *modes of adaptation* to one's surroundings, to *progressive growth* and development and to *distinctiveness*" (p. 47).

It may be argued that "progressive growth" is a matter of value as well and as such is inconsistent with Allport's value-free stance in defining personality. In response, I note that such inconsistency simply betrays Allport's strong concern for ethics, regardless of his posturing of value neutrality in keeping with ideas of political correctness at the time of writing. At any rate, the point I wish to make here is neither that psychology should re-introduce the term character, nor that we ought to be moralistic. There is no need to unlearn the lessons from the Lysenko affair or from the fate of psychology in China's cultural revolution. The problem is that in trying to keep values from interfering with objective fact-finding, psychologists have forgotten that human beings are concerned with the ideas of right and wrong, whether we like it or not. We cannot simply ignore the pervasive human tendency to assign credit and blame to actions and disregard the ethicolegal concept of personhood. To substitute personality for person is to throw away the baby with the bath water.

ON RESTORING PERSONHOOD TO ITS LEGITIMATE PLACE IN PSYCHOLOGY

It would be foolish to completely reject the application of natural science perspectives to psychology, for there are aspects of human nature that are explainable in terms of physics and biology. Cognitive psychology and evolutionary psychology will, no doubt, advance that cause. Physics and biology give us explicit metaphors for the study of humans—

machine and animal. The term *person*, by definition, designates those aspects of a human being whereby he or she is *not* a thing or an animal. The domain of personhood begins where that of physics and biology ends.

I shall not quibble here over the desirability of restoring the study of personhood to the mainstream of psychology; I would rather presume its legitimacy. No doubt the cognitive scientists and other enthusiasts of *Naturwissenschaften* (or the natural science approach) will oppose such a stand or ridicule it as regression to the level of folk psychology. Yet, as long as we live in a civil society regulated by law and a system of rewards and punishments, psychology will be incomplete without an adequate account of personhood. Indeed, under the influence of behaviorism, psychologists labored for half a century working out the laws of reinforcement, which in common language, means reward and punishment. Yet, behaviorists ignored the values that justify rewarding certain behaviors and punishing others. There is no reason to bury our heads in the sand when the issue of values arises. Again, this does not mean that we must give up the distinction between psychology and ethics and be moralistic. It simply means that we recognize humans as beings with rights and responsibilities capable of comprehending, creating, revising, following, as well as breaking norms of right and wrong—whatever they might be in a given community at a given time. Keeping this in mind, we should be able to find a place in our discipline for the study of those psychological processes that are involved in becoming and remaining part of a social ethos.

If the traditional rationale connecting personhood with the trilogy of mind is of any value, then the study of personhood implies the study of relevant aspects of cognition, affect, and volition. This suggests the usefulness restoring the trilogy in some form, in a way that it avoids past mistakes—like conceiving them as faculties, or placing them in separate compartments. We can think of the three processes as convenient fictions or heuristic devices without reifying them, or granting them ontic status. Granted that cognition and emotion continue to be topics of study, we may try to make sure that they are studied in a manner relevant and useful for the study of personhood.

The study of cognition in relation to moral judgment, along the lines of Piaget and Kohlberg, is clearly relevant in view of the ethicolegal concept of personhood. However, it must be noted that, given the inevitable interdependence of cognition, affect, and volition, overemphasis on moral reasoning, without attention to attendant emotions and subsequent action, makes such studies incomplete. It is hard to say whether the universalist conception of moral reasoning implied in Piaget and Kohlberg's approach is adequate; perhaps greater emphasis on the understanding of local moral order is needed. As pointed out by Solomon (1983), it is important to recognize the relation between emotions and values (pp. 267–270). Of the emotions, shame and guilt are clearly the most relevant emotions from an ethicolegal viewpoint. These emotions have been rightly considered inner sources of regulation of behavior. They were once the focus of psychoanalytical studies, and in Erikson's model, they are considered important in the development of personality in childhood. Whereas finding a place for the study of these emotions in psychology may not be a formidable job, restoring volition to a central place may call for a revolution.

Restoring volition implies accepting human agency, which in turn implies giving up what James called "hard determinism." There are some relatively recent trends of thought that point in this direction. For instance, back in the mid-1960s Popper (1966) elegantly pointed out how a position of hard determinism amounts to a hopeless fatalism. In the mid-1970s Rychlak (1977) tried to show how purposive behavior—or *telesponsivity* as he called it—can be conceptualized within the framework of a rigorous (as opposed to sloppy) humanism. More recently, in *Personal Being: A Theory for Individual Psychology*, Harré (1983) demonstrated how human agency can be conceptualized within a philosophically sophisticated framework. Most recently, Ansoff (1993) discussed, in an article in *Theory and Psychology*, finding a home for a psychology of volition. More instances of this type can certainly be found. If the trend continues, we will have an appropriate psychology of personhood.

If the naturalistic Zeitgeist was chiefly responsible for the disregard for personhood even among the strong upholders of *Geisteswissenschaften* (or the human science approach), like Allport in the yesteryears, then a major shift away from it is likely to be conducive to its restoration. The decline of positivism, combined with an interpretive turn in the social sciences, and the rise of constructionism and hermeneutics are perhaps the signs of change of Zeitgeist in that direction. Yet, we must also recognize countercurrents in the form of the increasing popularity of evolutionary psychology, cognitive science, and artificial intelligence. Regardless of which way the winds of Zeitgeist will blow, we may assert our belief in freedom and human agency. For, in the will to so believe, lies the true mark of personhood.

ACKNOWLEDGMENTS

I wish to thank Sue Driedger and Randal Tonks for their valuable suggestions on a previous draft of this paper.

REFERENCES

Allport, G. W. (1937). *Personality: A psychological interpretation*. New York: Henry Holt.

Allport, G. W. (1940). The psychologist's frame of reference. *Psychological Bulletin*, *37*, 1–28.

Allport, G. W. (1960a). Personality: Normal and abnormal. In G. W. Allport, *Personality and social encounter* (pp. 155–156). Boston: Beacon.

Allport, G. W. (1960b). Prejudice in modern perspective. In G. W. Allport, *Personality and social encounter* (pp. 219–235). Boston: Beacon.

Allport, G. W., & Vernon, P. E. (1931). A test for personal values. *Journal of Abnormal and Social Psychology*, *26*, 231–248.

Allport, G. W., Vernon, P. E., & Lindzey, G. (1959). *A study of values*. Boston: Houghton Mifflin. (Original work published by Allport & Vernon, 1931)

Ansoff, R. (1993). Finding a home for a psychology of volition. *Theory and Psychology*, *3*, 323–336.

Bakan, D. (1965). The mystery-mastery complex in contemporary psychology. *American Psychologist*, *20*, 186–191.

Bills, A. G. (1938). Changing views of psychology as a science. *Psychological Review*, *45*, 377–394.

Calkins, M. W. (1900). Psychology as a science of selves. *Philosophical Review*, *9*, 490–501.

Danziger, K. (1980). Wundt and the two traditions of psychology. In R. W. Rieber (Ed.), *Wilhelm Wundt and the making of a science of psychology* (pp. 73–87). New York: Plenum.

Eysenck, H. J. (1952). *The scientific study of personality*. London: Routledge & Kegan Paul.

Eysenck, H. J. (1954). The science of personality: Nomothetic. *Psychological Review*, *61*, 339–342.

Gilbert, A. R. (1970). Whatever happened to the will in American psychology. *Journal of the History of the Behavioral Sciences*, *6*, 52–58.

Harré, R. (1983). *Personal being: A theory for individual psychology*. Oxford, England: Basil Blackwell.

Hilgard, E. R. (1980). The trilogy of mind: Cognition, affection and conation. *Journal of the History of the Behavioral Sciences, 16*, 107–117.

Hilgard, E. R. (1987). *Psychology in America: A historical survey*. New York: Harcourt Brace.

Holt, R. R. (1962). Individuality and generalization in the psychology of personality: An evaluation. *Journal of Personality, 30*, 377–402.

Jones, W. T. (1969). *A history of Western philosophy: Hobbes to Hume* (2nd ed.). New York: Harcourt Brace.

Kant, I. (1987). *Critique of judgment* (W. S. Pluhar, Trans.). Indianapolis: Hackett. (Original work published 1790)

Kimble, G. A., & Perlmuter L. C. (1970). The problem of volition. *Psychological Review, 77*, 361–384.

Lazarus, R. S. (1982). Thoughts on the relations between emotion and cognition. *American Psychologist, 37*, 1019–1024.

Lazarus, R. S. (1984). On the primacy of cognition. *American Psychologist, 37*, 124–129.

Locke, J. (1959). *An essay concerning human understanding* (Vols. 1–2) (A. C. Fraser, Ed.). New York: Dover. (Original work published 1690)

MacDougall, W. (1923). *Outline of psychology*. New York: Scribners.

Mannheim, K. (1936). *Ideology and utopia: An introduction to the sociology of knowledge*. New York: Harcourt Brace. (Original work published 1929)

Popper, K. R. (1966). *Of clouds and clocks: An approach to the problem of rationality and the freedom of man*. St. Louis, MO: Washington University.

Reid, T. (1975). Of identity. In J. Perry (Ed.), *Personal identity* (pp. 107–112). Berkeley, CA: University of California Press. (Original work published 1785)

Russell, B. (1961). *Religion and science*. London: Oxford University Press. (Original work published 1935)

Rychlak, J. F. (1977). *The psychology of rigorous humanism*. New York: Wiley.

Rychlak, J. F. (1981). *Introduction to personality and psychotherapy* (2nd ed.). Boston: Houghton Mifflin.

Ryle, G. (1949). *The concept of mind*. Harmondsworth, England: Penguin.

Skinner, B. F. (1969). *Contingencies of reinforcement*. New York: Appleton-Century-Crofts.

Skinner, B. F. (1974). *About behaviorism*. New York: Knopf.

Solomon, R. C. (1983). *The passions: The myth and nature of human emotion*. Notre Dame, IN: University of Notre Dame Press. (Original work published 1976)

Taylor, C. (1980). Understanding in human science. *Review of Metaphysics, 34*, 3–23.

Trendelenberg, A. (1910). A contribution to the history of the word person. *The Monist, 20*, 336–363. (Original essay written 1870)

Watson, J. B. (1970). *Behaviorism*. New York: Norton. (Original work published 1924)

Winston, A. S. (1985). The use and misuse of Aristotle's four causes in psychology. In S. Bem & H. Rappard (Eds.), *Studies in the history of psychology and the social sciences: Vol. 4. Proceedings of the 1985 conference of CHEIRON, European society for the history of the behavioral and social sciences* (pp. 90–103). Leiden, Netherlands: Psychologish Instituut van de Rijksuniversiteit Leiden.

Wundt, W. (1897). *Outlines of psychology.* (C.H. Judd, Trans.). Leipzig: Wilhelm Engelmann.

Zajonc, R. B. (1980). Feeling and thinking: Preferences need no inferences. *American Psychologist, 35,* 151–175.

Zajonc, R. B. (1984). On the primacy of affect. *American Psychologist, 39,* 117–123.

CHAPTER 4

A Constitutive Understanding of Persons

Leendert P. Mos
University of Alberta
Edmonton, Alberta

Words are wise men's counters...but they are the money of fools.
—Thomas Hobbes, *Leviathan* (chap. 4, p. 18)

"Where there is power," wrote Michel Foucault (1976/1980), "there is resistance, and yet, or rather consequently, this resistance is never in a position of exteriority in relation to power" (p. 94). The pretext for what follows is in radical resistance to current scientific mythology in the strong sense that adherence to this view of knowledge leaves us mystified—the power of which is exemplified in Hobbes' nominalism which pervaded all forms of naturalism since the 17th century. However, if Foucault's anti-Cartesianism-cum empiricist, poststructuralism rejects the possibility that any resistance is inspired by something better—that it is "never in a position of exteriority in relation to power,"—the subtext of what follows rejects any such radical discontinuity between historical life orders or human natures. If truth and freedom in human affairs are produced by regimes of power, their unmasking in an "insurrection of subjugated knowledges" presupposes an understanding of the possibility of their transformation "in a move towards greater acceptance of the truth—and, hence, also...a move towards greater freedom" (cited in Taylor, 1984/1985f, pp. 179–180).

What grounds both the pretext and subtext of what follows is a rejection of objectivism, but also any poststructuralist vision of incommensurable life forms in an effort to recover a sense of what it means to become a person. My entry point to this endeavor comes by way of the phenomenon of self-deception, which presupposes an understanding of human nature that shares nothing with the false consciousness that emanates from an objectivist view of persons or a poststructuralist dissolution of our inwardness that would repudiate history in a never-ending quest of self-making. If nothing so presumptuous as an account of persons is attempted here, the implications of the following narrative bear the full weight of a historical, social–cultural sense of personal identity as a moral achievement.

It is not my purpose to engage in criticism, either of science or history. Unlike, for example, de Beauvoir (1949) who, in her devastating analysis of patriarchal mythology, polemically contrasted the fixed essence of mythical femininity with the diversity of flesh-and-blood women, such criticism is beyond the scope of this chapter. Moreover, such criticism of science and history is readily available elsewhere. Nevertheless, de Beauvoir's deep sympathy with women's plight under patriarchy—she wrote that, "overburdened, submerged, she becomes a stranger to herself because she is a stranger to the rest of the world" (p. 353)—may readily be echoed of the person under domination of a scientific model of human nature that has reigned, in various guises, since the time Hobbes deemed words to be "wise men's counters...but...the money of fools" (cited in Taylor, 1980/1985b, p. 249). Surely, de Beauvoir's indignation and outrage to the damage suffered by women under patriarchy is no less appropriate to the mutilation inflicted in our understanding of persons in psychology. Therefore, just as de Beauvoir lamented women's struggle to reconcile the contradictory demands of patriarchy which, on her existentialist view split off consciousness from the body, so must we lament any objectivist vision and its fragmented explanations of persons that is the achievement of science.

Of course, the latter was also Foucault's lament as he argued the savagery of domination by way of our institutions and practices, calling for "experimentation on ourselves" in a "sacrifice of the subject of knowledge" (cited in Taylor, 1984/1985f, p. 175). Yet, his was a lament without redemption; indeed, our victimization demands of us, in elaborate disguises, our collaboration. We are necessarily participants in the mechanism and techniques of discourses that manufacture truth and freedom, but the purported incommensurability of regimes of power, and the absence of any possibility of their transformation, can only enclose culture and history on itself. Neither culture nor history is of any significance to individual human activity. Without the possibility of understanding the patterns of history in relation to our individual human actions, desires, interests, and purposes, resistance, and the unmasking of illusions, however insightful, will not move us beyond where we are. As expositor of the human sciences, Dilthey, well-understood, the power of language can only be sustained in a continuous renewal of its individual expressions. Only in our interpretative articulation and understanding of life expressions do we constitute ourselves as persons; only in an understanding of the workings of history, is there the possibility of self-understanding and, therefore, any sense in resisting the workings of history in a move toward truth (e.g., Dilthey, cited in Rickman, 1976, pp. 170–245).

DECEIVING OURSELVES

It is our identity as persons and, therefore, also our sense of freedom, responsibility, and truth, that is at stake in the possibility of our being deceived by ourselves. In a remarkably prescient account of self-deception, Fingarette (1969) maintained that the paradox of self-deception—namely that the self-deceiver "in his heart" knows what he "sincerely denies"—has been sustained by an epistemological tradition that would appeal to belief and knowledge as well as to a moral conception that "ignorance exculpates" and "knowledge inculpates" (p. 136). Fingarette is one of those philosophers who would reposition the "cognition-perception family of terms" belonging to this tradition, notably all those terms belonging to the term *conscious* and its variants, within a more comprehensive "volitional-action" framework. From within this framework, Fingarette then unraveled the paradox of self-deception by reformulating it as a problem of becoming conscious (p. 34). Although he does not say so, this shift reflects a repudiation of the priority of the epistemological subject (Taylor, 1995) and, by implication, an adherence to an expressivist theory of language and an anthropology founded in a conception of personal agency (e.g., Taylor, 1977/1985a, 1983/

1985d).

From within this volitional-action framework, Fingarette's (1969) explication of self-deception begins with the "mystery" at the "center of Western philosophy," of becoming conscious. "I propose," he wrote, "a different model of explicit consciousness, that is, that we turn to a different but reasonably coherent set of imagery, metaphor, and idiom, in terms of which we shall portray what it is for us to be explicitly conscious of something" (p. 38). This different model is one of the "skill of saying what we are doing or experiencing," a purposive activity of the "exercise of the skill of spelling out" some "feature of the world as we are engaged in it." To spell out, "in close analogy to linguistic activity," is to become explicitly conscious and, conversely, in not spelling out one fails to become explicitly conscious of one's engagements—one's doing and experiences (p. 39). The failure to spell out one's engagements is, Fingarette claimed, the most visible feature of self-deception (p. 66), presumably to others.

Yet, failing to spell out one's engagements and so not becoming explicitly conscious of the manner in which one lives, is merely the most visible feature of self-deception because the more "fundamental maneuver" of not doing so is the "disavowal" of one's engagements as one's own. That is, self-deception turns on what Fingarette termed "personal identity," in becoming a person, as distinct from being an individual (p. 66). The emergence of personal identity in the course of individual development is an achievement of those purposive activities of avowal or disavowal, the expressions of which are evident in spelling out (or not) our individual engagements. Becoming a person—attaining a sense of personal identity   is then an achievement of a particular use of language in avowing those engagements as one's own. To avow one's engagements as one's own is to acknowledge, in both an enabling and capacity sense, those engagements as belonging to oneself as the agent of those engagements.

Fingarette (1969) distinguished between avowal as an inner act and its expression of spelling out as an outer act. He wrote that "overt conduct may manifest but cannot be an avowal or disavowal...the relation is analogous to that between the conduct which manifests a decision and the decision itself" (p. 71). If what is seemingly retained in this formulation is a distinction between the inner and outer, which is a remnant of the old cognition–perception framework, Fingarette also recognized that what is intrinsic to identity in becoming a person is the capacity for spelling out that identity, a capacity that assumes the "exercise [of] a peculiar authority, an authority intimately associated with one's existence as a particular person" (p. 72). Thus, typically, a person would deny any responsibility for those engagements that are disavowed while presumably acknowledging responsibility for those engagements avowed as belonging to oneself, to one's personal identity, and assuming the person values responsibility, to one's moral integrity (pp. 73–74).

Because the move into self-deception is understood in relation to personal identity, Fingarette claimed that self-deception is in a "genuine sense a subversion of personal agency." Or given that personal identity relies on that "peculiar authority" that permits persons to spell-out their identity and, assuming this includes an avowal of responsibility for their engagements, self-deception is a subversion of their moral integrity as well (p. 141). However, Fingarette warned that we must not confuse the movement in and out of self-deception with the movement in and out of responsibility. In the case of the former, we are concerned with personal identity; in the case of the latter, our concern is with moral integrity. If, in practice, we assume responsibility for what we avow, in the course of individual development, we might find that, for example, children are personal agents in having that peculiar authority to spell-out their identity, but they may not (on account of their immaturity) be able to assume responsibility for their avowed engagements. We might also find those who, because they do not express any concern or care for their engagements, also do not accept any responsibility for their engagements but are readily prepared, perhaps precisely because they do not express care or concern, to avow their engagements as their own. In contrast, there are those who are so deeply concerned about the burden of responsibility that they may be tempted, precisely for that reason, to disavow their engagements as their own. Fingarette claimed that moral agency presupposes personal agency, but also that the latter is not sufficient for the former and, of course, this claim dovetails well with his inner and outer distinction between avowal and spelling out. Both distinctions raise some profound questions for Fingarette's conception of spelling out as the most visible feature, and "avowal" as the most characteristic mark of personal identity and integrity, respectively.

Fingarette recognized some of these problems in his attempt to relate self-deception to Kierkegaard's double-mindedness and Sartre's bad faith. On choosing oneself, Kierkegaard maintained that the disparate moments of our individual lives are taken out of their aesthetic immediacy and, in ethical choice, are transformed and integrated into a spiritual unity that is the self. To choose one-self is to become a spiritual being, a unity of mind and body, and in choosing to become one-self one becomes a moral agent capable of accepting responsibility or not. This, in contrast to Sartre's claim that to choose oneself in good faith—in pure reflection— is to act conscious of one's radical freedom to be, and therefore, in choosing, one necessarily suffers the full weight of responsibility for one's choices. Evidently, Fingarette's distinction between personal and moral agency tempered Sartre's view of the person as a conscious being, free to choose and, in doing so, bearing full responsibility for one's choices. Yet, if Fingarette's distinction is more aligned with Kierkegaard's view of the person who, in choosing oneself, becomes prospectively a moral being, Fingarette's (1969) example of the sociopath (p. 148) as one who rejects or fails to understand responsibility but may nevertheless readily avow his engagements as his own, appears to set him at odds with Kierkegaard. If the sociopath, as Fingarette recognized, may be said to posses a "rather limited sense of personal identity," the example is an important one for his claim that self-deception turns on personal agency as distinguished from moral agency (p. 148). For Sartre, the sociopath is in bad faith unless he accepts responsibility for his antisocial engagements, and Fingarette, in his example, would seem to allow for that possibility. For Kierkegaard, the existential attitude of ethical choice, of choosing absolutely, must give way in a suspension of the ethical through faith as a continuing passion of the will to be oneself. Therefore, Kierkegaard conceives of the ethical of moral agency as but a moment in the passion to be one-self characteristic of personal integrity. Any attempt at reconciliation among these three positions on self-deception leads to intimations that becoming conscious allows for qualitative distinctions in spelling out, or in narrating, our personal identity.

It is the discrepancy between an individual's engagements and what he says about his engagements that is (for Fingarette) our access to an understanding of self-deception. Indeed, he claimed that it is this discrepancy that leads others to question a person's sincerity. Thus, the self-deceiver's apparent "insincere sincerity" is due to an ambiguity in the concept of sincerity, one that we may readily come to understand on Fingarette's (1969) view of spelling out as becoming conscious of one's engagements. Because what a person says may be sincere, or may give the impression of sincerity, the question arises of how we are to evaluate these sayings—these spellings-out—or, as Fingarette put the question, how are we to distinguish between "merely saying" and "sincerely saying" (p. 50)? That is, Fingarette recognized that not all saying is spelling out, and so, the question that is posed concerns the criteria that would enable others to judge when a person's sayings are indeed a spelling out of his engagements and therefore understood as sincere and when his sayings are not a spelling out his engagements and therefore understood as insincere.

In laying out the criteria of sincerity, Fingarette (1969) sets aside the common ascription of sincerity in terms of conformity between a person's engagements and his spelling out of his engagements. That is, the failure of such conformity, although suggestive of insincerity and, perhaps, self-deception, is not necessarily intentional or purposive and, therefore, on Fingarette's account self-deception is intentional and the apparent failure of conformity cannot be criterial of self-deception. One might have expected that Fingarette's volitional-action framework might have precluded any consideration of such a criterion of sincerity that, after all, relies on a comparison of one's spellings out with one's engagements and is therefore exemplary of the epistemological tradition he rejected. In any case, according to Fingarette, what we always mean when we ascribe sincerity "is conformity between what a person tells us and what he tells himself" (p. 52).

The ambiguity in the notion of sincerity is due to its having different criteria of fulfilment. Fingarette (1969) mentioned three criteria such that, when jointly fulfilled, they justify the ascription of sincerity and, when not, they justify the ascription of insincerity and possibly self-deception. The three criteria are (1) conformity between how a person spells out to his engagements for himself and others, (2) accuracy with respect to how a person spells out his engagements to himself, and (3) not being unintentionally wrong in the manner in which a person comes to spell out his engagements. It is important to note, even as Fingarette did not, that all three criteria essentially depend on our linguistic practices, that is, on the manner in which we spell out our engagements (p. 52). Even the notion of accuracy depends, because there is no comparison between language and the world (cf. Mos & Boodt , 1992), on how others would spell out a person's engagements (if they were so engaged). Accuracy, much like sincerity itself, is a communal affair, something I return to later. For now, an ascription of a deeper sincerity is justified, according to Fingarette, when Criteria 1 and 3 hold good, but Criterion 2 does not. Thus, when the self-deceiver tells others what he spells out for himself (and he is not unintentionally wrong in the manner of doing so), he gives the impression of sincerity. Yet, because he does not spell out his engagements accurately or in a manner that others might spell out his engagements as if they were so engaged, he gives the impression that the "story he is giving both himself and us is not unintentionally wrong but purposely wrong" (Fingarette, 1969, p. 53). Arguably, such sincere insincerity is then a judgment made of one who is self-deceived.

Fingarette's explication of the ambiguity of sincerity relied on an understanding of spelling out as being highly selective and purposefully at variance with how, in fact, the person is engaged. Evidently, this purpose need not be itself spelled out, just as the reasons for not accurately spelling out one's engagements may remain and, presumably, in the case of self-deception, are unarticulated. Consistent with his proposal that consciousness resides essentially in our articulatory practices, Fingarette relied on a preconceptual or pretheoretic and hence prelingual capacity of appraising one's engagements. However, the question arises as to how we are to understand this prereflective level of appraisal that is presumably reflexive with regard to our experienced engagements. In other words, how are we to understand the inner experience as lived, in relation to the outer as articulated or spelled out in consciousness of personal identity?

What is at stake in Fingarette's explication of self-deception—or better, his explication of self-deception as turning on an understanding of personal identity—is the adequacy of his conception of the volitional-action framework. In adopting this framework, Fingarette was not merely advocating a preference for one family of terms for another, rather in adopting this framework, he was reframing the conditions of our understanding of persons. In recent years, Taylor (e.g., 1989), perhaps more than anyone else, challenged our historical conception of human nature that would ground a perception–cognition epistemology. In particular, Taylor's (1995) critique of the received view of epistemology may be understood as a form of an immanent critique in an effort to recover a volitional-action conception of human nature that would serve the human sciences in a comprehensive vision of moral life (cf. Mos, 1996).

SIGNIFICANCE AND EMBODIMENT

Fundamental to this vision of moral life is a self-interpreting view of persons. Taylor was one of those who, in the tradition of Hegel (Taylor, 1975) and, later, Dilthey (1800–1890/1989a) began with what he termed the *agent's knowledge*. It is the notion that we are capable of understanding ourselves, our actions, desires, and intentions, in a way that is very different from the external view of an observer. However, this capacity for self-understanding is mediated through forms of expression. Prominent among these is the capacity to express ourselves in language; the interpretative understanding of these is constitutive of our personal identity. In the expressions of how we find ourselves—in how we are engaged—we transform, using Dilthey's language, our "reflexive understanding" of "lived experience" in a reflective articulation of our engagements (retaining Fingarette's word), and so become conscious of our thoughts, desires, feelings, purposes and actions. Knowledge of ourselves, in Taylor's view, is mediated by way of our expressions, such that our understanding of those expressions is not merely a way of becoming conscious of our engagements, but constitutive in realizing and clarifying our engagements.

Taylor (1983/1985d) directly confronted the question of what it is to become a person. He wrote, "A person is a being who has a sense of self, has a notion of future and past, can hold values, make choices, in short, can adopt life plans." A necessary condition for being a person is that it is "a being with his own point of view of things...who can be addressed and who can reply." Thus, what is characteristic of being a person, of being a "respondent," Taylor continued, is that "things matter to it in an original way;" persons as agents respond out of an original significance of things (p. 97). Among these matters of significance there are some that are "peculiarly human," and no agent could be sensitive to these peculiarly human significances that was not able to formulate them. It is in their formulation, or articulation, of peculiarly human significances that persons are distinguished from other agents. It is in the articulation of these peculiarly human significances that we become conscious of them and, indeed, that they are constituted. In our understanding of them, we are constituted as persons.

Taylor recognized that we cannot merely assert that persons are self-interpretative beings, and his own expository efforts to understand this claim all converged on the idea that psychic life can be understood only in the significations of our expressions. Our understanding of all that is inner of psychic life is constituted in those significations that are them-selves inescapably embodied as part of the texture of social and cultural life. Dilthey, in following Hegel, but shorn of metaphysical grounding, made much the same point, namely that our conception of mental life as much as our conception of the physical world emerges in a transforma-tion—in a reflective articulation—of our lived experience. A similar con-ception of our self-interpretative capacities is found in Husserl's later exposition of intentionality from within the context of the lived world. Whether from within a hermeneutical or phenomenological tradition, the concern is to derive our understanding of persons, including the so-cial and cultural life of persons together, from a more fundamental no-tion of agency. Differences among these positions are evident in their respective philosophical aims and starting points, but there is agreement that it is our capacity as agents, living out of the significances of our lives, that constitutes the necessary context from within which we ar-ticulate an understanding of who we are as persons.

There is an apparent circularity in this conception of understanding our lived experience. Dilthey initially wrote of it as a reflexive under-standing given together with lived experience. Only later, after resuming his intensive study of Hegel (Ermarth 1978; Makkreel, 1992) did he come to a full appreciation of his hermeneutical tradition—the understanding of lived experience is mediated not only in an imaginative reflection of the understanding of the expressions of lived experience in language, but also in all those social and cultural practices that characterize the historical world. It is the recognition that our self-understanding is me-diated by our participation in and understanding of the social–cultural world that signals Dilthey's hermeneutical turn away from a descriptive psychology—conceived of as foundational to the human sciences—to a conception of psychology as belonging to the human sciences, methodologically grounded in a hermeneutical conception of life.

If Dilthey's conception of expression is to be understood with reference to lived experience, namely the purposive structure of the "acquired psychic nexus" (Dilthey 1894/1977), this conception of expression owes much to Hegel's conception of "mind" as, citing Taylor (1983/1985e), "thoroughgoing activity" (p. 77). Mind as activity is a notion that is inseparable from its articulation and understanding as purposive or a notion in which "its articulation as a purpose exists in animating this action." This "basic, not further reducible distinction between action and what just happens is indispensable and ineradicable from our self-understanding as agents" (p. 79). The directness of activity—its sense of having a purpose—is part of what we mean by agency. Dilthey's recognition that lived experience is reflexively understood is captured in Hegel's claim that agents already have a sense of what they are doing, the articulation of which brings it to consciousness and thus, explicit understanding.

In founding our conception of the person in the notion of agency, Hegel not only overcame the dualism of mind and body (of the inner and the outer), but also formulated a conception of knowledge, including self-knowledge, that was mediated by an effort to articulate in language (in conceptual thought) our inarticulate sense or significance of our daily lives. Our articulation of our lived experience—of our lived world—in language is itself embodied (as a social praxis) in the activity of speaking. Moreover, in bringing the sense of our activities to significance in speech and therefore to consciousness, we transform those activities and experiences in bringing their inarticulate sense of purpose to explicit formulation. In so doing, the realization of their meaning and significance is never merely a privilege of the individual but belongs to the community of speakers.

One of the implications of a conception of mind as thoroughgoing activity (of agency) is that the mental is constituted in an inward reflection of what was originally external. The mental thereby becomes a category of activity, prominently, the activity of speaking. The *furniture of the mind*, as Taylor coined this phrase, is not a psychic datum of mental life, but constituted in a reflective understanding of our life expressions, embodied and fully situated in the world. Reposing on Dilthey's formulation, there is a distinction here between reflexive understanding of lived experience and the reflective expression of this experience first and fore-most in articulation as dialogically between us. This distinction goes over into Taylor's (1983/1985e) distinction, borrowed from Hegel, between the "effective" and "expressive" (pp. 87–88) aspects of our self-under-standing, in which the effective realization of our lives as lived is the basis for the expressive articulation of our lives as we come to under-stand ourselves, others, and the world in which we live.

Hegel conceived our self-understanding as something we do, an ac-tivity of reflection wherein we express and so constitute our desires, feel-ings, aspirations, and interests that are part of the ongoing life process or, in Dilthey's terms, "the experience of life." All that belongs to our self-understanding is a gradual achievement mediated in our reflective articulations or, more broadly, expressions. The understanding of these expressions is constitutive of the effective realization of a life process that exceeds our understanding in an ever greater demand for renewed expression and understanding. What is notable in this notion of the mind as activity is not so much its embodiment, which all transcendental per-spectives in some way share, but the absence of transparency and cer-tainty from the reflective understanding of our life expressions.

Moreover, if the genesis of the life of the mind is as it were a precipi-tate of what we are doing, of how we are engaged (especially in our articulations) then the sense of significance of our activities is also trans-formed in articulating their meaning. Coming to conscious understand-ing, as something we do, transforms the implicit significance of these activities in the expressive signification of our language. Tracing its roots to the late 17th century, Taylor (e.g., 1980/1985b) wrote, at length, con-cerning the conception of meaning that was at issue in this notion of language as expression. What is pertinent here is that expressivist theo-ries of meaning recognize expressive activities, as bodily activities that "aim to make plain in public space," Taylor (1983/1985e) wrote, "how we feel, or stand with each other, or where things stand for us" (p. 91). The expressive activity of speaking is not, in the first instance, depend-ent for its meaning (either on its signifying relation to thought or things), but only conceivable on the notion that expression is itself "primitive" (p. 91). That is, the activity of speaking, like that of all other activities, is at first, an unreflective bodily practice that only later attains its clarity in a mutuality of understanding (of signification) that enables us to articulate things for ourselves. So they come to serve as a medium of private thought. Our self-understanding may be conveyed and understood in our speaking of it, but it is constituted (made publicly evident) in our giving expression to it in the medium of language.

Hegel's conception of subjectivity reverses our idea of what it is to be an agent and, therefore, to become a person. The nature of agency—as individuals possessing the capacity for action—only becomes evident in our understanding of the nature of action. Agency is not necessarily restricted to individuals, nor is action necessarily the action of individuals; both may be attributed to our social institutions and cultural practices. Indeed, the achievement of self-understanding attained in our articulatory and discursive practices comes by way of others; not only in our speaking do we appropriate the articulatory practices of others, but we are necessarily participants in all the social–cultural objectifications that are our common heritage. Thus, if a reflexive understanding of life is our access to a conception of agency, then our self-understanding as persons resides in the reflective transformation of this understanding expressed in our discursive practices. Contrary to Hegel, but consistent with Dilthey, such understanding is anything but transparent or certain.

Taylor (1977/1985a) extended his explication of Hegel's fundamental conception of action in an exposition of feeling, emotion, and desire; he wrote, "saying properly what these are like involves expressing or making explicit a judgment about what objects they bear on" (p. 47). In articulating our feelings, emotions, and desires, it is assumed that our experience of these in a particular situation, or on a particular "occasion" (cf. Mos, 1995) of their experience, have an implicit sense of significance of the situation or occasion. "And that is why saying what an emotion is like involves making explicit the sense of the situation it incorporates" (Taylor, 1977/1985a, p. 49) or the sense of the occasion wherein we are engaged such that we do indeed experience the emotion. Thus, our emotions are not simply the manner in which we are moved in the situation; rather, saying what an emotion is like involves making explicit, the act of spelling out in an appraisal of the significance of the occasion of our being moved. On this account, saying what our emotions, feelings, and desires are is essentially dependent on spelling out the inarticulate sense of significance on the occasion of the experience. If the capacity to do so is what we mean by agency, then the manner in which we spell out our appraisals on the occasion in which we are moved may also reflect a deeper understanding of what it is to be a person.

What is distinctive about our being persons, according to Taylor (1977/ 1985a) is the "power of self-evaluation" (p. 16). What such self-evaluation amounts to is the capacity to distinguish the "qualitative worth" of our desires, feelings, emotions, thoughts, and purposes. Taylor wrote that:

> In this kind of case our desires are classified in such categories as higher and lower, virtuous, and vicious, more and less fulfilling, more or less refined, profound, superficial, noble and base. They are judged as belonging to qualitatively different modes of life: fragmented or integrated, alienated or free, saintly, or merely human, courageous or pusillanimous and so on. (p. 16)

What Taylor termed "strong evaluation" of our desires must be articulated in a "contrastive language" that characterizes the alternatives not as a choice among contingently incompatible desires or in terms of their consequences, but in terms of the meaning that is faithful to our reflective articulation of their significance on the occasion in which we are moved. "The strong evaluator," according to Taylor, "envisages his alternatives in a richer language," one wherein he can articulate his reflective choice among incommensurable alternatives in a manner that may well lead to a "conflict of interpretations" (p. 22; cf. Ricoeur, 1969/1974). Strong evaluation is the capacity to reflect on (and so, be more articulate about) our predicament. "So within the experience of reflective choice between incommensurables, strong evaluation is a condition of articulacy, and to acquire a strong evaluative language is to become (more) articulate about one's preferences" (pp. 24–25). Furthermore, to be so articulate about our desires is to evaluate our predicament in "greater depth;" it is to evaluate in a "struggle of interpretations" the moral stature of our identity as persons. "To characterize our desire or inclination as worthier, or nobler, or more integrated, etc. than others is to speak of it in terms of the kind of quality of life which it expresses and sustains" (p. 25).

If strong evaluation is constitutive of our identity as persons, as beings capable of giving expression to those peculiar human experiences of feeling, emotion, and desire that characterize us both in articulacy and depth, such strong evaluation does not preclude a "plurality of ways" of envisaging my predicament.

The choice between incommensurables, between what is higher and lower, is also constitutive of our conception of choice and responsibility. Choice and responsibility are intimately tied to our capacity for strong evaluations (as something we do) as activities bringing clarity to our experience. Our strong evaluations, as Taylor suggested, are "endorsed" and, hence, bear our responsibility, much as Fingarette claimed that we are responsible for those engagements avowed as peculiarly our own. To understand the manner in which strong evaluations imply personal identity, we only have to consider that if we were to repudiate or re-evaluate our strong evaluations, as we might in a renewed reflection on the occasion in which we are moved, or in conversation with someone whose evaluations on the occasion are very different, we may well place our personal identity at risk. If the articulation of the significance on the occasion in which we are moved implies strong evaluation, these may be more or less revealing, more or less faithful, and more or less truthful of how we live. It is in this sense that our articulations, in a struggle of our discursive practices, bear responsibility and suffer our freedom in that, on reflection, we might come to more fully understand ourselves and thus, the occasion in which we are moved or engaged. Freedom is then not for Taylor, as it is for Sartre, a "disengaged freedom" of radical choice, but is inextricably bound up with our capacity for strong evaluations. It is in these articulations of "our sense of what is worthy" (p. 35) that we constitute our moral dilemmas and it is from within our moral dilemmas that we choose—even, as Kierkegaard would, choose absolutely—in a manner that plunges the depth of what constitutes our identity as persons.

LIFE AND HISTORY

It was Dilthey who maintained that although life as lived is individuated and uniquely personal, it is also deeply implicated in the wider coherences of society and culture. According to Dilthey, the "standpoint of life" discloses that we are situated in a complex of relations that are constitutive of our historical world—of life. For Dilthey, life is this complex of social and cultural relations, immediately lived through as ineluctably significant in both its individual and communal dimensions. By writing of the "standpoint of life," Dilthey intended to find his starting point for all understanding of self, other, or the world in our lived experience. Reminiscent of Hegel, and in a tradition to which Taylor also appealed (reaching back through von Humboldt, Schleiermacher, and Herder), Dilthey maintained that we are deeply engaged in life before we come to understand it, and this engagement in life is a precondition for coming to know it (Ermarth, 1978, chap. 6; Makkreel, 1992, chap. 5).

Life is, for Dilthey, pre-eminently a biographical or historical phenomenon and cannot be identified with either consciousness or nature, even as it is grounded in the latter and fulfilled in the former as consciousness of ourselves and the world in which we live. It is from the standpoint of life that we come to know ourselves as temporal–historical beings, narratively relating our past, present, and future in a meaningful coherence of purpose and values. Dilthey maintained that in its temporal course, life as we live it and as we come to know it individually and collectively manifests "diremption," exemplified in the actual concrete oppositions between its transitoriness and the impulse for stability, the forces of nature and autonomy of the human will, and consciousness of finitude and limits and our capacity for transcending those limits. So that life lends us what Dilthey termed *corruptibility*: the "ominous side of our historicity" (Ermarth 1978, p. 115), which is the perpetual sense of incompleteness, frustrated effort, and revision of limits that leads to reflection and understanding, using a poststructuralist phrase, a *vouloir dire*—in wanting to be. According to Dilthey's view, life as lived possesses a structure that is immanently purposive, always moving beyond the present in an ever-expanding possibility of signification, of renewed understanding.

As individuals we participate in life in a special way in that we are engaged in life and, in being so engaged, we are obliged in varying degrees of consciousness and inclusiveness, to assume a particular attitude in and toward life. This attitude is not a theoretical stance, but a vitally interested immersion in life, out of which we come, through an imaginative articulation of how we live, to self-understanding. According to Dilthey, it is from this embodied standpoint in and toward life that one is as certain of the world as one is of oneself. Yet, this certainty is founded in what is an implicit, yet dynamically salient, interpretative standpoint of life. The individual is an inevitable biographical and historical coherence, part of life as a whole, which cannot be dissolved into a natural foundation. Dilthey's claim here is not unfamiliar to postmodern thought, namely that we become unique persons only in the social–cultural and, therefore, historical context with others. Individual life is never closed in on itself, but is continuous with those broader social–cultural coherences of history that characterize human life. This does not mean, as Dilthey came to realize, that these social and cultural coherences are all part of a person's lived experience, or encompassed in that person's reflective articulation and understanding of lived experience—as if the individual person was a microcosm of history. Rather, from birth, the individual is immersed in and appropriates those historical objectifications of our collective meaning, values, and ideals.

It was Dilthey's effort to understand these objectifications, or in a term borrowed from Hegel, *objective mind*, that led him to reformulate his conception of lived experience in a manner that anticipated many contemporary hermeneutical writings. He recentered his focus from a reflexive understanding of lived experience, such that a reflective understanding of lived experience is mediated by way of an understanding of its expressions, privileged among which is language, entirely inflected by social–cultural form. Dilthey (1880–1890/1989a, Bk. 6, Sect. 7) wrote: "In language, life relations are singled out by a process of articulation and form linguistic categories. These categories arise through a heightening of consciousness of life relations, by a process that separates them from the initially, connected whole of life" (p. 449). In this emphasis on the understanding of expressions, Dilthey proposed a dialectical relation between our reflexive, immediate, understanding of lived experience and a reflective discursive understanding of its expressions in what he termed the "experience of life" (Ermarth, 1978, p. 226).

This experience of life is lived experience, realized in a reflective understanding of its expressions as these belong to the social and cultural coherences of meaning and value that is their historical context. In fact Dilthey, in a move that is reminiscent of poststructuralist thought, maintained that lived experience, as interpreted in an understanding of its expressions, is itself constitutive of the lived experience. This is the process of becoming a person, during which lived experience and the experience of life are mutually implicated in the course of our lives, always reaching beyond the individual of lived experience and beyond our self-understanding in being embedded in those social and cultural significations constitutive of the historical world. Individual lived experience is deepened and expanded in our personal experience of life through a mutually engaged understanding of our articulated expressions and the objectifications of meaning and value that are our effective tradition and heritage.

With this revised conception of lived experience as the experience of life, essentially mediated in an understanding of our expressions, Dilthey suggested, much as Taylor (1980/1985b, p. 263) did in his discussion of the constitutive role of language, that our self-understanding, as indeed all understanding, proceeds through an understanding of others. To appreciate this insight is to appreciate that Dilthey understood history itself in terms of our expressions, namely those objectifications of life—of culture and society—that are constituted in our linguistic practices. In turn, objective mind is the horizon or atmosphere in relation to which we constitute our self-understanding as persons (see Ermarth, 1978, p. 278). Giving special consideration to language as the manifestation of the objective mind, Dilthey stressed that our linguistic practices condition our experience of life as much as experience conditions our discursive practices in giving expression to our lived experience.

It is in our linguistic practices that we constitute our standpoint as persons in and toward life. The reflexive understanding of lived experience is hereby not abandoned, as is so favored by poststructuralist semiotic thought; rather, it is the impenetrable depth of life that can be gauged only in bringing it to consciousness in a reflective understanding of its expressions, and in imaginative—Dilthey stressed here the "poetic"—articulations. Life, including our individual lives, is only available in a hermeneutical reconstituting of the "effective" processes, using Taylor's term in reference to Hegel, of our living it. Our expressions always move beyond their intended meaning in such a manner that they neither present nor represent experience as lived. Rather, our expressions, including our articulations, stand in a dialectical relation to who we are, in our strong evaluations, as persons. Our self-understanding is resolutely mediated by way of what is articulated as other, thus participating in what is common yet appropriating of what is unique.

As might be expected, Dilthey's understanding of choice and responsibility appeals to our capacity to respond to a multiplicity of possibilities, as these are mediated in our articulations of lived experience. Freedom is related to our self-understanding as persons, as the experience of responsibility not merely in our conscious accountability to others, but also as regret for one's own expression and interpretative understanding of those expressions. From the standpoint of life, we know ourselves to be both conditioned and unconditioned. We are conditioned and responsible in the manner of our expressions—our reflective articulation of experience—and unconditioned and responsible in an interpretation and re-articulation of those expressions in a renewed understanding that inescapably bears our responsibility in an emerging achievement of what Dilthey termed "character." Neither fate or necessity, nor the unlimited freedom of radical choice, but rather our freedom to choose comes to consciousness in those meaningful and valued expressions in which understanding in mutuality with others mediates our self-understanding in a constitutive movement to personal identity.

OTHERS ON DECEIVING OURSELVES

It was part of Fingarette's (1969) thesis on self-deception that "generally speaking, the particular features of an individual's engagement in the world need not be, and usually are not spelled out by him" (p. 40). The claim is that we are not generally explicitly conscious of our engagements, or features of our engagements, such as our aims, motives, attitudes, and purposes and that when we do spell out our engagements and so become explicitly conscious of them, there is special reason for doing so—reasons that presumably pertain to the avowal of our engagements as our own. Conversely, to not spell out our engagements is to avoid becoming conscious of them and, supposedly, the reasons for not doing so concern the disavowal of the engagements as our own. Fingarette wrote: "One of the marks which differentiates what is intrinsic to the identity of a person from what is not...is the peculiar capacity for spelling out that identity....It is the exercise of a peculiar authority...intimately associated with one's existence as a particular person" (p. 72). Now, if what is made explicitly conscious in an avowal of personal identity customarily bears the full weight or responsibility—under the assumption that personal identity is constituted in our strong evaluations—what is not spelled out and, hence, disavowed as belonging to personal identity, is necessarily denied the weight of responsibility. Nevertheless, Fingarette distinguished between personal and moral agency, where the latter, but not the former, implies the acceptance of responsibility for one's articulated engagements. The reason is that Fingarette recognized that holding someone responsible in the face of "genuine non-acceptance of responsibility," must fail in the "face of authentic unconcern" (p. 147).

Concerning the person who is self-deceived, Fingarette said that "even when normally appropriate he persistently avoids spelling out some feature of his engagement in the world" (p. 47). Implied here is that the self-deceiver chooses, on the basis of his implicit appraisal, not to spell out his engagement, and yet, he gives us the impression that he could do so, while he gives us the impression that he has somehow rendered himself incapable of doing. That is, either the self-deceiver is silent concerning his engagements or there is a discrepancy between how the self-deceiver is engaged and the manner in which these engagements are spelled out. However so conceived, this discrepancy remains closed in on an individual and may be contrasted with a relational view that depends in an evaluation of self-deception on whether and how others might choose to spell out the self-deceiver's engagements (as if they were so engaged). Fingarette, as we have seen, then tried to dissolve this appearance of insincere sincerity in his explication of the concept of sincerity. The self-deceiver is someone who tells others what he tells himself, and who is not unintentionally wrong about the manner in which he spells out his engagements, yet he somehow fails to spell out his engagements accurately. This state of affairs subverts both his personal identity and moral integrity.

Fingarette's reliance on the role of language in becoming explicitly conscious of how one finds oneself in the world and, hence, in the formation of personal identity, belongs to what Taylor termed the "expressivist" tradition. Thus, Fingarette understood well that in spelling out our engagements we not only bring to consciousness what is lived, but in so doing, we also realize and clarify in making public the manner in which we live, and so give form to our self-understanding. This is perhaps most evident in Fingarette's first criterion of sincerity, namely that there be conformity between what a person tells himself and what he tells others. An evaluation of this conformity essentially depends on the possibility that the articulations of our engagements, including what belongs to our inner life, is constituted within the public domain. In this sense, we may understand Fingarette's claim that spelling out is the most visible feature of avowal. Yet, in retaining too sharp a distinction between avowal and spelling-out, he also remained committed to a view of language that gives priority to a descriptive rather than an expressivist view of language, and thus, too sharp a distinction between the reality of experience and the expression of that reality of experience.

This is perhaps most evident in Fingarette's second and third criteria of sincerity, namely that the individual spells out his engagement such that it correctly reflects that engagement, and that he not be unintentionally wrong in doing so. These two criteria appear to perpetuate a thoroughly modern, epistemological conception of disengaged subjectivity and, in his adherence to the notion that spelling out is making public what is inner, a nominalist view of language as designatory and appellative. Of course, Fingarette clearly recognized that in spelling out, we become explicitly conscious and that the meaning of our articulations is grounded in an implicit sense of how we find ourselves in the world, yet his phenomenological view on the intentionality of experience (e.g., Smith & McIntyre, 1982), retained the descriptive or designatory priority of language. In this sense at least, phenomenology tends to a conception of language that differs little from those rationalist–empiricists who would deem it to be "wise men's counters" and the "money of fools."

Fingarette seemed to adhere, on the one hand, to a conception of intentionality characteristic of our immediacy in the lived world and, on the other, to a view of a language, in spelling out our engagements, that gives primacy to its designatory role in making explicitly conscious what is implicitly lived. However, this is an uneasy position, as many in the phenomenological tradition have come to realize, for in privileging the lived world, he failed to recognize that in our expressions, in our articulatory practices of speaking and understanding, we constitute and are constituted in the social and cultural objectifications of our historical world. (A similar impasse confronts those poststructuralists who would relegate all life to its significations without recourse to a standpoint of life.) It is remarkable that it was these insights that led Dilthey to abandon his descriptive psychology (1894/1977) and its foundational role relative to the other human sciences (1883/1989b) in favor of a hermeneutical understanding of life that was essentially a historical endeavor

(Boodt & Mos, 1993). Dilthey came to realize that our understanding of lived experience and, therefore, our self-understanding, was mediated by an interpretative understanding of its expressions, which were themselves embedded in the social and cultural coherences of historical life. If Dilthey was not, despite following his hermeneutical turn, always explicit about his conception of linguistic meaning, about the role of language, for example, in narrating our experience of life, he always profoundly agreed with von Humboldt's (1836/1988) claim that: "Man lives primarily with objects...as language presents them to him" (p.60). Dilthey understood the constitutive role of language as the finest instance of "reciprocity at work in mental life" (Ermarth, 1978, p. 278). We come to self-understanding in an understanding of our expressions, which are themselves appropriated from and embedded within those structures of objective mind that is our historical world.

It is this constitutive role of language that Taylor (1980/1985c) deemed to be at the core of the expressivist theory of language which, in turn, he made the cornerstone of his anthropology—his conception of persons. It is in the "contrastive web," borrowing von Humboldt's phrase, of language that we constitute, in a reflective articulation and strong evaluation, the contours, limits, and boundaries of those peculiarly human concerns that move us on any particular occasion. However, Taylor (1977/1985a) also retained something of the descriptive in contrast to the constitutive sense of language in his distinction between weak and strong evaluation, with which only the latter is characteristic of conditions of worth. Once we come to recognize that all our reflective articulations give expression to certain "standards" that "cannot be reduced to our behavior being controlled by them" (Taylor, 1980/1985c, p. 262), then it be can said that none of our engagements express such standards, have such meaning or values, unless they are constituted in our linguistic practices. Moreover, their being so constituted, interpreted, and understood is what we mean when we speak of the depth of psychic life or, using Dilthey's term, "character." Therefore if, as Taylor suggested, our capacity for agency requires that things really matter to us in an original way, that our lived experience (our engagements) are in some sense significant, then the reflective and imaginative articulation of those significances is constitutive of our being persons—that is, constitutive of our self-understanding in articulating the kind of person we aspire to be.

Dilthey clearly recognized that in the articulation of lived experience, we constitute our psychic life in becoming conscious of its meaning and value. Fingarette and Taylor both recognized that our capacity for doing so varies considerably and, to that extent, we may also expect our standing with respect to others, as well as our self-understanding, to exemplify those differences. Yet, it is especially Dilthey and Taylor who understood, in their adherence to an expressivist conception of language, that the activity of speaking, in expressing our peculiarly human concerns, opens up a "common vantage point," a public space, wherein our meaning and values are shared: They are now something "entre nous" (Taylor, 1980/1985c, p. 264). This is not making public what is private, as if language were merely a tool for communication, but in articulating our engagements, we constitute (embody) their meaning and value in dialogical or conversational context. Even as individual persons are not enclosed on themselves—Dilthey never relinquished his "lived experience"—the conversational context, our life with others, is always open to the wider social and cultural coherences of the historical life world.

It is from within this standpoint of life (this standpoint of the historical world) that we bring to consciousness our understanding, including our self-understanding as persons. The distinction that Fingarette made between personal and moral agency, as well as Taylor's distinction between weak and strong evaluations, belongs to those standards, or values, that inhere in the contrastive medium of language wherein we constitute the effective temporal course of the meaning of our lives. Avowal and disavowal and, therefore, responsibility and integrity, just as sincerity and insincerity and, therefore, the possibility of our being deceived, does not solely belong to our capacities as agents. Self-deception belongs to our personal identity, as Fingarette understood, but becoming a person belongs to those articulatory practices wherein we come to a conscious understanding of ourselves as a moral expression of social–cultural, historical life.

Finally, Fingarette's distinction between personal agency, or identity, and moral agency, or integrity, depends not on some special inner activity of mind but rather, as in Taylor's strong evaluations, choice, responsibility, and truth are articulated in our linguistic practices. It is in these practices that we constitute such standards and distinctions of meaning and value that are the marks of what is higher and lower in our character. If we distinguish between identity and integrity, as surely we might, such a distinction reflects a reliance on a dualism of disembodied consciousness, the transparency of our articulatory practices, and our disengagement from others. Instead, our self-understanding is deeply embedded in the efficacy of life as lived—in its individual and historical expressions: To live truthfully is to disclose our fidelity to our common, moral purposes.

REFERENCES

de Beauvoir, S. (1949). *The second sex* (H. M. Parshley, Trans.). London: Penguin.

Boodt, C. P., & Mos, L. P. (1993). Hermeneutics of lived experience: The foundations of a historical psychology. In H. J. Stam, L. P. Mos, W. Thorngate, & B. Kaplan (Eds.), *Recent trends in theoretical psychology, Volume III* (pp. 111–122). New York: Springer-Verlag.

Dilthey, W. (1977). Ideas concerning a descriptive and analytical psychology. In R. Zaner & K. L. Heiges (Trans.), *Descriptive psychology and historical understanding* (pp. 35–120). The Hague, the Netherlands: Martinus Nijhoff. (Original work published 1894)

Dilthey, W. (1989a). Introduction to the human sciences: Vol. II. Foundations of knowledge. In R. A. Makkreel & F. Rodi (Eds.), *Wilhelm Dilthey. Selected works, Volume 1* (pp. 243–391). Princeton, NJ: Princeton University Press. (Original work published 1880–1890)

Dilthey, W. (1989b). Introduction to the human sciences. Volume 1. In R. A. Makkreel & F. Rodi (Eds.), *Wilhelm Dilthey. Selected works, Volume 1* (pp. 55–240). Princeton, NJ: Princeton University Press. (Original work published 1883)

Ermarth, M. (1978). *Wilhelm Dilthey: The critique of historical reason.* Chicago: University of Chicago Press.

Fingarette, H. (1969). *Self-deception.* London: Routledge & Kegan Paul.

Foucault, M. (1980). *The history of sexuality: Vol. 1. An introduction.* New York: Vintage. (Original work published 1976)

Hobbes, T. (1904). *Leviathan* (A. R. Waller, Ed.). Cambridge, England. Cambridge University Press.

von Humboldt, W. von (1988). *On language. The diversity of human language structure and its influence on the mental development of mankind* (P. Heath, Trans.). Cambridge, England: Cambridge University Press. (Original work published 1836)

Makkreel, R. A. (1992). *Dilthey. Philosopher of the human studies.* Princeton, NJ: Princeton University Press. (Original work published 1975)

Mos, L. P., & Boodt, C. P. (1992). Mediating between mentalism: The conventionality of language. In C. Tolman (Ed.), *Positivism in psychology: Historical and contemporary problems* (pp. 185–216). New York: Springer-Verlag.

Mos, L. P. (1995). Aesthetic qualities, expressive properties, and the "deep structure" of taste. In I. Lubek, R. van Hezewijk, G. Pheterson, & C. Tolman (Eds.), *Trends and issues in theoretical psychology* (pp. 359–366). New York: Springer-Verlag.

Mos, L. P. (1996). Immanent critique of experience: Dilthey's hermeneutics. In C. Tolman, F. Cherry, R. van Hezewijk, & I. Lubek (Eds.), *Problems of theoretical psychology* (pp. 368–377). Toronto: Captus University Publications.

Rickman, H. P. (Ed.) (1976). *W. Dilthey: Selected writings*. Cambridge, England: Cambridge University Press.

Ricoeur, P. (1974). *The conflict of interpretations. Essays in hermeneutics* (D. Ihde, Ed.). Evanston, IL: Northwestern University Press. (Original work published 1969)

Smith, D. W. & McIntyre, R. (1982). *Husserl and intentionality. A study of mind, meaning, and language*. Dordrecht, the Netherlands: D. Reidel Publishing Company.

Taylor, C. (1975). *Hegel*. Cambridge, England: Cambridge University Press.

Taylor, C. (1985a). Self-interpreting animals. In C. Taylor (Ed.), *Human agency and language. Philosophical papers, Volume 1*. (pp. 15–44). Cambridge, England: Cambridge University Press. (Original work published 1977)

Taylor, C. (1985b). Language and human nature. In C. Taylor (Ed.), *Human agency and language. Philosophical papers, Volume 1* (pp. 215–247). Cambridge, England: Cambridge University Press. (Original work published 1980)

Taylor, C. (1985c). Theories of meaning. In C. Taylor (Ed.), *Human agency and language. Philosophical papers, Volume 1* (pp. 248–292). Cambridge: Cambridge University Press. (Original work published 1980)

Taylor, C. (1985d). The concept of a person. In C. Taylor (Ed.), *Human agency and language. Philosophical papers, Volume 1* (pp. 97–114). Cambridge, England: Cambridge University Press. (Original work published 1983)

Taylor, C. (1985e). Hegel's philosophy of mind. In C. Taylor (Ed.), *Human agency and language. Philosophical papers, Volume 1* (pp. 77–96). Cambridge, England: Cambridge University Press. (Original work published 1983)

Taylor, C. (1985f). Foucault on freedom and truth. In C. Taylor (Ed.), *Philosophy and the human sciences. Philosophical papers, Volume 2* (pp. 152–184). Cambridge, England: Cambridge University Press. (Original work published 1984)

Taylor, C. (1989). *Sources of the self. The meaning of the modern identity*. Cambridge, MA: Harvard University Press.

PART II

AESTHETIC DIMENSIONS OF PERSONHOOD

CHAPTER 5

Understanding the Depth Metaphor in Aesthetic Experience: Pressing the Limits of Psychological Inquiry

Don Kuiken
University of Alberta
Edmonton, Alberta

At times, what is missing in psychological inquiry seems unmistakably clear to me. During these moments, what is missing does not need to be "found" by developing a more apt methodology, by securing a more compelling epistemology, or by articulating a refined ontology. No, at these times it seems as simple as going "there," as straightforward as walking into the next room. The most recent occasion for this extravagant confidence was when I had been listening to Mahler's "Kindertotenlieder," which on my recording by Dame Janet Baker includes the less well-known "Rückertlieder." These melancholy songs have become friends, partly because I am drawn to their rich chromatic style, partly because I have studied them to amplify some thoughts about mourning and creativity, and partly because, in recent years, I have experienced bereavement first hand. Yet, on this occasion, one of the songs, "Ich bin der Welt abhanden gekommen," came home to me with a clarity that was different than before, especially where Mahler's orchestration adds a subtle and somber complication to the otherwise sentimental closing lines of Rückert's verse. As I listened, Mahler's musical sense of being "allein...in meinem Lied" became freshly available as an echo of myself, as I was at the time of listening, as I have been as an occasionally melancholy tenor, and as I had been several months earlier during a particularly significant period in my bereavement. During this musical moment, had anyone been there to inquire, I could have said, "Listen here...and here..." and then talked about myself in what would have been, I think, an uncommon depth.

It seems disconcertingly obvious that psychologists are almost never "there" to inquire during such moments. They could—but they almost invariably do not—situate themselves to study people during their deepest reflections on lived experience. And, that is regrettable. During my moment with Mahler, I could have offered commentary on my life in a way that, at the time of this writing, I cannot. I could have offered a relatively rich portrayal of what matters in my life, but no one—certainly no psychologist—was there to inquire. Perhaps anyone present, even a psychologist, would not have known how to inquire, and perhaps I would have quickly shifted from confident openness to complicated reluctance. But, the pragmatics of interpersonal affairs—and neither epistemology nor ontology—constitute the most formidable obstacle to psychologists' inquiry into moments like mine with Mahler. This is why I have become increasingly impatient with philosophical attempts to examine the limitations of psychological studies. Philosophers (and the theoretical psychologists who draw heavily from them) seem nearly as reluctant as mainstream experimental psychologists to actively shape the circumstances that would allow concrete exploration of the depth of human experience.

"Concrete exploration" is an important phrase here. It is crucial that psychologists create or locate situations that enable individuals to express the depth of their lived experience. That is, people must be given the opportunity to present through some medium, usually language—the experiential fullness and complexity of life events. Moreover, the investigator must be able to articulate an understanding of the individual's expressions that remains faithful to their fullness and complexity. If those conditions are not met, depersonalization is, by my definition, inevitable. *Depersonalization* in psychological research *is* the failure to locate and understand expressions of the depth of human experience. Defined in this way, much depends upon how the depth metaphor in that phrase is spelled out—and such explication is the primary objective of this chapter.

THE DEPTH OF AESTHETIC EXPERIENCE

An appropriate focus for examination of the depth metaphor is aesthetic experience, especially if, as I submit, an experience is not aesthetic unless it invites depth. To suggest that aesthetic experience inherently invites depth is neither essentialistic nor stipulative. Rather, its epistemic force is comparable to saying that an animal is not a bird unless it has wings. Both claims require qualification (and perhaps apologies to graphic designers and penguins), but in a manner that generally reflects the complexity of empirical statements. Also, claims about aesthetic experience and about birds differ in the clarity and precision with which they can be justified, but that is a separate issue. Despite these limitations, my moment with Mahler—and my firm impression that others find such moments among their experiences of art—persuade me that it is important to reconsider the status of the depth metaphor in our conception of aesthetic experience.

I say "reconsider" because attempts to identify the constitutive features of aesthetic experience were largely abandoned about 30 years ago. It is usually suggested that abandoning this effort was a considered decision, justified under the scholarly circumstances. After all, in an extension of Wittgenstein's analysis, Weitz (1956) had persuasively argued that aesthetic concepts are inherently open, that is, there are no necessary and sufficient conditions for the use of an empirically descriptive term like aesthetic experience. Unless such a concept is closed by stipulation, there are always unforeseeable exceptions to any purportedly defining conditions (e.g., an experience may be aesthetic and yet lack depth). Although certain paradigm cases may unambiguously instantiate a concept, the inclusive conditions of a term's use depend upon a complex of family resemblances.

Weitz's family resemblances argument has usually been used to demonstrate the futility of the definitional task, rather than to initiate consideration of the network of resemblances that shape the use of aesthetic concepts (Mandelbaum, 1965). Some scholars have taken this as a newly justified opportunity to examine how certain experiences are deemed aesthetic only within certain sociohistorical contexts (cf. Sass, 1994). Their studies have strengthened the impression that analyses of such open concepts as aesthetic experience will not provide determinate results. Yet, from the argument that a concept is open, it does not follow that it is arbitrary, and Wittgenstein himself remained unclear about the extent to which open concepts were indeterminate. Moreover, the level of determinacy for open concepts may itself be an empirical issue, rather than a matter of principle (cf. Schwartz, 1977).

If so, without succumbing to either a rigid essentialism or to an a priori historicism, it may be appropriate to (a) empirically reconsider the depth to which experiences of art occasionally invite us, (b) examine whether such depth is an aspect of the kind of experience referred to as aesthetic, and (c) articulate the possibility that the depth of aesthetic experience might provide a focus for psychological research that is not depersonalizing.

Contextualizing the Present Project

Explicating the depth metaphor in aesthetic experience is more than describing how the term *aesthetic experience* has been used. Instead, it requires empirically exploring actual aesthetic events, unveiling their resemblances, articulating the patterns in those resemblances, and so forth. Without concrete exploration of actual aesthetic events, there is great risk of conceptual atrophy, rather like trying to improve understanding of a poem without repeatedly reading it. Yet, as indicated by a century of methodological exploration in psychology, empirical study of important human phenomena seems an attractive option until you actually try it— and find yourself in the Procrustean bed of positivism. Can the present project be empirical without being positivistic?

One problematic remnant of positivistic science in psychology is the notion that definitions of empirical concepts either arbitrarily specify a technical term or explicate a term already in use within a language community. However, in either case, such conventional terms often provide arbitrary class concepts (e.g., defining classes of animals according to color), in contrast to natural class concepts that depend upon numerous resemblances cohering across different levels of individuation (e.g., as in the definition of a species). To avoid the limitations of arbitrary class concepts, empirical studies of the depth of aesthetic experience should include efforts to develop natural classes. In what follows, I examine a single account of an aesthetic experience (my own) in order to articulate the depth metaphor in that context. Doing so is like examining a single bird to articulate whether—and in what sense—birds have wings. The comparative examination of additional accounts would be needed to carry this project forward and to clarify whether aesthetic experiences constitute a natural kind of experience, with depth as one of its distinctive attributes.

Another problematic remnant of positivistic science is the notion that operational definitions of empirical terms enable discrimination by any person with the requisite sensory apparatus. Such democratization of definitional practice purportedly ensures the objectivity of investigative efforts. However, such definitional requirements would, if consistently practiced, preclude investigation of phenomena that are only discriminable by small numbers of specially trained or especially discerning observers. To avoid such constraints upon the phenomena legitimately within our purview, empirical studies of the depth of aesthetic experience should allow that sometimes only certain individuals are reliably able to make the distinctions that define a concept. Given the complexity of the connoisseur's task (e.g., the identification of a certain kind of intimacy that contributes to the depth of an aesthetic experience), the development and communication of empirical findings often converge with hermeneutic endeavors. In what follows, explication of the depth of aesthetic experience in the selected account requires some discerning judgments. Whether these judgments are reliably shared by even a few individuals remains an open question. Carrying this project forward entails continued attention to whether some level of connoisseurship should be defended against the democratizing concreteness of ordinary definitional practice.

A third echo of positivistic science is the notion that, optimally, empirical investigations are experimental ones. Justification includes the long-standing adulation of causal induction, as well as the more modest notion that experimentation allows controlled observation. However, insistence on experimentation may limit empirical studies to those phenomena that are amenable to such control. Phenomena, the occurrence of which cannot be manipulated (e.g., deeply moving aesthetic events), are then unnecessarily excluded from study or artificially miniaturized in the laboratory. Empirical studies of aesthetic experience should allow that access to these aperiodic or occasional phenomena is often dependent upon a review of complex and elusive autobiographical accounts, such as the one that follows.

AN AESTHETIC EVENT—WITH DEPTH?

Experiencing Within the World of the Art Object

Consider the following (partial and personal) account of an aesthetic event:

> I am not quite sure what made me open my volume of *Van Gogh: A Retrospective* (Stein, 1986). It was partly so that I could decide whether to develop some lecture notes concerning Van Gogh's artistic "enterprise" (a term used by Gruber [1989] to describe the network of activities and projects through which an artist attempts to achieve certain aesthetic goals). I was somewhat reluctant to develop these notes, because important aspects of Van Gogh's "enterprise" concerned sorrow (in his words, "not sentimental melancholy but serious sorrow," letter to Theo, July, 1882; Roskill, 1983, p. 156). Since I had experienced two deaths in my family in the preceding year, and since reflection on those losses had affected my mood in preceding days, presenting such sorrowful material in my class risked indiscretion.

> And yet, to some extent I opened the Van Gogh volume precisely *because* of my mood during the preceding days. I wanted to spend time with the images of miners, gleaners, and other "outcasts" who were so important to Van Gogh—and in some vaguely similar ways to me. In several respects, I already "knew" what I would find as I wandered through the book: solemn, isolated figures with a hint of earth-bound strength. So, mostly I browsed, occasionally settling on one of the paintings or on a commentary about Van Gogh by people who knew him personally (e.g., Theo Van Gogh, Paul Gauguin) or respected him posthumously (e.g., Roger Fry, Paul Klee). And, I browsed in a double-minded manner, alternately musing about the lecture possibilities and about something in Van Gogh's paintings that seemed related to my own personal life.

> That began to change when I focused on those aspects of Van Gogh's "enterprise" that reflected his admiration for Millet. After considering Van Gogh's "Two Women Working in a Peat," a portrayal of arched, straining backs echoing Millet's "The Gleaners," I shifted to two versions of Van Gogh's "Sower with Setting Sun," both reminiscent of Millet's "The Sower." One version (the 1888 canvas located in the Kröller-Müller Museum) presented a sower much like one in "The Sower, after

Millet." However, the sower in the second version (the 1888 canvas in the Foundation of E. G. Bührle Collection) was a significant departure from both of these. There were superficial resemblances: the right arm poised for scattering seed, the right leg asserting the next stride, and shadows formed by the setting sun. But the differences were more striking: the sower's orientation toward the viewer, the posture supporting his sowing motion, and the depth of the shadows he cast. I stopped wandering through the book and began to concentrate on the second painting, with its darker, more somber connotations. In doing so, thoughts about lecture notes were forsaken almost entirely; I began to sense myself as somehow "there" with that painting, single-mindedly absorbed in it alone. (personal account)

In this account, forsaking thoughts about future lectures and instead becoming "single-mindedly absorbed" in the second version of "Sower with Setting Sun" is an experiential boundary crossing, a transition from experiencing the world surrounding the painting to experiencing the world within the painting. Traditionally this boundary crossing is described as adopting a "disinterested" attitude toward the work of art, that is, beginning to reflect on the work of art for its own sake rather than for other more practical purposes (Stolnitz, 1960). Although this view fits details in the preceding account, the pivotal (and more general) feature of this transition is that the locus of experiencing is changed from the world outside the work of art (e.g., the world of students and lectures) to the possible world constituted within the work of art (e.g., the world of the sower and setting sun).

Changing the locus of experiencing to the world within the work of art is much more than an attentional shift. To say that the work of art becomes the locus of experiencing means that the world embodied within the work of art becomes the realm that is explored, felt, remembered, and understood. For example, exploring and understanding *this* sower, *his* fields, *these* shadows, and so forth, becomes paramount. Moreover, besides presenting objects and events within that possible world, a particular framework for exploring and understanding that world is also embodied in the work of art. For example, the sower is seen from a particular perspective and at a particular distance, implicitly locating the viewer and offering a particular way of seeing that approaching figure. Thus, becoming absorbed in the world constituted by the work of art is more than an attentional adjustment by which one enters another place and time; it involves participation in a mode of experiencing that is itself embodied in the work of art.

Also, changing the locus of experiencing to the work of art is not simply a suspension of disbelief in the reality of the world presented there. Rather than abstention from activities that negate belief, the work of art invites participation in activities that establish belief. Art invites such participation by embodying aspects of experiencing that constitute a persuasively present world, and making a work of art the locus of experiencing means participating in such reality-constituting activities. Film provides an especially accessible example. The cinematic medium obviously can invite the viewer to constitute a separate space and time, a separate and possible place. It can do so with a visual "realism" that mirrors the "accuracy" of photographic reproduction and with a temporal "realism" that reflects the clock-like regularity of a camera mechanism. However, this is only one (rather limiting) cinematic option. Film can embody a range of other activities that persuasively contribute to the lived reality of the cinematic world, including the active allocation of attention (e.g., the moving camera), shifts between perception and memory (e.g., flashbacks), the simultaneity of reflection and perception (e.g., voice-over), and so on (Berleant, 1991). The viewer's participation in the experiential complexity of these activities gives the cinematic world its reality in a manner that seems comparable to that by which the experiential complexity of a dream becomes real. Both embody many of the perceptual and reflective adjustments by which experiencing gives reality to a possible world.

Of course, the preceding comparison of art with dreaming underlines the importance of acknowledging differences between the modes of experiencing supported by various media (if we can call dreaming a medium for the moment). Each medium embodies different components of those activities through which we experience and constitute the reality of possible worlds: the apparent "otherness" of objects "seen" in dreams, the "solidity" provided by chiaroscuro in painting, the "completion" of feeling moments in musical cadenzas, the "lightness" sensed in a dancer's pirouette. Yet, regardless of differences in medium, works of art in general provide opportunities for participating in activities that make a possible world seem actual.

Changing the locus of experiencing to the world within a work of art seems a viable way to identify the beginning of an aesthetic event. Nonetheless, the emergence of experiencing within the realm established by the art object is neither sufficient to define aesthetic experience nor to characterize its depth. Experiencing within the world of the art object frequently remains as mundane as an everyday dream, as familiar as an everyday conversation. It is the direction that experiencing takes that marks the depth of aesthetic events. One aspect of that direction can be illustrated by continuing the earlier account.

Accentuating Felt Meanings Within the World of the Art Object

The sower in Van Gogh's painting is approaching the viewer, not directly but obliquely. So we would not encounter each other beyond a passing glance, as already is suggested by the downward direction of his posture and gaze, by his absorption in sowing. Also, he is closer than I am to the tree that echoes his deep shadow, confirming that this is HIS space, not mine.

He is continuing his sowing during dusk, which seems to fit his silent dedication, and deepening shadows add somber stillness to the fields in the background. The sky and sun have touches of amber that subdue their glow, subdued but not cold. As I focus on the fields, for a moment I sense my centre of gravity "behind" the sower, in the middle of those fields. While there, I focus on the dark blue, red, and orange that reflect from the surface, and I remember a childhood fascination with the iridescence of freshly plowed earth. For reasons not entirely clear to me, I start to feel a shared ownership, that this is OUR space.

I return to the figure of the sower, but now the phrases that describe him seem partly to be about him *and* me. The metaphoric force of "looking downward," being "deeply shadowed," feeling "subdued but not cold," etc., sharpen the mood. I am not sure whether those feelings are in me or in the painting. (personal account)

In several ways, this account of the experienced world of the painting underlines the importance of felt meanings in aesthetic events: the sense of the sower's possession and self-absorption ("this is HIS space"), the perceived mood of the setting (the "somber stillness [of] the fields"), the tangibility of being located in a place ("my centre of gravity [is] 'behind' the sower"), and the explicit reference to emotional feeling (metaphorically being "deeply shadowed"). Taken together, these comments seem an initial step toward depth in aesthetic experiencing within the world of the sower. Acknowledging that possibility is compatible with a broad spectrum of analyses in aesthetics, even with the formalist proposal that feelings in art may have no counterpart in everyday living (cf. Fry, Hanslick). At least that is so if we differentiate between two general forms of felt meaning: personal feelings and the felt presence of objects or events. *Personal feelings* are grasped as inner tension and include (a) *felt-engagement*—the experience of inner tensions related to positions, postures, or actions vis-à-vis the environment (e.g., the felt exertion in an overt or imagined action), and (b) *felt emotion*—the experience of inner tensions related to the basic emotions (e.g., fear, anger, sadness). Whereas personal feelings are experienced as inner tensions, even when directed toward something outer, outer objects themselves have perceptible tensions that contribute to their felt presence. In ways that can be supplemented by but not reduced to empathic identification, tensions that constitute the presence of other objects, persons, and places can be directly felt. Consider the off-center circle in Fig. 5.1a. Compared to the circle in Fig. 5.1b, it does not seem at rest; rather it seems to be drawn toward the center (or perhaps the side) of the square. Such tension is localized in the figure and not in the viewer, perhaps because at least some aspects of an object's perceived presence depend upon the integration of visual, vestibular, and kinesthetic modalities at the very core of object perception (cf. Arnheim, 1974; Marandez, Stivalet, Barraclough, & Walkowiac, 1993; Merleau-Ponty, 1971).

Both personal feelings and the felt presence of objects of events are accentuated in the possible world constituted during an aesthetic event. The incipient movement of the sower's arm, the stillness of the fields: these tensions constitute the felt presence of the world of this painting. Anticipating the oblique encounter, imaginatively entering the space in the fields: these tensions constitute a form of personal engagement in the world of the painting. Deepening the metaphoric shadows that resonate between the painting and viewer: such tensions constitute richly contextualized emotional feelings. The relations among these feelings

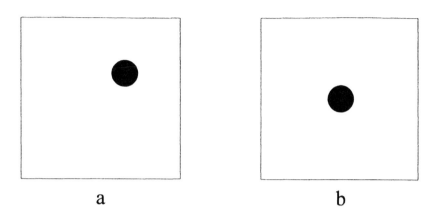

FIG. 5.1. An example of visual tension (adapted from Arnheim, 1954/
1974). Reprinted with permission of the University of California Press.

are complex, and no easy formula for their expression will suffice. Yet, in general, felt meanings in this broad sense are accentuated during aesthetic events.

Suggesting that the depth of aesthetic experience is partly contingent upon the accentuation of felt meanings still allows that such feelings are not necessarily embodiments of feelings with which we were acquainted prior to the aesthetic event. For example, the felt presence of the sun and sky in Van Gogh's painting may not correspond to any viewer's feelings about sunsets, the felt presence of a particular musical structure may be almost entirely intrinsic to that structure, and so forth. Nonetheless, by embodying a possible world with its own time and space, the work of art becomes a locus for felt meanings and for their transformation.

Transformations of Felt Meanings Within the World of the Art Object

Being "deeply shadowed" by a "subdued but not cold" sun seems peculiarly compelling. But, when I give full attention to the sun again, the phrase "subdued" does not seem an apt descriptor at all. Some more tortured elocution, like "honied fire" or "molten honey," goes further toward making that feeling "hold still" in my experience. In fact, saying "molten honey" captures the "coagulation" of the sun's energy well enough to make its temperature seem to drop a little. The heat of this sun is heat in another sense.

As the temperature drops, I am drawn back to the cool, shadowed foreground, back to the visual plane of the sower and tree. The tree now stands out even more than the sower himself. Like the sun, the tree is a mixture of something warm and something cool. Its shadows are cool with their touches of blue, and yet there is a warmth to its visible shaded side that I hardly noticed before. Besides the rust-red, blossom-like leaves at its top, there are similar colors in the lower part of the trunk. These pick up the burnt orange in the sun and sky. Where a moment before there seemed mostly cool shadow, there now is a hint of warmth, almost like glowing embers, almost inside the tree.

My eye moves up the tree again, and this time I stop at the gnarled protrusions, remnants of broken or trimmed—in some sense injured—branches. They almost bleed with a warmth that seems to come from inside the tree. Some of the "molten honey" is in the tree; it also glows. In fact, the boldest leaves (or are they blossoms?) are those that sprout directly from the gnarled protrusion that is in the deepest shadows—and closest to the sower.

Suddenly the sower seems to be in the deepest shadows of all. In his figure, there seems hardly any of the bleeding, burning warmth that was in the tree. And, yet, now I come back to him with something more than I had before reflecting on the sun and then on the tree. Now, more than before, it seems important that he is a sower. Somewhere inside him—even more deeply hidden than in the tree—is another kind of bleeding, burning warmth: a focused purpose, a solitary passion for his sowing. I am sure that there is something like that in him, and I am bolstered in that impression as I see—for the first time—the hint of a stride in his walk, of poise in his sowing motion. Not only is he a sower, but there also is some of that subdued, bleeding, warmth in his pensive action. For a moment, I feel like I am residing in the most interior world of Van Gogh's painting. (personal account)

As suggested by this account, the depth of aesthetic experience also involves the transformation of felt meanings. These transformations dissolve familiarity and conventionality and provide something "more."

Even without specifying what that "more" entails, the very presence of such transformations is a symptom of the depth of these experiences. The transformations of felt meaning occur at two levels. First, in the details of an aesthetic event, there are modest mutations of felt meaning. For example, the "subdued" amber tones in the sun, when seen as "molten honey," become fixed as an aspect of the sun's felt presence (by making its felt presence "hold still") and yet alter the feeling somewhat (by making "the temperature drop a little"). What seemed vaguely familiar about the sun is now sensed in a more distinct and rather unexpected way.

Such mutations of felt meaning can frequently occur within an aesthetic event, and sometimes their recurrence resembles variations on musical motifs: each successive variation carries forward something slightly "more" than was there before. In the present example, finding an amber "coagulating" coolness in the sun's warmth is followed by an almost contrapuntal discovery of the "bleeding, burning warmth" in the tree's cool shadows. The same motif is amplified further when, in the "deepest shadows of all," the sower's "solitary passion for his sowing" becomes another form of "bleeding, burning warmth."

A second level of analysis is suggested when one of the transformations more thoroughly alters the meaning of the entire aesthetic event. The discovery of the "bleeding, burning warmth" in the tree's cool shadows is seemingly such a pivotal transformation. After identification of the "bleeding, burning warmth" in the tree, the commentary on the sower's "solitary passion" seems a derivative development, albeit an important one. It is as though, as Ingarden (1983) suggests, this pivotal transformation completes a Gestalt; other aspects of the possible world embodied by the art object become construed within that conception of the whole.

Existential Inclusiveness of the Transformed Felt Meanings

The interior world of Van Gogh's painting is where, for a few moments at least, I not only reside but live. As I sense the metaphorically "bleeding warmth" in the isolated sower and then review the repetition of this feeling complex in the tree and sun, I sigh and feel myself sag slightly, as if bodily settling into something that IS, not only in the life of the sower but in life as I know it. And the sorrowful, isolated, vitality that IS also seems pervasive, so much so that it is in the sower, in the tree, in the sun, in the fields, in the iridescence of the plowed soil. And, for now at least, it is also in iridescence of the soil from my farmboy youth; it is in the figure of my father cultivating corn in the dust at dusk and singing, and it is also in the mixture of sorrow and solitary passion that has marked my bereavement. These parts of my world were, to oversimplify, just additional aspects of the sower's world. (personal account)

Memory plays an important role in understanding the depth of aesthetic experience. Most obviously, experiencing the felt meanings of a work of art depends upon implicit memory, in much the same way that my present experience of this warm, purring creature on my lap implicitly depends upon some residue of my past experiences with cats. That is, an experiential residue informs my recognition of and expectations of this familiar being. Similarly, experiencing felt meanings in the possible world of "Sower and Setting Sun" depends implicitly on memories for field workers, setting suns, plowed fields, gnarled trees, and so on. Even when such experientially shaped recognitions and expectations are transformed from a familiar to an unfamiliar form (e.g., a familiar golden sunset becomes like "molten honey"), implicit memories—perhaps now nonprototypic ones—nonetheless inform that experience.

However, the depth of an aesthetic experience is not dependent upon the sheer fact that implicit memories play a role in experiencing the world of the work of art. Rather, the depth of aesthetic experience depends upon explicit memory. However, the explicit memories that contribute to depth are only those that have been transformed during experience within the possible world constituted by the work of art. For example, in the preceding account, there is an important difference between the original and the concluding recollections of the "iridescence of plowed soil." In the first instance, that memory seems merely an association, as though an object within the possible world embodied by the work of art simply evoked remembrances of something from another possible world. But, in the second instance, there seems to be no division between the two worlds. That is, the plowed soil of the viewer's youth is imbued with felt meanings *arising from transformations that occur within the aesthetic event.* The "iridescence of plowed soil" has acquired the sower's and the tree's "bleeding, burning warmth," and, to that extent, personal recollection of the plowed soil is within the transformed felt meaning of the experienced world of the work of art. As Dufrenne (1953/1973) suggests, "it is not the past by itself which has depth...[but] the meeting within myself of the past and present" (p. 400). The "present" in his statement is best understood as memory for the transformed felt meanings, arising within the ongoing aesthetic event.

The confluence of the remembered past and the aesthetic present accounts for the existential quality of aesthetic events. The depth of an aesthetic event becomes *existential* when the person inclusively remembers; the past and the aesthetic present are subsumed by the same conception. Effectively the person is saying, "These transformed meanings are my experience, present and past. The felt meaning of this aspect of my living is as I am experiencing it within this aesthetic moment." Also, when the remembered past involves self-relevant memories, the confluence of remembered past and aesthetic present becomes an intimate moment. Effectively the person is saying, "These transformed meanings are my personal experience, present and past. The felt meaning of who I am is as I am experiencing it within this aesthetic moment." Finally, because felt meanings have been transformed, intimate and existential aesthetic events uproot superficiality—and require the courage to consider change in one's sense of self. The person is effectively saying, "These transformed meanings are my personal experience, present and past. I now realize that the felt meaning of who I am is as I am experiencing it within this aesthetic moment."

PSYCHOLOGICAL STUDIES OF HUMAN DEPTH

The depth that is characteristic of aesthetic experience, in short, involves (a) changing the locus of experiencing to a possible world constituted by the work of art; (b) accentuation of felt meanings within that world; (c) a transformation of felt meanings within that world, dissolving familiarity and suggesting something "more;" and (d) a confluence of the transformed aesthetic present and a remembered past (existential inclusiveness) within a moment of courageous intimacy. Each aspect of this description begs for elaboration and qualification, but I think in the same way that we have had to elaborate and qualify statements about birds having wings. I suggest that this experiential pattern describes a natural kind, the intricacies of which need to be discovered, clarified, and substantiated much like we have had to articulate the nature of birds (cf. Kuiken, Wild, &

Schopflocher, 1992). This suggestion might seem anachronistic in a climate of combined positivist and postmodern nominalism, but no a priori claim about the futility of the results of this project will suffice. Ultimately, it will be decided empirically, by expanding the concrete examination of aesthetic events and by determining whether the pattern defining aesthetic experience coherently holds over a subset of those events.

Moreover, this empirical enterprise is one in which psychologists might well be involved. Psychologists should be able to create—or at least locate—aesthetic events within which such depth is possible. Moreover, by being alert to the fragility of these moments, they should be able to support individual expression of their experienced depth. That would mean tolerating and nurturing the articulation of felt meanings, offering an opportunity to express changes and transformations of feeling, and encouraging careful presentation of the existential inclusiveness of the aesthetic event.

Is that feasible? In psychology, perhaps the only serious attempts to systematically study events possessing such experiential depth have been by clinical psychologists, but their attempts have often been subverted by pragmatic concerns about therapeutic efficacy. It is tempting to entertain what a nonclinical depth psychology would look like. Would it be possible to develop a social psychology that is faithful to moments of human interaction possessing depth in the sense described here? Would it be possible to shape a developmental psychology that is faithful to the depth of transitional events in people's lives? These and similar possibilities have not been thoroughly pursued.

The recurrent malaise about psychological studies runs deep precisely because psychological investigators shun the depth of the human realms with which they are concerned. This is more than wordplay. Malaise about psychologists' endeavors would dramatically diminish if we were at least assured that they regularly lived their investigative lives in situations that explore human experience in its depth. Sometimes this thought seems naive, but not so during moments like mine with Mahler and Van Gogh. Then it seems a step toward psychological studies that respect the experiential depth we repeatedly find when we turn to art and literature. The fruits of such studies might be both vulnerable and rich in the same way that studies in the humanities often are, but they would not be depersonalizing.

REFERENCES

Arnheim, R. (1974). *Art and visual perception: A psychology of the creative eye.* Berkeley: University of California Press. (Original work published 1954)

Berleant, A. (1991). *Art and engagement.* Philadelphia: Temple University Press.

Dufrenne, M. (1973). *The phenomenology of aesthetic experience* (E. S. Casey, A. A. Anderson, W. Domingo, & L. Jacobson, Trans.). Evanston, IL: Northwestern University Press. (Original work published 1953)

Gruber, H. E. (1989). The evolving systems approach to creative work. In D. B. Wallace & H. E. Gruber (Eds.), *Creative people at work* (pp. 3–24). New York: Oxford University Press.

Ingarden, R. (1983). Aesthetic experience and aesthetic object. In P. J. McCormick (Ed.), *Selected papers in aesthetics* (pp. 107–132). Washington, DC: Catholic University Press.

Kuiken, D., Wild, T. C., & Schopflocher, D. (1992). Positivist conceptions of induction and the rejection of classificatory methods in psychological research. In C. Tolman (Ed.), *Positivism in psychology: Historical and contemporary problems* (pp. 47–56). New York: Springer-Verlag.

Mandelbaum, M. (1965). Family resemblances and generalizations concerning the arts. *The Philosophical Quarterly, 2,* 219–228.

Marandez, C., Stivalet, P., Barraclough, L., & Walkowiac, P. (1993). Effect of gravitational clues in visual search for orientation. *Journal of Experimental Psychology: Human Perception and Performance, 19,* 1266–1277.

Merleau-Ponty, M. (1971). *The phenomenology of perception* (C. Smith, Trans.). London: Routledge & Kegan Paul.

Roskill, M. (Ed.) (1983). *The letters of Vincent Van Gogh.* London: Fontana.

Sass, L. (1994). Psychoanalysis, romanticism, and the nature of aesthetic consciousness—with reflections on modernism and post-modernism. In M. Franklin & B. Kaplan (Eds.), *Development and the arts: Critical perspectives* (pp. 31–56). Hillsdale, NJ: Lawrence Erlbaum Associates.

Schwartz, S. P. (1977). Natural kind terms. *Cognition, 7,* 301–315.

Stein, S. A. (1986). *Van Gogh: A retrospective.* New York: Park Lane.

Stolnitz, J. (1960). *Aesthetics and the philosophy of art criticism.* Boston: Houghton-Mifflin.

Weitz, M. (1956). The role of theory in aesthetics. *Journal of Aesthetics and Art Criticism, 15,* 27–35.

CHAPTER 6

Pictures of People: How the Visual Arts Might Inform a Psychology of Persons

John B. Conway
University of Saskatchewan
Saskatoon, Saskatchewan

Psychological representations of humans, including those offered by personality psychologists and clinicians, often enough are found to be wanting. Consider a personality description that might be provided by a psychologist using the now widely recognized Five Factor model for personality traits. Following Goldberg's (1981) simplified characterization of the Big Five personality factors, a person would be described in terms of five bipolar factors: active or passive; agreeable or not; responsible or not; crazy or sane; smart or dumb (p. 161).

Although such a trait description may offer a rudimentary caricature of the public persona of an individual—the sort of impression one might form on first meeting a stranger (see McAdams, 1992)—it is a representation of persons that is static, simplistic, shallow, impersonal, lifeless—in a word, a *depersonalized* rendering of humans. Trait descriptions also completely neglect life context, as if humans could be examined in a vacuum.

By way of contrast, the portrayal of a person in a good piece of literature typically leaves us with a far better sense of knowing that person than might be provided by a personality trait assessment. Why this is so, how literary and psychological renditions of humans compare, and how literature might contribute to our understanding of humans are questions that frequently arise, but questions that are seldom seriously pursued (see, Laszlo, 1992; Potter, Stringer, & Wetherell, 1984; Vygotsky, 1968/1971).

In this chapter, a related question is explored: "How might the representations of persons offered in the visual arts compare with and inform our psychological representations of persons?" The only other work that I know of that has directly addressed this question is by Beloff (1985, 1994); some of Arnheim's (1966, 1986) essays are also relevant. In considering the several fine art photographs of people that are reproduced on the following pages, my goal is to explore ways in which we might enrich, enliven, broaden, and humanize our representations of persons in psychology. The lament "Where is the person in personality research?" rings as true today, to my ears and also to Paranjpe's (chap. 3, this volume), as it did when Carlson (1971) voiced it more than 25 years ago. The visual arts, I believe, can illuminate something of what is absent in a depersonalized psychological representation of humans.

Artists have been representing humans for a very long time. For almost as long, scholars have thought that art can offer us insights about humans, about the inner life of both artists and viewers. That art can inform us about the inner life of humans is a traditional view in aesthetics, elaborated by Hegel (1975) and Tolstoy (1930) among others and more recently associated with an expression theory of art (Collingwood, 1938; Dewey, 1934). The theory, simply put, asserts that art is the expression of emotion.

Social scientists are not used to thinking about art as providing insights about the inner, emotional life of persons. By way of introduction to this way of thinking about art let me say a little more about just what art is following a contemporary expressionist view. Danto (1981) developed perhaps the best-known contemporary aesthetic theory in which he grappled with the question of what art is and what distinguishes art from nonart. In summarizing Danto's theory of what art is about, Carroll (1993) concluded:

> The most salient differentia between art and non-art is...that art expresses points-of-view about its subjects. Moreover, these points-of-view are something that flow from the very being of the artist. And, finally, the audience's reception of the artwork involves taking on the artist's point-

of-view in interpretive acts in which one explores the subject of the artwork in virtue of the artist's fundamental (existential, so to speak) metaphors. In a rough way, this recalls the expressionism of someone like
Tolstoy, however startling that may sound. For the artwork derives from
the very being of the artist, incarnating her point-of-view and attitude in
metaphorical structures whose engagement by spectators enables them
to share her point-of-view and attitude...Points-of-view or ways of seeing the world are usually transparent to us because we inhabit them. By
embodying them in artworks, what is transparent and unnoticed becomes
opaque and salient. Art, then, serves the purpose of making consciousness aware of itself. Thus, in a way that parallels many expression theories, Danto locates the point of art in the externalization of subjectivity in
such a way that the artist and the rest of us are able to examine it. (p. 87)

Danto (1993) endorsed this reconstruction of his theory, commenting
that:

[it is] quite the best account I can imagine...and it is to Carroll's text that
I would send anyone who sought a statement of what I might have
achieved. In fact, I learned things from Carroll that I had not in the least
appreciated, such as the degree to which my theory might be classed as
an expressionist theory, involving the objectification of points-of-view,
a concept that has come to seem to me more and more important. (pp.
205–206)

It is intriguing to consider the extent to which art, as construed by
Danto, and psychology might share some similar purposes in their quests
to represent humans. Might not a psychology of persons strive to "make
consciousness aware of itself," to make subjective experience external
in such a way that the psychologist and "the rest of us are able to examine it." Might not the "point-of-view" or "way of seeing the world" that
is offered by a psychologist "flow from the very being" of that psychologist.

Turn to a consideration of several classic fine art photographs of people. In commenting on these photographs, I attempt to draw some com-
parisons between artistic and psychological portraits of humans, and I
explore how art might inform efforts to bring the person back into personality psychology.

As viewed by a psychologist, Fig. 6.1, photographed by Helen Levitt

FIG. 6.1. Helen Levitt, "New York, c. 1942," reprinted with permission from the Laurence Miller Gallery, New York.

(1965) may be seen to capture some of the well-known essentials of attachment theory (e.g., Bowlby, 1988). The little girl, having ventured out to explore the novelty and excitement in the street, has apparently been frightened, maybe humiliated, by the force of the water rushing from the open fire hydrant and perhaps also by the bluster of the older children across the street. Not yet grown-up enough to join with the older children in so bold an adventure, she returns, shaken and crying, to her mother. Her mother, the safe haven, welcomes the child with apparent sensitivity, affection, and enjoyment. The photograph portrays the dynamics of attachment quite nicely: a child using the caregiver as a secure base from which to explore the world; a responsive, affectionate caregiver in interactional synchrony with the child; a child located in the midst of a developmental progression moving from an early secure attachment to the caregiver to the independence of middle childhood and beyond.

Agee (1965), in an essay introducing Levitt's photographs, expressed his feelings about this picture more lyrically:

I do not know of any image so completely eloquent as [Fig. 6.1], of all that is most gracious, great, and resplendent of well-being and of loveliness, that loving servitude can mean, and bring in blessing. No one could write, paint, act, dance, or embody in music, the woman's sheltering and magnanimous arm, or tilt and voice of smiling head, or bearing and whole demeanor; which are also beyond and above any joy or beauty which a child could possibly experience or embody. (p. xv)

Agee would not, could not, have been so moved by learning of research in modern attachment theory. What is it about a picture such as this one that can be so moving?

Levitt's photograph is somehow evocative. It evokes an emotional response, an emotional truth. All of the emotions potentially felt and, to some degree, expressed by the child and the mother in this photograph may be kindled in the viewer—not each emotion in each viewer. Yet, in a compelling picture such as this one, one that is evocative of important human emotional experiences, viewers experience the principal emotions connoted in the picture. Certain viewers place an emphasis on certain emotions, other viewers on other emotions, each in resonance with their own emotional life history.

Important emotional experiences, such as those about attachment, are etched in memories of our lived experience. They are our feelings about our childhood and children, about parents and caregivers, and about being a caregiver. These feelings are evoked when we see this image, just as those same feelings are evoked when we conjure up certain episodic memories from our lives, memories of scenes that have come to represent attachment themes for us.

Clients in psychotherapy are not helped much by being told by their therapists about attachment theory, or even by hearing about how their particular problems originated in certain difficulties in attachment. This knowledge makes no sense at all until a client has come to know and re-experience the emotions involved. This typically occurs in therapy as clients remember and talk about episodes from their lives that are infused with attachment themes. It seems to be this kind of emotional awareness about attachment themes that is so readily evoked in Levitt's picture and that cannot be similarly evoked by abstract theory or research.

Walker Evans, a great American photographer, described the essential emotional impact of a picture in these words:

The real gift and value in a picture is really not a thought; it is a sensation that is based on feeling....We are overly literary, really, although I am very much drawn to literature; but I cannot recommend that as an approach...because words are abstract things, and feeling in a sense has been abstracted from them. (Caplan, 1976, p. 23)

Referring to visual aesthetic experiences as feeling-based, or as emotionally evocative, is quite vague. To be more particular, I know of no better elaboration of the psychological features of aesthetic experiences than Kuiken's (chap. 5, this volume) explication of his depth metaphor.

To regard photographs as feeling-based, as emotionally evocative, as promoting deep aesthetic experiencing (following Kuiken), or as embodiments in art of subjective points of view about humans (following Danto), such views challenge the notion that photographs are straightforward, objective records of the external world. In some limited respects, it can be said that a photograph is a realistic and objective representation of the world, but a photograph is also undeniably a construction of the maker and of the viewer. Photography, very much like psychology, is profoundly influenced by objective and subjective views of the world.

Consider the pictures of passengers riding the New York subway in "New York Subway 1938–41," by Walker Evans (1982, Fig. 6.2). These illustrate how close a photograph might come to providing an utterly objective record of a person. Evans made hundreds of such candid portraits with a small, quiet camera hidden beneath his coat and a long cable release extended down his sleeve.

Evans' aim was to record a random variety of human beings who "came unconsciously into range before an impersonal fixed recording machine...and [were] photographed without any human selection for the moment of lens exposure" (Evans, 1982, p. 160). Although he acknowledged that these photographs did not represent such "ultimate purity," he claimed "that this series of pictures is the nearest to such a pure record that the tools and supplies and the practical intelligence at my disposal could accomplish" (p. 160). Today, I suppose that ultimate purity could readily be achieved by having hidden video cameras record people unaware at almost any place and time.

FIG. 6.2. Walker Evans, "New York, Subways, 1938-41," composite, copyright Walker Evans Archive, The Metropolitan Museum of Art, New York.

Such utterly candid portraits would seem to represent an objective record of humans. A candid record of a person, in contrast to a posed portrait, is not contaminated by the self-dramatization of the individual or by any projections or other preoccupations of the photographer.

As objective a representation of a person as it is possible to obtain, the candid photograph may tell us very little of psychological interest about a person. To make psychological sense of a photograph of a person requires an interpretation that necessarily goes beyond the naively objective record.

Some psychologists have tried to restrict themselves to an utterly objective account of humans. For example, Duncan and Fiske (1977) published a volume of analyses of the audio–video recording of the behavior of two people in a 10-minute interaction. They analyzed every conceivable bit of objectively observable nonverbal behavior displayed in search of interactional patterns (e.g., so much eye contact initiated by one person is followed by an increase or decrease in talking time by the other person). They eschewed any interpretations beyond the patterns of correlations found among objectively measured behaviors.

To make some psychological sense of Duncan and Fiske's research participants, or the women on the subway photographed by Evans, requires some interpretation. What do the facial expressions, or body postures and gestures, captured in these photographs mean? What might they reveal about the person? Although answers to such questions entail interpretations that go further beyond the record than radical empiricists allow, there is now ample psychological research available to support the idea that facial expressions and other nonverbal displays reveal something of the language of emotional expression (e.g., Darwin, 1872/1965; Ekman, 1993; Gifford, 1994).

What psychological sense can be made of the 16 faces captured by Evans's camera? Perhaps the best that can be said of these photographs, from a psychological point of view, is that they are indeed a more or less objective record of these women on the New York subway in about 1940. As such, Evans' subway photographs speak to the social practices of the day, to the way women presented themselves in public at the time, but they do not speak to the individual personalities of these women.

In contrast to Evans' objective social record of people, there are a great many portrait photographers and painters who believe that they are able to reveal something fundamental about the personal qualities of their subject in a portrait (see Jussim, 1989). Karsh (1967), the Canadian photographer, spoke about his ability to reveal the inner qualities of a subject with a confidence greater than many psychologists might claim:

> All I know is that within every man and woman a secret is hidden, and as a photographer it is my task to reveal it if I can. The revelation, if it comes at all, will come in a small fraction of a second with an unconscious gesture, a gleam of the eye, a brief lifting of the mask that all humans wear to conceal their innermost selves from the world. In that fleeting interval of opportunity the photographer must act or lose his prize. (p. 10)

Those many psychologists who would disagree with Karsh would assert that portraits reveal little but the photographer's own penchants and beliefs, just as a Rorschach test says more about the clinician rendering the interpretation than it can ever reveal about the client being assessed.

The polarity between objective and subjective epistemic values in psychology (e.g., Conway, 1992) has its parallel in photography. Szarkowski (1978) described the "two cultures" in photography plainly using the metaphors of a mirror and a window: Some photographs are windows through which one can more or less plainly view the world, other photographs function more like mirrors, reflecting back a portrait of the artist who made it (p. 25).

Consider another picture, a more subjective one. Figure 6.3 is a famous photograph by Dorothea Lange (1982) who, while working for the U.S. Farm Security Administration, documented the plight of rural people during the depression. The mother and her children, huddled in a lean-to on the edge of a field of peas that had been frozen in the cold March weather, were hungry and desperate. The woman asked no questions as Lange took a few photographs. The picture was seen in newspapers and magazines around the world and was instrumental in gaining popular and political support for New Deal relief efforts. This picture established, beyond a doubt, the power of a photograph to move and persuade people. Psychiatrist Coles (1982) said of Lange's portraits of people suffering during the depression, "She made us look at them, look into their faces" (p. 41).

FIG. 6.3. Dorothea Lange, "Migrant Mother, Nipomo, CA, 1936," copyright the Dorothea Lange Collection, The Oakland Museum of California, The City of Oakland. Gift of Paul S. Taylor.

Coles (1982), as a good social scientist, worried about balancing subjectivity and objectivity in photographs that were meant to be social documents. Is Lange's photograph of the Migrant Mother a documentary record, an artistic interpretation, or both? The artist and photographer Robert Adams (1994) observed that the subjective or objective dichotomy is not often on the minds of artists. Rather, Adams suggested that Lange "was after an objective vision of truths that cannot be discovered by scientific observation" (p. 120).

That there could be truths about humans that may be revealed in a work of art—but that cannot be discovered by science—is an idea that is utterly alien to most social scientists. How could an artistic vision be objective? What truths might be found in art that are not available to science?

A photograph is an objective documentation of the visual facts before the camera. The Migrant Mother undeniably looked just as she is represented in this picture at the moment Lange released the camera's shutter. In this sense, a photograph, more obviously so than a painting, is an objective vision.

Whether this photograph is representative of anything beyond the objective record of the instant is another matter. Art, like science, aims to make the specific universal. In this sense, both art and science seek universal truths. To achieve this, representational artists, again like scientists, are acutely sensitive to and responsive to what is before their eyes. Through their technique and craft, artists re-present what is there in a way that is universally recognized and experienced by others as true. The truth, unlike in science, is an utterly subjective truth. It is a truth grounded in human experience, not in objective facts. We recognize the qualities of suffering, desperation, as well as courage and beauty, in the Migrant Mother from our own lived experience. Lange herself, largely because of her own personal qualities and life experiences, was especially responsive to the pride, courage, and need for independence of people who suffered injustice; she remarked, "I many times encountered courage....and I have learned to recognize it when I see it" (Lange, 1982, p. 131).

The kind of truth about humans shown in this picture is surely different from scientific truth. Rather, it is a truth akin to what Bruner (1986) called "narrative truth." A good picture, like a good narrative account, is not about the question of empirical truth—what is really out there—but rather a picture is about the broader question of the meaning of experience. The truth of a picture is in principle problematic; believability, compellingness, truthfulness, or ringing true to experience, are the hallmarks of good pictures and narratives.

A good portrait shows us something about the person—his or her inner life or character. Yet, as Bunnell (1993), a historian of photography, reminded us:

> We must not fail to realize that this is a multiple interpretation; the subject's own, the portraitist's, and the viewer's. The portrait exists simultaneously for all three but differently in each case. The individual participants are required to interpret each other by actually asking what they know of themselves. (p. 88)

These very same words, I believe, may also be used to describe a psychological portrait of a person. The portrayal of an individual by a psychologist, one of any theoretical persuasion, is also subject to multiple interpretations. Any interpretation of a person, including the assessment of the psychologist, is grounded in what the interpreter knows of his or her own self. It is rare in psychology that such relativism and subjectivism is appreciated. This, then, is something that art can remind us about; that is, that psychological interpretations of persons, like those rendered by artists, are infused with subjectivity and open to multiple interpretations.

Although not easy to look at, Diane Arbus' (Arbus & Israel, 1972) photograph of identical twins (Fig. 6.4) may be even more difficult to forget. "What disturbs people more than the subjects of [Arbus's] pictures, is the intensity of their power to dominate us, to literally stop us in mid-life and demand we ask ourselves who we are" (Bunnell, 1973, p. 129). If this is so, then time spent looking at a photograph by Arbus might have much the same effect as does a visit to a good psychotherapist. Also like psychotherapy, it is difficult to say just how it is that Arbus' twins affects us, what it is about the picture that haunts us.

There is, in my experience, a profound sense of ambivalence in looking at this and other pictures by Arbus. I am fascinated and repelled. The twins are real, but unreal; they appear identical, but different; they are

FIG. 6.4. Diane Arbus, "Identical Twins, Roselle, NJ, 1967," reprinted with permission from the Estate of Diane Arbus 1971.

freakish, yet normal. Does looking at the picture reveal something important about humans, about myself, or does it reveal nothing at all? In the end, it is perhaps this very ambivalence that is remarkable. Indeed, photography critics have either praised her work (e.g., Bunnell, 1973) or condemned it (see Sontag, 1978, pp. 27–48).

Arbus photographed freaks and deviates of all sorts, and part of what is compelling about her photographs is the opportunity to stare directly, even intimately, at what one should not.

In contrast to the people riding the subway that Evans photographed, Arbus' subjects were fully aware of being photographed. She spent considerable time with her subjects, got to know them, gained their confidence, reassured them, sometimes became friends with them. That her friendly, even intimate, portraits were typically of freaks is unsettling. She posed a subject, awkwardly and stiffly in the way a portrait painter would, and then she recorded them, looking straight into her camera with the harsh lighting of a flash, as like in a snapshot. This clash of styles is unsettling. Her subjects "seem like images of themselves" (Sontag, 1978, p. 37), more surreal than real to be sure. Arbus' subjects revealed something of themselves to her. The something that typically caught Arbus' eye was that which was strange, askew, bizarre, or abnormal about her subjects.

It is the surreal rendering of that which is strange about a person that gives Arbus' portraits their compelling psychological force. Her portrait of the identical twins is a surrealist juxtapositioning of incongruities on many levels: portrait or snapshot; Arbus as sympathetic friend or cruel voyeur; the twins as both normal and freakish, lovely and grotesque, symmetrical and ambivalent, two and one. Images such as this that are paradoxical in an unsettling, haunting way, are "glimpsed only deep within the self, where the landscape is symbolic rather than actual" (to borrow words that Westerbeck & Meyerowitz, 1994, p. 156, used in describing a surreal quality in Cartier-Bresson's photographs). For Arbus, identical twins represented a paradox that haunted her, that is, the paradox of creating a separate identity in a body that is virtually indistinguishable from that of your twin's (Bosworth, 1984, p. 281).

What does any of this have to do with a psychology of the person? The aim of that surrealist art that explores the abnormal in humans is similar to the aim of depth psychotherapy. The Surrealist movement, much influenced by Freud, was viewed as a means of reuniting the conscious and unconscious realms of experience so completely that the world of dream and fantasy might be joined to the everyday rational world in "an absolute reality, a surreality," according to Andre Breton (as cited in *Encyclopaedia Britannica*, 1994, Vol. 11, p. 412), the poet and spokesperson for the movement. Looking hard at Arbus' portrait of the twins may lead to an exploration, largely tacit at first, of what may be strange, secret, and paradoxical in ourselves. Such an exploration is the crux of depth psychotherapy.

Some are skeptical about the significance of Arbus' photographs, and some are also wary of psychotherapy. Having already declared myself to be ambivalent about Arbus' photographs, I am also ambivalent about the value of psychotherapy. On the one hand, I believe in the value of the depth psychology quest for greater self-understanding through exploration of the inner world, a world which is partly hidden from our awareness and in which troublesome secrets and paradoxes may be found. On the other hand, there are a great many false projects masquerading as the real thing; in both the worlds of art and psychology, there are projects that pretend at being genuine explorations of the inner world. For example, there are many photographs of freaks in the style of Arbus that are just that, photographs of freaks and nothing more. Similarly, there are many therapies and therapists today that claim to reveal what is hidden in a person that are just plain silly, or worse, fraudulent. It is the many false projects that, understandably, give rise to skepticism. It is a fine line between art and psychology that leads to self-understanding on the one hand, or self-deception on the other hand.

I turn now to Nicholas Nixon's (1988) series of pictures of the Brown sisters (Figs. 6.5, 6.6, and 6.7). The pictures are not as unsettling as Arbus', the faces are more hopeful and more beautiful, yet I find these portraits equally as compelling and revealing. If I were to take up Rogers' (chap. 7, this volume) implicit challenge to find meaningful images for the covers of personality textbooks, Nixon's series of photographs of the Brown sisters would be among my selections.

Nixon has taken annual portraits of his wife, Bebe, and her three sisters over many years. They agreed on two constants: a single picture would be chosen to represent each year and an unvarying line-up (from left to right: Heather, Mimi, Bebe, Laurie). In 1975 the sisters ranged in age from 15 (Mimi) to 25 (Bebe) years old.

These are family pictures, though not like any you or I would take. We cannot, of course, read into these family pictures any of the many and varied meanings that they hold for the family. For the sisters, these annual pictures are rich in reminiscences, each portrait holding a chapter's worth of memories that together make up the stories of their lives. It

FIG. 6.5. Nicholas Nixon, "The Brown Sisters, 1975," reprinted with
permission from the Zabriskie Gallery, New York.

may be that we construct our life stories on a series of such episodic
memories, vivid images of emotionally laden scenes from our lives.

There are two features of these portraits that strike me as especially
relevant for the study of persons. First, as portraits taken regularly over
many years, the series as a whole is able to show something of the course
of life over time. The lives of persons over time has not been much studied in psychology, although a growing body of longitudinal empirical
work in personality is now available (e.g., Heatherton & Weinberger,
1994) and some psychobiographical studies of persons' lives, still sadly
suspect in the mainstream, are emerging in the discipline (Elms, 1994;
Runyan, 1982). In the psychological study of personality, considerable
emphasis is placed on documenting continuity over time in the lives of
individuals: Longitudinal researchers find that personality traits may
change very little in individuals once they reach adulthood;
psychobiographers typically emphasize central motives, dynamics,

FIG. 6.6. Nicholas Nixon, "The Brown Sisters, 1980," reprinted with permission from the Zabriskie Gallery, New York.

scripts, or stories that bring coherence and continuity to the complexities of lives over time.

Nixon's systematic series of photographs of the Brown sisters, with the fixed sibling relation of the four women in a row and the unvarying interval of time, might be turned to for some additional support for continuity in the lives of persons over the years. Some continuity may be seen here, but Galassi (1988) astutely argued for another view, one that personality psychologists might consider with care:

> The series presents a fluid image of time, complex with eddies and pools, swells and calms. Each portrait, stable in isolation, is qualified by a rich store of resemblances and differences, which cannot be reconciled to a single linear narrative. Age, identity, family relation are not pictured as fixed qualities but as pliable threads within a fertile and provisional view of experience. (p. 25)

FIG. 6.7. Nicholas Nixon, "The Brown Sisters, 1985," reprinted with permission from the Zabriskie Gallery, New York.

A portrait, either photographic or psychological, is usually thought of as a representation of one person, a person isolated from any context so as to better reveal the unique inner personality of the individual. In picturing the four sisters together, Nixon's portraits represent something really quite different from a portrait of any one sister alone. In these portraits, each woman is characterized in relation to her sisters and also as an individual. This is how it is for each of us. We are both individual and social beings, both agentic and communal; we both define ourselves and are defined by others, as Tolman (chap. 1, this volume) so persuasively argued. In the psychological study of persons, this dialectic between the individual and the social world is typically neglected in favor of an exclusive focus on either the individual person or the social world.

Finally, there is a quality to these portraits that is difficult for me to articulate. I find them especially coherent, complete, and also comforting and hopeful. Adams (1981) would say that these are true and beautiful pictures whose structure and form reveal something of the order and wholeness of life (p. 23). He is right. Here, formalist theory in art may have something worthwhile to offer. Beauty is a preoccupation of much art. As understood by such photographers as Adams (1981, 1994) and Szarkowski (1978, p. 25), beauty in photography, in all art, is that formal integrity that pays homage to the affirmation of life and its meaningfulness. To affirm life—to deepen our appreciation of it, to foster our love of it, to sustain us in the living out of our lives—is an important function of art.

To affirm human life and find meaning in it would also seem to be a worthy goal for a psychology of persons. There is, perhaps, something of psychological beauty represented in these pictures. I think that it has to do with seeing these women pictured over the years and seeing them together. The plain fact that we have here 11 years of living is redemptive. These four women have endured, matured, lived. This reassures us and gives us comfort. These four women have not lived alone, they have had each other. Intimate relatedness with other human beings surely is life affirming, something of psychological beauty if you will.

Before concluding this chapter, I "change lenses" for a "final frame" and consider an altogether different point of view about persons, one that finds representation both in the art world and in psychology. I have taken for granted that people have personalities, perhaps not singular true selves, but that humans have inner lives, subjective selves that may be explored, revealed, made manifest, externalized, or embodied in representations by artists and by psychologists alike, each in their distinct ways.

The whole idea of the person or the individual, let alone any notion of the inner self, has been thoroughly deconstructed by postmodern critics in social science such as Gergen (1991) and Shotter (1993). In the postmodern view, lives are like texts, narratives that continue to be written and rewritten. Texts are nothing but patterns of words, pictures, signs, and other sorts of representations. There is nothing real about them, and they cannnot be said to be true, good, or bad. Texts have no inherent or stable meanings. So, it also is with human lives that, like texts, have no inherent meanings. People may think that their lives mean something or that they understand themselves, but people are mistaken. A deconstructionist reading of a text or of a life exposes the many inconsistencies and contradictions.

People construct selves in and through the sharing of texts in discourse. Identities are made through talk in a social context. As Shotter and Gergen (1989) put it, "the primary medium within which identities are created and have their currency is not just linguistic but textual; persons are largely ascribed identities according to the manner of their embedding within a discourse—in their own or in the discourses of others" (p. ix).

Gergen (1991) cited an Arabian poet: "Identities are highly complex, tension filled, contradictory, and inconsistent entities. Only the one who claims to have a simple, definite, and clear-cut identity has an identity problem" (p. 155). So, for postmodern scholars, what we are left with is what Gergen (1991) called a "pastiche" personality and a "relational" self. We are social chameleons, our personalities assuming this and then that coloring depending on where we are and who we are with. In Gergen's words:

> One's own role thus becomes that of a participant in a social process that eclipses one's personal being. One's potentials are only realizable because there are others to support and sustain them; one has identity only because it is permitted by the social rituals of which one is a part; one is allowed to be a certain kind of person only because this sort of person in essential to the broader games of society. (p. 157)

For a striking representation of this view of the individual and personal identity as socially constructed, consider two photographs (Figs. 6.8 and 6.9; for two others see Gergen, 1991, pp. 152–153) by the artist Cindy Sherman (1993). I take these two from the body of her work which includes several hundred images of mostly women, a veritable repertory company including women of varying age, class, occupation, state of mind, state of body. In Sherman's photographs, we recognize some familiar roles: woman as career girl, dishwasher, victim of battering, centrefold, fashion plate, and so forth. Now, first-time viewers of her photographs are usually taken aback to discover that all of the images are of only a single woman, each is a picture of the artist herself.

In Sherman's pictures, there is an embodiment in artwork of the so-

FIG. 6.8. Cindy Sherman, "Untitled Film Still, # 21, 1978," reprinted with permission from Metro Pictures, New York.

cial construction of personhood. Sherman played the role of each of these women; she donned the masks. Although she played each of these women, as any white woman could, she was in no sense any of these women (Beloff, 1994, p. 498). Who is the real Cindy Sherman? Well, as postmodernists in psychology would have it, there is no real Cindy Sherman, just as there is nothing real about any person. Our lives have no inherent or stable meanings. Metaphors for our lives, such as those portrayed by Sherman, are created from time to time, fashioned in the social discourse in which we partake. When the social milieu changes and we find ourselves located in another social discourse, the metaphor for our life is likewise changed.

Beloff (1994) wondered, rhetorically, "Is the implication of this art work that all our selves are shadows? That the social floods individuality, personality and psychology?" (p. 499). Indeed, this is the implication, both of social constructionist thinking in psychology and the impli-

FIG. 6.9. Cindy Sherman, "Untitled Film Still, # 3, 1977," reprinted with permission from the author and Metro Pictures, New York.

cation of Sherman's poststructuralist art work.

However, I cannot fully embrace such a radical deconstruction of the person in which the social eclipses all that is individual. Social constructionist critiques of the person can sometimes be as depersonalizing as radically reductionist biological accounts of persons. Still, both social and biological accounts are necessary in any ultimate understanding of humans. To somehow join the social and the biological together with the individual is a grand undertaking indeed, one that House and McDonald (chap. 8, this volume) have wrestled with.

In this chapter, I have neglected the social and entirely ignored the biological in favor of the individual, psychological nature of humans. In these reflections on ways in which artistic representations might inform a psychology of persons, my aim has been to broaden and humanize the study of the individual in psychology.

CONCLUSION

A psychology of persons finds itself amidst the dialectic between objective and subjective perspectives. In a psychological portrait of an individual, there is more of the subjective than is typically appreciated, including the subjective feelings of the psychologist offering the interpretation. Like a portrait by an artist, a psychological portrayal is always open to multiple interpretations. To be evocative, believable, and compelling, psychological understandings of persons must ring true to lived experience—must be grounded in important emotional truths in the lives of humans. Ambivalence and paradox are inescapably a part of human experience and should be accepted as such. Our quest for order and formal integrity in psychological renderings of persons can be life affirming and can bring meaning to life in a way that is similar to how formal beauty in a work of art can affirm life. The inner life of humans is best studied over time and as that life is embedded in the social context that envelopes each individual.

A thoughtful look at how visual artists have represented humans can be revealing for psychologists or other social scientists. Visual art is interested in things that cannot easily be put into words or otherwise made abstract. The lived experience of humans, our central emotional experiences, are difficult to capture in words. At best, lived experience is captured by language that is figurative—metaphorical not literal. The following are some rather humbling thoughts of Beloff's (1994) about words and images:

> We must acknowledge at least, that [visual artists] have communicated their ideas more directly, more subtly and, of course, more elegantly, than one ever could in words. Words are not only pedestrian but provide closure. They seem to sum things up. This is presumptuous and it is not what I want my work to do. The images are always open—for more exciting new meanings. As in the best conceptual analyses more questions should be raised than answered. (p. 499)

REFERENCES

Adams, R. (1981). *Beauty in photography: Essays in defence of traditional values.* New York: Aperture.

Adams, R. (1994). *Why people photograph.* New York: Aperture.

Agee, J. (1965). Essay in *Helen Levitt: A way of seeing.* New York: Horizon Press.

Arbus, D., & Israel, M. (1972). *Diane Arbus*. New York: Aperture.

Arnheim, R. (1966). *Toward a psychology of art*. Berkeley: University of California Press.

Arnheim, R. (1986). *New essays on the psychology of art*. Berkeley: University of California Press.

Beloff, H. (1985). *Camera culture*. Oxford, England: Blackwell.

Beloff, H. (1994, November). Reading visual rhetoric. *The Psychologist*, 495–499.

Bosworth, P. (1984). *Diane Arbus: A biography*. New York: Avon Books.

Bowlby, J. (1988). *A secure base*. New York: Basic Books.

Bruner, J. S. (1986). Two modes of thought. In J. Bruner (Ed.), *Actual minds, possible worlds* (pp. 11–43). Cambridge, MA: Harvard University Press.

Bunnell, P. C. (1973). Diane Arbus. *Print Collector's Newsletter*, *3*, 128–130.

Bunnell, P. C. (1993). *Degrees of guidance: Essays on twentieth-century American photography*. Cambridge, England: Cambridge University Press.

Caplan, L. (1976) (Ed.). Walker Evans on himself. *New Republic*, *175*, 23–27.

Carlson, R. (1971). Where is the person in personality research? *Psychological Bulletin*, *75*, 203–219.

Carroll, N. (1993). Essence, expression, and history: Arthur Danto's philosophy of art. In M. Rollins (Ed.), *Danto and his critics* (pp. 79–106). Oxford, England: Blackwell.

Coles, R. (1982). Essay in *Dorothea Lange: Photographs of a lifetime* (pp. 9–43). New York: Aperture.

Collingwood, R. G. (1938). *The principles of art*. New York: Oxford University Press.

Conway, J. B. (1992). A world of differences among psychologists. *Canadian Psychology*, *33*, 1–24.

Danto, A. (1981). *The transfiguration of the commonplace*. Cambridge, MA: Harvard University Press.

Danto, A. (1993). Responses and replies. In M. Rollins (Ed.), *Danto and his critics* (pp. 193–216). Oxford, England: Blackwell.

Darwin, C. (1965). *The expression of the emotions in man and animals*. Chicago: University of Chicago Press. (Original work published 1872)

Dewey, J. (1934). *Art as experience*. New York: Minton.

Duncan, S., & Fiske, D. W. (1977). *Face-to-face interaction*. Hillsdale, NJ: Lawrence Erlbaum Associates.

Ekman, P. (1993). Facial expression of emotion. *American Psychologist*, *12*, 384–392.

Elms, A. C. (1994). *Uncovering lives: The uneasy alliance of biography and psychology*. New York: Oxford University Press.

Encyclopaedia Britannica (1994). Chicago: Encyclopaedia Britannica, Inc.

Evans, W. (1982). *Walker Evans at work*. New York: Harper & Row.

Galassi, P. (1988). *Introduction to Nicholas Nixon: Pictures of people*. New York: Museum of Modern Art.

Gergen, K. J. (1991). *The saturated self: Dilemmas of identity in contemporary life*. New York: Basic Books.

Gifford, R. (1994). A lens-mapping framework for understanding the encoding and decoding of interpersonal dispositions in nonverbal behavior. *Journal of Personality and Social Psychology*, *66*, 398–412.

Goldberg, L. (1981). Language and individual differences: The search for universals in personality lexicons. In L. Wheeler (Ed.), *Review of personality and social psychology* (Vol. 2, pp. 141–166). Beverly Hills: Sage.

Heatherton, T., & Weinberger, J. (Eds.). (1994). *Can personality change?* Washington, DC: American Psychological Association.

Hegel, G. W. F. (1975). *Aesthetics: Lectures on fine art.* (T. M. Knox, Trans.). London: Oxford University Press.

Jussim, E. (1989). The psychological portrait. Essay in *Karsh: The art of the portrait* (pp. 87–112). Ottawa: National Gallery of Canada.

Karsh, J. (1967). *Karsh portfolio.* Toronto: University of Toronto Press.

Lange, D. (1982). *Dorothea Lange: Photographs of a lifetime.* New York: Aperture.

Laszlo, J. (1992). The psychology of literature: A social-cognitive approach. In G. C. Cupchik & J. Laszlo (Eds.), *Emerging visions of the aesthetic process: Psychology, semiology, and philosophy.* Cambridge, England: Cambridge University Press.

Levitt, H. (1965). *Helen Levitt: A way of seeing.* New York: Horizon Press.

McAdams, D. P. (1992). The five-factor model in personality: A critical appraisal. *Journal of Personality, 60,* 329–361.

Nixon, N. (1988). *Nicholas Nixon: Pictures of people.* New York: The Museum of Modern Art.

Potter, J., Stringer, P., & Wetherell, M. (1984). *Social texts and context: Literature and psychology.* London: Routledge & Kegan Paul.

Runyan, W. M. (1982). *Life histories and psychobiography.* New York: Oxford University Press.

Sherman, C. (1993). *Cindy Sherman 1975–1993.* New York: Rizzoli International Publications, Inc.

Shotter, J. (1993). *Conversational realities.* Newbury Park, CA: Sage.

Shotter, J., & Gergen, K. J. (Eds.). (1989). *Texts of identity.* Newbury Park, CA: Sage.

Sontag, S. (1978). *On photography.* New York: Farrar, Straus and Giroux.

Szarkowski, J. (1978). *Mirrors and windows: American photography since 1960.* New York: Museum of Modern Art.

Tolstoy, L. (1930). *What is art?* (L. Maude & A. Maude, Trans.). London: Oxford University Press.

Vygotsky, L. S. (1971). *The psychology of art.* (Scripta Technica, Inc., Trans.). Cambridge, MA: MIT Press. (Original work published 1968)

Westerbeck, C., & Meyerowitz, J. (1994). *Bystander: A history of street photography.* Boston, MA: Bulfinch Press.

CHAPTER 7

The Look of Depersonalization: Visual Rhetoric in Personality Textbook Covers

Tim B. Rogers
University of Calgary
Calgary, Alberta

The title of this volume, *Toward a Psychology of Persons*, suggests an underlying optimism regarding the possibility of reframing psychology's project to bring the individual back into psychological discourse. There appears to be an implicit sense that studying this topic can, perhaps, lead to new understandings of the person that would do greater justice to the subject than is currently evident in mainstream psychology. For the most part, this optimism appears to have been warranted. In this volume, we find proposals to relocate the explanatory action to the social world from its currently privileged intrapsychic locus (see Tolman, chap. 1; Smythe, chap. 2; House & McDonald, chap. 8; Shotter, chap. 10). We also find suggestions that detailed explorations of nonlinguistic phenomena may provide a means of escaping the current metatheoretical straightjacket that has resulted in ejecting the person from psychological theory and discourse (e.g., Kuiken, chap. 5; Conway, chap. 6). Constraints on possible changes are also articulated (Stam, chap. 9). Despite its form, the need for change has remained constant throughout the evolution of this volume.

This chapter is concerned, in its own way, with the possibilities of change within psychological discourse. It confronts the very complex topic of the current forces that would make any revisions to the status quo (no matter how warranted) exceedingly difficult. It is concerned with some of the institutional resources currently marshaled in defense of the mainstream positions that expel the person from our discipline. Specifically, this chapter addresses the manner in which the contemporary view is literally marketed to members of the discipline, as well as to students. Here, we find a curious nexus of content, contradictions, and commercialism.

The present analysis draws from the others in the volume, as it instantiates the idea of relocating the explanatory locus into the social world. It also deals with partially nonlinguistic phenomena and articulates some of the constraints that frame any attempt to get people back into psychology. Like Paranjpe (chap. 3, this volume), the starting place for this analysis is a brief glimpse at history.

The invention of the modern mental test, starting with Binet's methods of measuring higher mental processes (circa 1905), did much more for psychology than provide it with a convenient, institutional-friendly technology from which it could launch its quest for disciplinary and scientific legitimacy. The emergence of this technology ushered in a major reconceptualization of several of the fundamental ideas typically associated with psychology. Foremost, for our purposes, is the manner in which the mental test, among other things, stimulated the redefinition of the study of individual differences and hence the theoretical formulation of the person.

Prior to Binet's innovations, the challenge of studying individual differences had been the description of individuality or the analysis of typological patterns (Danziger, 1987, p. 11). The acceptance of the mental test, with its inherent quantitative character and normative turn, resulted in defining the person with reference to an aggregate of individuals. The knowledge generated from this reconceptualization was framed by the performance of other folks, rendering conceptualizations of the person dependent on qualities shared with others rather than attributes unique to the individual.

This need for normative descriptive variables meant, among other things, that the characteristics, along which persons differed, had to be viewed as common to and salient for the description of everyone. These universal variables that, happily for our disciplinary forebears, emerged from the standardized administration and scoring of a psychological test, had to be thought of as transhistorical—regardless of the manner in which they might interact with unique patterns of individuality, context, relational medium, and a wide range of other potential mitigating conditions. Thus, not only was the person submerged in an ocean of aggregated, faceless individuals, but he or she was also forced to demonstrate his or her uniqueness along a restricted set of dimensions that were not necessarily selected to optimize the demonstration of his or her individuality.

The investigative practices that emerged in the service of this approach to the person were the antithesis of individuality and uniqueness. They focused on conformity by setting up norms by which individuals could be evaluated. Indeed, the exact variables chosen in this normative enterprise were selected not because they were socially neutral or optimized the expression of individuality, but because they provided information that could be used in the prediction and control of individuals by whatever institutional forces were sponsoring the knowledge-generation activity. Through all of this, the constant quest for scientific legitimacy, framed in terms of the pursuit of quantitative and typically positivist knowledge forms, persisted. An additional aspect of this emerging disciplinary matrix was the adoption of a basic, naive realist position that emphasized the ascendance of objective, empirical data, reflective of a single incontrovertible reality.

Once established and institutionalized, this approach to the person became taken for granted in the proceedings of psychology. Disciplinary norms marginalized any attempts to stray from this fundamental view. Formulations that could not be forced into this paradigm were devalued and debunked. Even in the positivist traditions, the challenge to normative practices sounded by the call to idiography were met with astonishing silence and, in some cases, outright hostility (e.g., Bem & Allen, 1974 vs. Chaplin & Goldberg, 1984). Several generations of psychologists have cut their scientific teeth on this fundamental perspective, and its taken-for-granted character has become so entrenched that to query its premises is typically an invitation to remove oneself from disciplinary discourse.

The main focus of this chapter is on the mechanisms that are used to sustain this particular view that might be described as a "personless view of persons." What are the institutional strategies that foster the unquestioned acceptance of this particular and peculiar perspective? How are neophytes recruited to this view? What institutional forces are at play when the view is challenged? Answers here provide interesting insights into the communities of scholars that are involved in studying people.

In asking these questions, we are brought face-to-face with issues of rhetoric—defined here as the processes of persuasion inherent in any communicated message. In this case, then, we are concerned with the rhetorical strategies that are used to maintain the contemporary mainstream view of persons that shears them of their individuality, describing them as a faceless aggregate of abstract constructions.

RHETORIC IN PSYCHOLOGY

The study of rhetoric is problematic for mainstream psychology, as the vast majority of the discipline is framed in a rhetoric of realism. The problem here is that this form of rhetoric denies that it is rhetorical—rather, it claims to represent the facts. The inherent truth value of its propositions are thought to speak for themselves, thereby making it possible to believe that rhetoric is not part of the business of doing psychology. Most psychologists view themselves as being in the business of truth, not in the practice of salesmanship. Yet, rhetoric is here and it is significant.

Several domains of social science have begun to peel away this arhetorical stance. For example, the contributors to Clifford and Marcus' (1986) watershed volume, *Writing Culture*, emphasized the complex interplay between literary, rhetorical, and historical influences on the production of ethnography. Of particular interest was the demonstration of how the manner in which ethnography was written—the styles and aesthetics adopted in the discipline—served to reproduce the theoretical and political perspectives of the writers. This signaled the importance of rhetoric in sustaining specific theoretical and ideological positions—despite earlier ethnographic pretenses of writing objective truth.

This concern with the rhetorics of text has also begun to surface in psychology. For example, Bazerman (1987) noted the manner in which various components of practice in the discipline served to reinforce the philosophy of behaviorism. With special attention to the experimental report and the APA-style manual, he demonstrated the manner in which discursive practices function as rhetoric in the promotion of one specific theoretical position (see also Billig, 1994). There appears to be an emerging understanding of the place of rhetoric in psychology, but much remains to be done.

RHETORIC SUSTAINING THE PERSONLESS VIEW OF PERSONS

Several writers in psychology explored rhetorical mechanisms used to promote the personless view of persons. Gigerenzer (1987) argued that the elimination of the individual in most of psychological writing is the result of the adoption of standardized statistical procedures. The exclusive use of mean-based statistics, which background individual variability, is seen as primary inspiration for the personless texts that are so typical of the molar psychological subdisciplines. Billig (1994) carefully examined several issues of the *European Journal of Social Psychology* and teased out a number of rhetorical devices that were used to sustain what he called the "depopulation of psychological texts." Of note was the calculated use of vagueness both in terms of subject specification and language as agents in the promotion of the personless view of persons.

Thus far, rhetorical analysis in personality has emphasized verbal, textual, and linguistic strategies. In the grand tradition of the Durkheimian linguistic turn, we tend to emphasize words in our quest for understandings. This chapter explores the rhetoric psychologists use to sustain the depersonalized view of persons by considering a nonverbal strategy. By doing this, it is possible to complement the more linguistically based approaches to this complex topic. It provides an alternative perspective to the strategies used to maintain a personless view of the person and also serves to document the extent to which this vision permeates disciplinary proceedings.

The subject to be considered here is the artwork that appears on the covers of textbooks, intended to teach neophytes the nature of the personless view of persons contained in its covers. Here, we find one of the few places where the discipline attempts to crystallize its basic beliefs into a single visual image. Such artwork is very revealing not only of the view of the discipline held by the members, but it also clearly reflects on the complex marketing and institutional frameworks that sustain the discipline. Such an analysis complements our understandings,

especially as the visual mode of rhetoric has become increasingly dominant in nearly all mass communication (see Griffin, 1992). This observation has not escaped the attention of contemporary scholars like Gergen
(1994) who indicated, "because visual media are rapidly replacing print
as the major means of broad communication, a premium should be placed
on the future development of visual resources" (p. 414). Surprisingly,
the visual component of persuasion has remained relatively unexamined
(Craig, 1992) and perhaps the present study can help to redress this imbalance at least to a degree. When combined with the chapters by Conway
(chap. 6, this volume) and Kuiken (chap. 5, this volume), it can be seen
that an important component of any attempt to consider change in the
study of persons may have to consider the visual as well as the linguistic.

An Example

A paradigm example of the utility of examining textbook cover art comes
from the third edition of a fairly popular introductory psychology book
by Wade and Tavris (1993). As shown in Fig. 7.1, we find a powerful
instantiation of the submergence of the person within a matrix of universal variables; the matrix is conveyed by a grid of intersecting pathways,
with each element of the grid framing a set of tiers leading downward.
The strangely out of place, faceless, E.T.-like figures lounging near the
intersect of two variables, illustrate the place of the person in the discipline. Small and overshadowed by the right-angled, seeming mathematical, and manufactured background, these people are clearly subservient
to the organizational schema. The people are all oriented away from each
other isolated, as it were, on the grand steps of normative psychological theory. This rendering is a provocative representation of the depersonalized view outlined earlier, whereby the variables become the essential feature and the people become secondary—even out of place.

Wade and Tavris (1993) were clear in their endorsement of this vision
of psychology:

> We cannot begin to thank Saul Bass for once again giving us a unique
> and stunning cover design, and for adding immeasurably to the visual
> impact of the new edition with a series of striking part-opening illustra-
> tions. Saul's work conveys the mystery, the challenge, the risk, and the
> rewards in thinking critically and creatively, and represents art and psy-

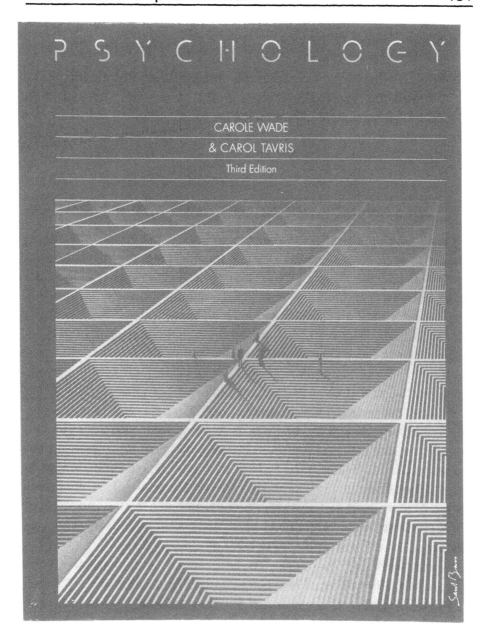

FIG. 7.1. Cover from Wade & Tavris (1993). This cover was designed
by Saul Bass and is reprinted with the permission of his estate. It is
predominantly black and grey in color with the title *Psychology* rendered in yellow-orange. The author names and edition number are white.
The bottoms of the tiered "pits" shade into the same yellow-orange used
with the title.

chology at their best. (p. xxii)

To the extent that this image represents "art and psychology at their best," so too must the place of the person in this image be congenial to the discipline. This example indicates that the examination of textbook cover art provides an interesting window on the world view of the persons creating and marketing the literature between the covers of psychology texts.

PERSONALITY TEXTBOOK COVER ART: A GENRE

Of particular concern for the present analysis is the art that appears on covers of textbooks intended to teach the contemporary psychological view of the person. Most of these can be found in the corner of the discipline known as personality or adjustment, although domains such as psychological testing and social psychology can, in a sense, be considered closely allied. What follows is based on examination of the covers of recent texts in these areas.

Recent personality textbook covers show what might be considered a genre in that almost all of them share a number of highly significant and distinctive properties. They are all rendered in expensive four-color printing, glossy, laminated (as opposed to using a removable dust jacket), highly professional, and polished. Perhaps the most important of these common characteristics is the style of the visual image appearing on the cover. The covers involve some kind of abstract, relatively nonrealist art as the predominant visual image. Indeed, ranging from impressionism through to some cubism, almost all of the covers would be subsumed under the sometimes problematic label of modernist art.

The artwork on most of these covers is abstract and modernist. Some (e.g, Aiken, 1993; Allen, 1994; Burger, 1992; Mischel, 1993; Ryckman, 1989) involve abstract images that make no effort to represent people. For example, the cover of Mischel (1993), the most popular and authoritative text in the field, consisted of several multicolored swatches arranged vertically on the extreme left and right hand sides of a stippled white background. No clear content emerges from these swatches. This image was not created especially for the text, as it is a 1959 oil painting by Sam Francis, entitled "White Line," drawn from the National Gallery of Art in Washington, DC. The relatively small textual entries (title, edition number, and author) are removed from the image being embedded in a purple/blue frame surrounding the image that dominates the cover. This cover is fairly typical of many of the current personality texts.

Another set of covers involves representations of people, but again they are clearly abstract (e.g., Feist, 1994; Hjelle & Ziegler, 1992; McAdams, 1990, 1994: Phares, 1991; Singer, 1984). For example, the cover of Hjelle and Ziegler (1992) presented a highly abstract image of a leftside profile of a face, eyes closed, and several wisps of hair drooping across.

Several books included variations on impressionist renderings (e.g., Fadiman & Frager, 1994; Feshbach & Weiner, 1986; Monte, 1991). Three books incorporated photos of idealized sculptures of faces (Pervin, 1989, 1993; Scheier, 1992). Finally, one outlier was simply a series of letters on a cover (Peterson, 1992).

The orientation of the face on covers containing representations of persons warrants mention as well. In the vast majority of these covers the image is not looking at the viewer, but rather is gazing off into the distance. The degree of contact between the image and viewer, called *paraproxemics*, is thought to convey the degree of real-life content in the image with greater contact reflecting a more lifelike positioning (see Meyrowitz, 1986). It appears that many of the images on these covers, then, have been selected to connote a relatively unlifelike positioning— adding to the abstract, contentless character of the image.

EMERGENCE OF THE MODERNIST GENRE OF TEXTBOOK COVERS

This genre of cover art seems to have emerged in the 1960s. For example, undergraduate personality texts in the early 1960s (e.g., Hall & Lindzey, 1957; Stagner, 1961) had text-only covers with no visual images.[1] By the mid-1960s, however, abstract–modernist images were becoming the norm. Byrne (1966) and Madison (1969) were examples. Interestingly both of these covers had matte rather than the glossy finishes characteristic of contemporary covers. Later editions of the classic Hall and Lindzey (1970, 1978) had text-only covers, but were sold with dust jackets with an abstract–modern image. The emergence of slick,

---

[1] Stagner (1961) had a dust jacket, but I believe that it was text only as well.

glossy, laminated covers, along with the use of abstract–modern images appeared to be associated with rapid increases in the size of the personality textbook market, correlated with the arrival of post-war baby boomers in the university system.

It should also be noted that these covers and their attending images were relatively ephemeral. Because of buy-back-used-book schemes and the desire to keep up to date, revised editions of texts are usually prepared on 4 or 5 year schedules. Each revision received a new cover to clearly distinguish the new version from the old, making the numbers of such images quite large.

There are clearly a number of intriguing questions that surface when we examine this genre of textbook cover. For example, "why would a textbook writer, working in a field dominated by a realist epistemology, select or approve a fundamentally nonrealist image to convey what was to follow?" "Why would a marketer select an image that seems so far removed from the subject matter—at least on the surface?" "What are the rhetorical functions served by this genre of textbook cover?" "Why, given the almost infinite possibilities of using photos of actual people, has a domain that purports to provide understandings of real people selected a style of image that hides and masks the reality of persons within stylized abstract forms?" Although there may be relatively straightforward answers to some of these questions, it becomes necessary to explore the uniqueness of this textbook cover genre both in and outside of psychology before proceeding to address them.

OTHER SUBFIELDS OF PSYCHOLOGY

An examination of textbook covers in fields allied to personality, such as psychological testing, reveals fundamentally the same cover genre. However, in testing, any pretense of representing people on the cover is lost (e.g., Aiken, 1988, 1989; Anastasi, 1988; Cronbach, 1990; Gregory, 1992; Kaplan & Saccuzzo, 1989; Walsh & Betz, 1990). For example, the cover of Anastasi (1988), the most popular and long-standing contemporary testing text, is a colored montage of rectangular swatches. There are three exceptions: Murphy and Davidshofer (1988) had a text-only cover; Cohen, Montague, Nathanson, and Swerdlik (1988) employed a colored photo of test-related materials (no people); and Rogers (1995) used a simple photo of braidwork to represent the approach employed to present testing. In all cases, no representations of people occurred on the covers of testing texts.

Social psychology texts share this genre as well. Of over 20 recent texts, all but one showed cover art that could be described as abstract–modernist, although many of the created covers attempted to suggest groups of individuals rather than the lone figure characteristic of the personality texts. The one exception consisted of three actual photos of interacting people (Vander Zanden, 1987). This one example aside, social psychology texts clearly subscribed to the abstract–modernist genre previously outlined.

Interestingly, other subfields of the discipline do not share this genre— at least to the extent demonstrated in personality, social psychology, and testing. For example, many developmental psychology texts use photographic representations of children or adults with Santrock (1994) serving as a good example. Even in cases where nonphotographic art work is employed, it tends to be representative of the subject matter (e.g., the impressionist rendering of two little girls on the cover of Bernat, 1992, is highly representative compared to the personality and testing texts).

One subfield of psychology—neuropsychology—appears to have evolved a cover genre comparable to personality in its pervasiveness. This neuropsychology tradition involves high-tech photomicrographs of various parts of animal physiology, such as stained brain slices and CAT scan or MRI computer screen output (e.g., Kandel, Schwartz, & Jessell, 1993; Kolb & Whishaw, 1990; Pinel, 1993). Notice, however, that this genre is, in contrast to personality, highly concrete and representative, although the design quality of the images conveys an abstract aesthetic to the uninitiated.

In general, it appears that personality, testing, and social psychology employ the abstract–modernist genre of cover art to a much greater extent than do other subfields of psychology.[2] Although abstract art appears in other subfields of psychology, it has not achieved the strong positioning demonstrated in personality.

---

[2] The observations here are restricted to the North American context. Several European-oriented publishers such as Gaetan-Martin (Montreal, Paris, and Casablanca) have adopted modernist art covers for all of their volumes, cutting across a wide variety of domains including person-related psychology.

OTHER DISCIPLINES

Textbook covers in disciplines outside of psychology do not show the almost exclusive commitment to abstract–modernist images demonstrated in personality. For example, many sociology texts contain photographic images of groups of people. The created art that appears on covers tends to be much more representative of the content of the discipline than, say, that shown in Mischel (1993).

In physics, psychology's long-standing model of the proper science, textbook cover art tends to be highly representative. Photographic and created art can be found in this area, but in all cases, it is highly representative and concrete in its content. One "Dali-esque" surrealist piece of cover art revealed its realist roots in the placement of photographic images of physics-related objects (i.e., clocks, mathematical formula, etc.) in the cells created by a formless three-dimensional array.

Applied fields like engineering tend to have little cover art work, with many examples of text-only covers. As in physics, any cover art work is highly concrete and representative.

Biology texts, like neuropsychology, tend to employ photos of relevant subject matter (e.g., montages of animals for zoology, photomicrographs of various plant parts for botany). There was one impressionist rendering of a forest grove on a botany text, but, as with the developmental psychology texts, the image selected was highly representative of the book's content.

In general terms, it appears that the modernist–abstract genre of textbook cover is relatively unique to the person-related subdisciplines of psychology. Although the use of this genre can be found in many other areas, both in and outside of psychology, the frequency of use in the personality domain is noteworthy.

MARKET CONSIDERATIONS

It must be noted that the markets for the psychology texts are not trivial. The industry estimates that yearly sales of psychological testing books is greater than 150,000. Personality is a much more popular and more frequently taught course, yielding a market that is easily five times as large as testing. When you add a probably comparable market for texts in abnormal psychology, it becomes clear that large stakes are involved in person-related psychology textbook marketing. This helps to explain why the personality field has moved toward slick, laminated, multicolored textbook covers (in contrast to other, less popular fields where text-only covers can still be found). It also indicates that considerable financial resources are available to generate these covers and that the emergence of the abstract–modernist genre has been sustained by significant financial input. This gives all the more reason to consider this aspect of institutional proceedings important.

Another marketing concern is the sales target for a textbook. These books are an interesting indirect market, as the professor selects the book, and students must then purchase it if they hope to succeed in the course. Thus, even though it is the students' dollars purchasing the book, it is the judgment of the adopting professor that controls the sales process. Of course, it is typically active members of the subfield represented in the book that end up teaching the relevant courses and making the adoption decisions. It follows, then, that the primary market for the book is the professor, not the student. Thus, the good marketer develops cover images that function as advertisements to attract professors to their product. Adoption decisions are typically made by active members of the disciplinary subfield, so the cover images must serve to draw them toward the product. At the very least, the cover images must not repulse the would-be adopting professors—else sales would be compromised. How better to do this than to create visual images that the professors find representative and appealing?

TWO TYPES OF VISUAL EXPLANATION

The abstract–modernist cover art shown in person-related subfields of psychology is descriptive in the sense that it provides visual information about the conception of the person to follow. However, description is not as important as intended explanatory functions served by the cover, and it is here that some interesting observations can be made. In discussing photographic images, Barrett (1990) suggested two levels of explanation. The first involves images that are intended as extensions of the scientific method—using photographic images as tools in the pursuit of positivist knowledge. For example, to resolve a controversy about whether or not a trotting horse always had one foot on the ground, the turn-of-the-century British photographer Muybridge devised a scheme that allowed for taking numerous photos of a trotting horse at different places in the trotting cycle. The resulting photos revealed that horses did, indeed, leave the ground, thereby making a contribution to understandings of biomechanics.

Much of the cover art in natural scientific domains can be seen as intending this kind of explanation. For example, the abstract-seeming photomicrograph of a stained brain slice in Kolb and Whishaw (1990) was intended as a realist explanation or extension of an aspect of the content that follows. So too can the photographic images of children and adults on the covers of many developmental psychology and sociology texts be seen as an attempt to provide this kind of visual explanation. In this case, the image functions as what Szarkowski (1978) called a "window on the world."

Barrett (1990) also suggested a second kind of explanation in photographic images that he labeled interpretive: "Interpretive photographs, like explanatory photographs, also seek to explain how things are, but they do not attempt scientific accuracy, nor are they accountable to scientific testing procedures. They are personal, subjective interpretations more like poetry than a scientific report" (p. 59).

Seen as more like mirrors than windows per Szarkowski (1978), this type of explanatory image is self-expressive and revealing of the people who created it. It is clear that the abstract–modernist art work found on the covers of personality texts falls more into this second category of explanation. Here, we find images that interpret a specific view of the person in the abstract, modernist, featureless formulations appearing on the covers. A different type of visual explanation has been adopted here with, contrary to institutional propaganda, the person-related subfields adopting a more figurative, less scientific, mode of explanation.

WATERING THE COVER FRONT

It is necessary to go beyond this distinction between explanatory and descriptive visual images to understand the meaning of textbook covers. Simply, a cover is much more than an image. There is a complex relationship between the cover art, the rest of the cover (e.g., colors), the textual entries, and a wide range of other aspects of the specific book. Several lines of argument have been presented that begin to explore the complicated relations between covers and texts. In general terms, this work is framed by concerns about the manner in which the cover provides a context for the acceptance, valuation, and meaning of the material between the covers.

In discussing the romance novel, Radway (1984) stated:

> A good cultural analysis of the romance ought to specify not only how women understand the novels themselves but also how they comprehend the very act of picking up a book in the first place. The analytic focus must shift from the text itself, taken in isolation, to the complex social event of reading where a woman actively attributes sense to lexical signs in a silent process carried on in the context of her ordinary life. (p. 8)

After arguing that the material in romance novels is imaginary, and that readers are clearly aware of this, Radway (1984) went on to indicate that there are some very important constraints on book covers that sound, at least on the surface, like the realist types of explanation noted earlier.

> Indeed, they [readers] believe so strongly in the autonomous reality of the fictional world that they are positively indignant if book covers inaccurately portray the heroine or the hero. A good cover....is one that implicitly confirms the validity of the imaginary universe by giving concrete form to that world *designated* by the book's language. As Ann [an interviewee] patiently explained, a good cover is dependent on the artist's "having read the book and at least if you're going to draw the characters, have the right color hair." Favorite covers include several "factual" vignettes, again because these portrayals give credence to the separate, real existence of the fictive universe. (p. 109)

The rhetorical function of these "realist images" is clear: "most romance readers are forced to choose their books on the basis of covers, blurbs, and familiarity with an author" (p. 166). So too is the possibility of reader manipulation rendered explicitly in Radway's work:

> When a book like *Purity's Passion* sports a highly romantic, dreamy portrait of a man kissing a woman chastely on her forehead and says only on the back cover that "her innocence could last no longer....Her bold desires could burn forever....Her woman's heart would love but once," the prospective reader has no way of knowing that the book contains re-

peated rapes of a heroine who enjoys the sexual stimulation despite her
lack of consent. (pp. 166–167)

The challenge for an effective cover, then, appears to be to capture the
essence of the following text, as opposed to conveying a truthful representation of what follows. Thus, by Radway, romance novel covers function as more interpretative than explanatory.

These ideas are nicely contained in McGann's (1983) notion of the
bibliographic environment, which suggests that all aspects of the physical book, place of publication, physical form, cover, and the institutional
structures surrounding its production and marketing have an important
effect on literary meaning. His view of the importance of the physical
attributes of the book, which involve the cover, is clear in his argument
that physical form is in fact crucial in establishing protocols of reading.

Ted Bishop explored this relation between the physical and literary
components of a book in two projects. The first explored the changes in
the covering of James Joyce's *Ulysses* (Bishop, 1994). He documented
an almost isomorphic transition between the literary stature of the book
and the manner in which it was covered. This novel was first published
as a magazine serial. When formatted as a book, the jacket designs started
out very simply, such as the 1922 first edition that was text only. This
was followed by a series of highly visual representations as the impact
of the book spread. Finally, having achieved the status of a "classic,"
Ulysses was covered using Joyce's portrait, creating an understated, low-
impact cover. Covers, then, serve to define the intended interpretation
and valuation of the material between the covers.

Bishop's second project (Bishop, 1995) involved exploring the covering of *little magazines*—small press publications that were frequently
the first place in which eventual classics were published (*Ulysses* was
initially published in one of these). In this domain, we find the emergence of a conflict between the commercial motives of the small presses
and their desire to maintain low prices and a sense of literary value.
Bishop said, "if you are publishing literature and you seem to be trying
too hard to make a profit, by trading reputation for dollars, you will lose
your reputation—and thus ultimately lose dollars, or at least the chance
of dollars" (p. 4). As might be expected, the choice of cover is critical to
defining the commercial but not commercial middle ground demanded

in this particular publishing context. Bishop's examination of little magazine covers revealed a wide range of art and graphics work that clearly reflected the position of the publishers on this commercialism dimension. For example, *Egoist* adopted a highly conservative cover, making it look more like an academic journal than a magazine. This served to enhance the noncommercial dimension of the publication by foregrounding ideas.

The research by Radway and Bishop began to demonstrate the complexity one inherits in attempting to explore book covers. In the context of personality texts, the emergence of a cover genre signals a relative stability in the bibliographic environment. The publishers and professors involved in this enterprise appear to have come to an agreement about the types of covers that are acceptable, with modernist art work being predominant. So too have the relatively meager textual entries on the cover (e.g., title, subtitle, edition number, author) become normative. Of interest now is an exploration of the manner in which this negotiated genre of book cover serves the needs of the major stakeholders in the textbook publishing business.

TEXTBOOK COVERS AS RHETORIC

In what way do these abstract covers serve rhetorical functions in the discipline? How does the adoption of interpretive rather than descriptive explanation affect these rhetorical processes? A good place to begin here involves examining, at least briefly, current thinking in the field of visual rhetoric.

There are several relevant families of theories in this domain. In advertising, the current favorite hangs on the notion of metaphor (e.g., Kaplan, 1990, 1992). However, the positivist roots of this approach, as it is currently articulated in the advertising literature, suggested looking elsewhere. Simply, the metaphor notion in advertising gently seduces its proponents away from considering the social–political dimensions of the rhetoric, directing attention, instead, toward its psychological–cognitive properties.

An alternative that appears more congenial to a social analysis is *semiotics*—the study of signs. Semiotics itself began with a relatively modernist, structural perspective in which concern focused on universal, deep structures of meaning, typically adopting a Marxist perspective (e.g.,

Williamson, 1978). More recent views, however, have begun to bring semiotics back into the contextualized, social world (see Manning & Cullum-Swan, 1994). These poststructuralist views of semiotics provide an effective lever for understanding visual rhetoric in psychological text-book marketing.

A major gain of semiotics is voiced by Tolman (chap. 1, this volume). He noted that Volosinov considers consciousness to take "shape and be-ing" from the signs created by a group in its day-to-day social inter-course. An explanation of the psychological, then, hinges on a semiotic analysis of the social environment. This relocation of explanatory locus not only provides a potentially rich theoretical system (e.g., see Smythe, chap. 2, this volume), but also resolves some of the long-standing issues of dualism (see Tolman, chap. 1, this volume).

The first step in a semiotic–rhetorical analysis of the personality text domain involves identifying the various publics involved. For our present purposes, we consider three fundamental communities—the professors, the student body, and outsiders. The semiotic and rhetorical devices ob-served in these communities are somewhat different and warrant sepa-rate consideration.

Professors

Structuralist and semiotic approaches to advertising (e.g., Williamson, 1978) typically define the *sign* as the object used to promote a given product. The *sign* is, analytically, thought to consist of the *signifier*, which is the material object and the *signified*, which is its meaning. Thus, the sign Is, in reality, the thing plus meaning.

In the case of textbook covers, it is important to realize that both the art work and the linguistic messages on the cover constitute the signifier—not the visual image alone. With personality text covers, the signifier then becomes the visual image plus its juxtaposition with the book title and related information. The textual entries on these covers are typically quite terse, including a short title and subtitle, the author name, and the edition number. Color selection and title location typically give the tex-tual information a privileged place on the cover. When a reproduced image of the kind found on personality text covers is bracketed with carefully selected verbal text, the resulting argument has nothing to do with the image's original meaning—the words quote the image to confirm the intentions of the creator (see Berger, 1972, pp. 28–29). Thus, the signifier in textbook covers is the complex interplay of text and image that takes on a life of its own, independent of the denotative meaning of the image.

The mechanism of rhetoric in a textbook cover involves creating a connection between the elements in the signifier. This connection is not necessarily rational, but rather depends on "a leap made on the basis of appearance, juxtaposition and connotation" (Williamson, 1978, p. 19). The meanings associated with one component of the signifier are, by visual proximity and allied processes, thought to flow between elements. Textbook covers, then, are "constantly translating between systems of meaning, and therefore constitute a vast meta-system where values from different areas of our lives are made interchangeable" (p. 25). A rich social analysis emerges when we realize that the meaning systems involved are unique to specific communities—with the constructed meanings of these covers varying greatly as a function of the community to which the viewer belongs.

For a professor looking at a book cover as part of making an adoption decision, there are some immensely complicated meaning–value systems at play. The title of the book connotes a complex set of meanings that has been partially captured in Kuhn's (1970) notion of the disciplinary matrix and Danziger's (1990) ideas of investigative practices. Of course, the personless view of persons, the inherent empiricist and realist epistemology and ontology, and a wide range of ideas, values, and investigative practices are all part of this meaning system for personality scholars and instructors. Many denotative and connotative meanings are stimulated by this simple textual entry. Additionally, issues of disciplinary status are enacted by the author names. The longevity, and presumably its allied acceptability to the subfield, are captured in the edition number, leading to a complex set of meanings associated with the textual entries on the cover.

The meaning systems associated with the visual image are equally complicated and can only be understood by examining the lived cultural experiences of the professors making the adoption decision. Of course, there are tremendous cohort and individual differences here. Many of my mainstream colleagues view the modernist–abstract art selected for personality textbook covers as a socially acceptable genre of art, one that has been sanctioned and accepted by elite culture by virtue of its appearance in national galleries and other high-status institutions. Generally, modernist art abandoned the merely decorative in its search for essentials of form and color (Gergen, 1992, p. 19), and presumably these textbook covers recapitulate that quest for the essentialized version of the person. Not only does this signal the modernist turn of the personality project, but it also serves as a clear instantiation of the personless aspect of this view.[3] Perhaps perceived by would-be adopters as being at the leading edge of creative endeavor, this genre of image walks a thin line between being "hip" or "in touch" or "avant garde" on the one hand, but not too outrageous or too "old fashioned and commonsensical" on the other hand. Additionally, the cover art connotes financial value as this form of socially accepted image has, in the past, been sold at rather high prices.

For professors, the rhetorical turn in these covers relates to the association of a socially accepted, valuable, elite art form with the disciplinary matrix associated with personality. After all, if art like that on the cover hangs in prestigious national galleries, certainly the substance of work reflected in the title of the book must deserve the equivalent fate. So what follows in the text must also be valuable. Additionally, the choice of relatively safe artistic representations (not too radical, but not overly representative) becomes part of the meaning translations embedded in this genre of textbook covers. So, from the professors' perspective, the key association in these textbook covers becomes the socially sanctioned and valuable character of the artistic genre employed with the disciplinary matrix revealed between the covers.

This aspect of rhetorical practice is clear in cases when already sanctioned abstract art is borrowed from elite sources and placed on a cover (e.g., Aiken, 1993; Allen, 1994; Burger, 1992; Mischel, 1993; Ryckman, 1989). These contentless images that initially seemed so strange now make considerable sense when viewed in terms of their rhetorical purpose. This art work has passed muster with elite society and is valuable, thus, clearly the content in the book, as revealed in the cover, must be as well.

---

[3] Presumably, if a postmodern text ever exists (and it may not; see Kvale, 1992), it would employ a more heterogeneous image, perhaps through collage or pastiche.

It seems reasonable that the selection of this genre of art in the creation of text-specific images is directed by this same desire to associate elite art forms and value with the disciplinary matrix presented between the covers (Fadiman & Frager, 1994; Feist, 1994; Feshbach & Weiner, 1986; IIjelle & Ziegler, 1992; McAdams, 1990, 1994; Monte, 1991; Pervin, 1989, 1993; Phares, 1991; Scheier, 1992; Singer, 1984). In these cases, the content of the image (typically a single face) is rendered in the conventions of this genre of art to make the link between the genre and the substance to follow more explicit.

There is no claim here that this association between the high status and fiscal component of the image and the text is necessarily being made consciously by the authors, marketers, or professors considering adoption. Rather, the argument is that there is a complex intermixing of meaning systems that culminates in this correlation between status or value and content. This unconscious aspect of visual rhetoric has been understood since the beginnings of the advertising field (see Scott, 1908). Positive affect toward job security, contribution to society, and the proper place of psychology in the social fabric are captured and strengthened in this association, making the rhetorical process very effective.

To this point, we have examined some of the rhetorical reasons why abstract–modern images have been employed on personality textbook covers. A more difficult problem involves determining why the field has so consistently shunned realistic covers—especially images drawn from realist schools of painting or, even more appropriately, photographs of actual people. Such images would denote the nature of the subject matter in much greater fullness and richness and provide incredible variety (see Conway, chap. 6, this volume). To the extent that colleagues in the more scientific domains of the discipline have adopted this genre of cover (e.g., neuropsychology), along with its attending higher status form of visual explanation, it seems even more surprising that the personality area has not moved to a more realist image form.

Reasons for adopting abstract cover art appear to rest in the observation that realistic styles of graphic image do not provide the personality domain with the needed rhetorical edge. Realistic paintings from the premodern oil-painting era connote old-fashioned and historical traditions that the modernist versions of psychology would like very much to avoid. The association with old, traditional art would conflict with the domain's constant striving to be current and up to date. This type of image would not provide an effective rhetorical lever.

Photographs—color or black and white—are not entertained for a different reason. These realist images have become so closely associated with the everyday, commonsense communication, such as newspapers and television, that they too do not provide the sought after elitist turn. The fear that the knowledge in personality might be simple common sense renders photographic covers rhetorically ineffective. Images representative of primitive or folk-art traditions would also be rejected for this reason.

Finally, images from the neorealist schools of painting (e.g., Bateman, Pratt, etc.) in Canada and, to some extent surrealist styles, have yet to attain the social status associated with the older, more accepted versions of postimpressionist art. This, in combination with the arguments against photographic-type imagery, blunts their potential rhetorical utility.

In summary, an important component of the rhetoric of these covers lies in the correlation between the socially sanctioned and fiscally valuable component of the image style and the disciplinary matrix of the personality field. This association creates feelings of social approval, value, and elitism in the community of professors examining these texts. This helps to explain, at least partially, why such nonrepresentational image styles have become the norm in the field.

Students

The second level to be considered here is the rhetoric involved in selling the content of standard personality courses to students. The professor is unlikely to adopt a text that does not facilitate these rhetorical processes so such considerations are relevant to the overall market success of the book.

In the natural sciences, especially with the explanatory types of images indigenous to their art work, covers serve as a kind of puzzle or promise that contributes to the persuasive message regarding the book content. For example, in a photomicrograph of a brain slice (as in Kolb & Whishaw, 1990), the puzzle or promise reads, "You don't know what this is right now, but if you read the book carefully you will learn what it is and all about it, and thereby become a more educated person." Solving the riddle of the cover instantiates the achievement of knowledge and self-improvement that is promised by the educational program. It is a promise of the enlightenment to follow.

Yet, the personality domain is quite different as the art work employs an interpretive (rather than explanatory) style of image. The puzzle or promise rhetorical vehicle characteristic of natural science covers is not as clearly evident—another rhetorical strategy appears to be in evidence.

Perhaps the most important observation here relates to student motivation for taking a person-related psychology course. Many students enroll in such courses with a natural interest in understanding how people, particularly themselves, work. The rhetoric used to promote the course and to help sustain its particular approach tends to take advantage of the fact that most students are just beginning to achieve adulthood and independence. The natural insecurities and uncertainties born of relative inexperience create a context ripe for messages focusing on a promise of future self-understanding. Quoting from Berger's (1972) *Ways of Seeing*:

> The purpose of publicity[4] is to make the spectator [student] marginally dissatisfied with his present way of life. Not with the way of life of society, but with his own within it. It suggests that if he buys what it is offering, his life will become better. It offers him an improved alternative to what he is. (p. 142)

The natural insecurity of the individual student is the root dissatisfaction involved in our case. The rhetoric in the textbook cover can then effectively be written as, "If you buy what is pictured here, your life will be improved and you will become a better person." Within the cover, then, we find a promise of improved self-understanding for general interest students and perhaps advancement for those considering a psychological career, with the image informing an interpretation of the verbal entries on the cover.

Yet, what is pictured on the cover from the student's perspective? Again, there are tremendous variations here, but in discussions with students, at best, the image is described as picturing a novel, perhaps unex-

---

[4] This quotation is from a British source in which the word *publicity* implies what North Americans call *advertising*.

pected, vision of the person. It is clearly abstract and nonrepresentative, but at the most important level, it is original and unanticipated.

The meaning system associated with the abstract–modern image on the cover is transferred to the content of the book. This serves to inform the student that something unique and unexpected is contained in its covers. This abstract something on the cover is not what would be expected from common sense or experience, but something rather different. It signals the need for a willing suspension of disbelief, as it clearly requires a bit of work to discover what this strange picture actually means. In all, this is a rather effective piece of rhetoric because it does quite a bit of persuasive work for the professor.

Meaning transmission occurs from the text to the image as well. The only vaguely understood word—*Personality*—on the text cover serves as a cue to the correct interpretation of the visual image (see Kaplan, 1990; Pollay & Mainprize, 1984). The textual component of the cover embodies the desire for self-improvement and the unique, unexpected image is then seen to stand for promised resolution of that dissatisfaction.

It would seem that the choice of an abstract image here is no accident. Advertisers have known for some time now that images facilitate unquestioning acceptance of communication—after all, seeing is believing. Advertisers indicate that "the likelihood that the viewer will consciously question the intentions of a image's creator(s) depends to a large extent on the image's genre" (Messaris, 1972, p. 194). More ambiguous and less explicit images are less prone to having their intentions questioned. Thus, the abstract–modernist images on personality text covers appear to have been selected to minimize the chances of students discovering the intentions of their creators. The full force of the rhetoric in these covers is quite impressive.

The Outsider's Perspective

Of course, to the outside observer, what is being clearly communicated here, and supported by these rhetorical devices, is the personless view of persons outlined earlier. Here, we see the ideological component of the textbook covers. The abstract, featureless, contextless approach to the person is clearly embedded in this cover genre, albeit in a way probably not noticed by the students or the professors. The abstract character of the image conveys the ascendance of the formal organizational system that dwarfs the persons within it (see Fig. 7.1). The featureless aspect of the image clearly communicates the submergence of the person into a sea of faces created by the normative approach in the domain. The contextless component of the image telegraphs the positivist and empirical metatheory and epistemology to follow. Yet, from the perspective of the students and professors encountering these signs, these characteristics are not in evidence. Rather, the message is read differently by both students and professors. This is accomplished by the clever juxtaposition of the meaning systems associated with abstract–modernist representation, the emotional needs of both the student body and the professors, and the preliminary textual jargon offered on the cover.

The failure of viewers to make the link between the abstract image and the empty vision of the person to follow is an example of a relatively typical phenomenon in the advertising domain. Indeed, it is exactly this failure to connect that allows for the insertion of ideology in this medium: "The form of advertisements, and their processes of meaning through our acceptance of implications in that form, constitute an important part of ideology. Non-senses (the illogical juxtaposition of, say, a face and a bottle) become invisible" (Williamson, 1978, p. 29). In such instances, the observation that the correlating object (the cover image) and the promised product (increased self-understanding for students, and elite status for professors) have no inherent similarity escapes the attention of the viewers. However, when the two are placed together, the image and emotion become linked together in the minds of the observers— and here lies the rhetorical turn of textbook covers. Messaris (1972) argued that visual images can be used to make implicit claims that would meet with great resistance if put into words (p. 181) and it seems likely that this, too, is a significant aspect of the rhetorical mechanisms involved, giving us some purchase on the manipulative character of these rhetorical devices.

CONCLUSIONS

It must be stressed that no claim is being made here that the cover is the only input that goes into a decision to adopt a particular text. Furthermore, it is not implied that the selection of the text is the only rhetorical device employed by professors to promote the personless view of persons. Clearly, inspections of tables of contents, sampling the writing style, agreement with methodological and theoretical biases, perusal of the visual support in the text, assessments of teachability, availability of ancillary materials (up to and including bribes of high-tech hardware, such as laser disk readers), and a wide range of other factors are part of the adoption decision. In addition, there is much more than the cover that goes into promoting and sustaining the depersonalized view of persons in the student group. Lectures, reading assignments in the text, lab or tutorial projects, exams, implicit bribes of future career potential, personal styles, competencies of the professors, and a wide variety of other factors all contribute to the rhetorical practices used to promote this perspective. To be sure, a thorough analysis of this entire constellation of factors is beyond the scope of a chapter such as this and I confess my biases and selectivity in choosing to look at a visual component of this complicated process.

The choice to focus on textbook cover art was taken in the belief that it is an effective way of understanding the current status of the depersonalized view of persons. There seems to be little doubt that there is a tremendous amount of rhetorical energy being invested in the maintenance of this view of the person. Be it the sophisticated understandings of the textbook marketers, the generations of successful selling of psychology to both the disciplinary community and society at large or the unquenchable need our students feel for self-understanding, there is an incredible array of resources, and hence, power involved in this enterprise. The extent and subtlety of these rhetorical processes are a bit intimidating to anyone who has determined to try and resist this mainstream perspective. In a sense, almost all of the communities involved in the psychological study of persons conspire against making even the slightest dint in the depersonalized view.

The power structures laid bare by this analysis of textbook covers are most clearly represented in the dominance of the professors over the students. The rhetorical properties previously outlined are all writ on the power imbalance between these two parties and have the effect of strengthening the position of the dominant party. Professors have all of the knowledge and power in this situation and have developed a number of devices to maintain it—despite the institutional propaganda that defines their jobs as giving it away.

With personality text covers, the use of an abstract–modernist genre to communicate what follows to the student can be seen as another example of the use of obfuscation to help maintain this position of power (see Billig, 1994; Rogers, 1987, for several other examples). Keeping students in the dark as long as possible by correlating the field with a relatively incomprehensible image helps retain the privileged position of the professor. When we add to this the observation that the professor is actually spending the students' money in textbook selection, the substance of this power imbalance becomes quite visible, and the rhetorical devices employed here can be readily seen as serving the political and ideological aims of the professors. These rhetorical devices, then, become more than incidental strategies to help professors teach their personality courses. Rather, they become part and parcel of a wide-ranging social system that is designed to keep the powerless as such.

Of course, to the extent that the knowledge created, using the personless approach to persons, has almost always been applied in the service of the sponsoring institutions rather than individuals (e.g., see Danziger, 1990), these rhetorical systems become quite significant. The aggregated, abstract vision of the individual is a particularly effective way for powerful institutions to maintain control of the social fabric. By reinforcing this individualized, yet featureless, vision of the person, those who deviate from the grand aggregated vision can readily be constructed as the source of social problems. Blame for deviance, then, rests on the individual and society is saved harmless and blameless. Deviant individuals, that is, those who do not fit into our normative scheme (see Fig. 7.1), can then be blamed for their acts—regardless of the contextual and social factors that contributed to their occurrence. The rhetoric embedded in the adverts that are textbook covers contributes, in its own small way, to this state of affairs.

Perhaps by rendering these rhetorical processes visible, it is possible to empower some of the publics involved in this enterprise. The mere act of exposing the incongruity of abstractness with a true understanding of persons that lies at the heart of these advertisements may help students to see through the persuasive messages with which they are being bombarded. However, some research indicates this is unlikely, as knowledge of manipulation does not necessarily produce a negative reaction to the message (see, e.g., Messaris, 1972). By initiating discussion within the psychological community about the rhetoric of the images and the formally stated intentions of the discipline, it might have an impact upon the monolith that confronts anyone hoping to induce change in the field. Yet, these are concerns that will have to await further work.

For me, the most intriguing aspect of this overall analysis is the clear manner in which textbook covers are almost literally "seen" as different by the communities involved with these signs. To most students, they are seen as novel, unanticipated renditions of the person promising improved self-understanding. To adopting professors, they are seen as avant garde visual images that connote social sanctioning, monetary value, and acceptance by an elite culture. To the critical community, they are amazingly frank and accurate images of the lack of richness and intellectual bankruptcy of the depersonalized view of persons. Yet, all three groups are looking at the same fundamental images. The contextual meaning systems that each brings to bear, and the linkages made by virtue of the juxtaposition of visual and textual materials, yield radically different readings pending the mythologies and social needs brought into the interpretive act.

None of these three interpretations is necessarily privileged over the others, but each represents the manner in which visual images can and do interact with complex meaning systems and ideologies. The main strength of the visual medium is the relative ease of understanding these ideologies. Hopefully, this first pass at unpacking these complex visual signs has, at least, offered a sense of the potential promise of this approach.

This chapter is a first step at developing an analysis of visual rhetoric in the disciplinary matrix of psychology. It is congenial to the major thrust of this volume because it locates the explanatory action in the interpersonal world. The meanings of the images are seen as constructed by the various viewing communities, each bringing its own vested social, political, material, and aesthetic interests into the viewing context. Following the lead of visual sociologists like Harper (1994), this chapter suggests viewer-dependent variations of meanings of the cover images, with the rhetorical power being tied to these varying contexts. The distribution of power between the various viewers is also revealed in this analysis, but this is only a first step; more systematic collaboration with the various communities and individuals involved is necessary in order to fulfill the promise of this approach. An interesting next step would be to conduct a series of "image elicitation" interviews with professors and students, using the covers to guide unstructured discourse (e.g., Collier, 1967; Gold, 1991). This approach (see also Manning & Cullum-Swan, 1994) offers promise of further understanding of differential meanings as a function of class, personal elements, role relationships, and group membership. In such studies, hopefully, more evenly constructed conversations could be presented.

ACKNOWLEDGMENTS

I would like to thank Brian Rusted, Hank Stam, and Ted Bishop for their helpful comments on earlier drafts of this chapter. In addition, thanks goes to the many WCTP discussions that have added, in many ways, to this chapter.

REFERENCES

Aiken, L. R. (1988). *Psychological testing and assessment* (6th ed.). Boston: Allyn & Bacon.

Aiken, L. R. (1989). *Assessment of personality*. Boston: Allyn & Bacon.

Aiken, L. R. (1993). *Personality: Theories, research and applications*. Englewood Cliffs, NJ: Prentice-Hall.

Allen, B. P. (1994). *Personality theories*. Boston: Allyn & Bacon.

Anastasi, A. (1988). *Psychological testing* (6th ed.). New York: Macmillan.

Barrett, T. (1990). *Criticizing photographs*. Mountain View, CA: Mayfield.

Bazerman, C. (1987). Codifying the social scientific style: The *APA Publication Manual* as behaviorist rhetoric. In J. S. Nelson, A. Megill & D. N. McCloskey (Eds.), *The rhetoric of the human sciences* (pp. 125–144). Madison: University of Wisconsin Press.

Bem, D. J., & Allen, A. (1974). On predicting some of the people some of the time: The search for cross-situational consistencies in behavior. *Psychological Review, 81*, 506–520.

Berger, J. (1972). *Ways of seeing*. Harmondsworth, England: Penguin.

Bernat, T. J. (1992). *Child development*. New York: Harcourt Brace.

Billig, M. (1994). Repopulating the depopulated pages of social psychology. *Theory and Psychology, 3*, 307–335.

Bishop, E. L. (1994). Re:covering Ulysses. *Joyce Studies Annual, 5*, 22–55.

Bishop, E. L. (1995). *Re:covering modernism: Format and function in little magazines*. Unpublished manuscript, University of Alberta.

Burger, J. M. (1992). *Personality* (3rd ed.). Monterey, CA: Brooks/Cole.

Byrne, D. (1966). *An introduction to personality: A research approach.* Englewood Cliffs, NJ: Prentice-Hall.

Chaplin, W. F., & Goldberg, L. R. (1984). A failure to replicate the Bem and Allen study of individual differences in cross-situational consistency. *Journal of Personality and Social Psychology, 47,* 1074–1090.

Clifford, J., & Marcus, G. E. (Eds.). (1986). *Writing culture: The poetics and politics of ethnography.* Berkeley: University of California Press.

Cohen, R. J., Montague, P., Nathanson, L. S., & Swerdlik, M. E. (1988). *Psychological testing: An introduction to tests and measurements.* Mountain View, CA: Mayfield.

Collier, J. (1967). *Visual anthropology: Photography as a research method.* New York: Holt, Rinehart & Winston.

Craig, R. L. (1992). Advertising as visual communication. *Communication, 13,* 165–179.

Cronbach, L. J. (1990). *Essentials of psychological testing* (5th ed.). New York: Harper & Row.

Danziger, K. (1987). *Psychology for whom?* Paper presented at the University of Saskatchewan.

Danziger, K. (1990). *Constructing the subject: Historical origins of psychological research.* Cambridge, England: Cambridge University Press.

Fadiman, J., & Frager, R. (1994). *Personality and personality growth* (3rd ed.). New York: HarperCollins.

Feist, J. (1994). *Theories of personality* (3rd ed.). New York: Harcourt Brace.

Feshbach, S., & Weiner, B. (1986). *Personality* (2nd ed.). Lexington, MA: D. C. Heath.

Gergen, K. J. (1992). Toward a postmodern psychology. In S. Kvale (Ed.), *Psychology and postmodernism* (pp. 17–57). Newbury Park, CA: Sage.

Gergen, K. J. (1994). Exploring the postmodern: Perils or potentials. *American Psychologist, 49,* 412–416.

Gigerenzer, G. (1987). Probabilistic thinking and the fight against subjectivity. In L. Kruger, G. Gigerenzer & M. S. Morgan (Eds.), *The probabilistic revolution* (Vol. 2). Cambridge, MA: Harvard University Press.

Gold, S. J. (1991). Ethnic boundaries and ethnic entrepreneurship: A photo-elicitation study. *Visual Sociology, 6,* 1–19.

Gregory, R. J. (1992). *Psychological testing: History, principles, and applications.* Boston: Allyn & Bacon.

Griffin, M. (1992). Introduction to a special issue on visual communication. *Communication, 13,* 163–164.

Hall, G., & Lindzey, C. S. (1957). *Theories of personality.* New York: Wiley.

Hall, G., & Lindzey, C. S. (1970). *Theories of personality* (2nd ed.). New York: Wiley.

Hall, G., & Lindzey, C. S. (1978). *Theories of personality* (3rd ed.). New York: Wiley.

Harper, D. (1994). On the authority of the visual image: Visual methods as the crossroads. In N. K. Denzin & Y. S. Lincoln (Eds.), *Handbook of qualitative research* (pp. 403–412). Thousand Oaks, CA: Sage.

Hjelle, L. A., & Ziegler, D. J. (1992). *Personality theories: Basic assumptions, research, and applications* (3rd ed.). New York: McGraw-Hill.

Kandel, E. R., Schwartz, J. H., & Jessell, T. M. (1993). *Principles of neural science* (3rd ed.). Norwalk, CT: Appleton and Lange.

Kaplan, R. M., & Saccuzzo, D. P. (1989). *Psychological testing: Principles, applications, and issues* (2nd ed.). Monterey, CA: Brooks/Cole.

Kaplan, S. J. (1990). Visual metaphors in the representation of communication technology. *Critical Studies in Mass Communication, 7*, 37–47.

Kaplan, S. J. (1992). A conceptual analysis of form and content in visual metaphors. *Communication, 13*, 197–209.

Kolb, B., & Whishaw, I. Q. (1990). *Fundamentals of human neuropsychology* (3rd ed.). San Francisco: Freeman.

Kuhn, T. S. (1970). *The structure of scientific revolutions* (2nd ed.). Chicago: University of Chicago Press.

Madison, P. (1969). *Personality development in college.* Reading, MA: Addison-Wesley.

Manning, P. K., & Cullum-Swan, B. (1994). Narrative, content, and semiotic analysis. In N. K. Denzin & Y. S. Lincoln (Eds.), *Handbook of qualitative research* (pp. 463–477). Thousand Oaks, CA: Sage.

McAdams, D. P. (1990). *The person: An introduction to personality psychology.* New York: Harcourt Brace.

McAdams, D. P. (1994). *The person: an introduction to personality psychology* (2nd ed.). New York: Harcourt Brace.

McGann, J. (1985). *Historical studies and literary criticism.* Madison: University of Wisconsin Press.

Messaris, P. (1972). Visual "manipulation": Visual means of affecting responses to images. *Communication, 13*, 181–195.

Mischel, W. (1993). *Introduction to personality* (5th ed.). New York: Harcourt Brace.

Monte, C. F. (1991). *Beneath the mask: An introduction to theories of personality* (4th ed.). New York: Harcourt Brace.

Murphy, K. R., & Davidshofer, C. O. (1988). *Psychological testing: Principles and applications.* Englewood Cliffs, NJ: Prentice-Hall.

Pervin, L. J. (1989). *Personality: Theory and research* (5th ed.). New York: Wiley.

Pervin, L. J. (1993). *Personality: Theory and research* (6th ed.). New York: Wiley.

Peterson, C. (1992). *Personality* (2nd ed.). New York: Harcourt Brace.

Phares, E. J. (1991). *Introduction to personality* (3rd ed.). New York: HarperCollins.

Pinel, J. P. J. (1993). *Biopsychology.* Boston: Allyn & Bacon.

Pollay, R. W., & Mainprize, S. (1984). Headlining of visuals in print advertising: A typology of tactical techniques. In D. R. Glover (Ed.), *Proceedings of the 1984 Convention of the American Academy of Advertising* (pp. 24–28). Lincoln: School of Journalism, University of Nebraska-Lincoln.

Radway, J. (1984). *Reading the romance: Women, patriarchy, and popular literature.* Chapel Hill: University of North Carolina Press.

Rogers, T. B. (1987). Hearing the unsaids: An essay on the role of folkloristics in metapsychology. In H. Stam, T. B. Rogers, & K. J. Gergen (Eds.), *The analysis of psychological theory: Metapsychological perspectives.* New York: Hemisphere.

Rogers, T. B. (1995). *The psychological testing enterprise: An introduction.* Monterey, CA: Brooks/Cole.

Ryckman, R. M. (1989). *Theories of personality* (4th ed.). Monterey, CA: Brooks/ Cole.

Santrock, J. W. (1994). *Child development* (6th ed.). Madison, WI: Brown and Benchmark.

Scheier, C. (1992). *Perspective on personality* (2nd ed.). Boston: Allyn & Bacon.

Scott, W. D. (1908). *The psychology of advertising.* Boston: Small, Maynard and Company.

Singer, J. (1984). *The human personality.* New York: Harcourt Brace.

Stagner, R. (1961). *Psychology of personality* (3rd ed.). New York: McGraw-Hill.

Szarkowski, J. (1978). *Mirrors and windows: American photography since 1960.* New York: Museum of Modern Art.

Vander Zanden, J. W. (1987). *Social psychology* (4th ed.). New York: Random House.

Wade, C., & Tavris, C. (1993). *Psychology* (3rd ed.). New York: HarperCollins.

Walsh, W. B., & Betz, N. E. (1990). *Tests and assessment* (2nd ed.). Englewood Cliffs, NJ: Prentice-Hall.

Williamson, J. (1978). *Decoding advertisements: Ideology and meaning in advertising.* London: Marion Boyars.

PART III

CRITICAL PERSPECTIVES ON THE PERSON

CHAPTER 8

Realist Brains and Virtual Conversations: Morals, Molecules, and Meanings in Social Constructionism

D. Vaden House
Institute for Christian Studies
Toronto, Ontario

Marvin J. McDonald
Trinity Western University
Langley, British Columbia

Most of the problems involved in philosophical interpretations of the social sciences tend to center on the supposed conflict between the methodological requirements of science and the individuality and freedom of human beings. This science–person conflict can take many forms. On the one hand, it might be contended that because of the individual variability of humans, human freedom or intentionality, subjectivity of human motivation, or the value-laden character of social research, human science is an impossibility. A contemporary representative of this position is Neil Postman for whom social inquiry is not science, but a form of moral theology (Postman, 1988).

On the other hand, it might be contended that science consists in discovering the underlying causal mechanisms of everything (including humans) or that science consists in discovering universal laws that determine all individual existence and that there is no place in science for human intentionality or human freedom. Thus, these purported features of humans are specious and all references to them should be eliminated.

The concept of the person is a highly beleaguered one in psychology. Most contemporary mainstream psychology deals with human cognition, emotion, and personality in terms of neuroanatomy, genetic conditioning, functionally defined modules, and so on. In all these cases, the distinctively human processes of thinking, feeling, meaning, and evaluation are referred for explanation to subpersonal components understood in terms of brain parts and processes or functional modules. These bottom–up strategies in psychology often try to explain personal behavior by appealing to features of human biology (e.g., genetic make-up or brain function). Dennett (1978) found it unintelligible that a psychological theory could be anything but a subpersonal theory.

Some top–down strategies try to understand human behavior as a function of some more inclusive entity (e.g., social system or conversation) of which individual humans are components. The first strategy explains humans as constituted by their biological components; the second understands humans constituted as components of a larger system.

The usual assumption is that constitution entails determination: The action of humans is fully or exhaustively determined by how they are constituted (by their subunits) or by their being constituent parts or subprocesses of a larger social system. In other words, human behavior is seen, in some sense, as the outcome of biological forces, social forces, or both. Traditionally, the idea of the person has been intimately linked to our ideas of agency and moral responsibility. However, both the subpersonal, molecular psychologies and suprapersonal, cultural psychologies are thought to make traditional discourse about persons as moral agents extremely problematic. Rosenberg (1988), for example, talked of two kinds of invisible hands, thereby suggesting that persons might be the passive products of either molecular or genetic determination on the one hand, or of social forces on the other hand. Similarly Glover (1990) spoke of the skepticism about human agency borne of the suspicion that we are entirely the product of various social pressures or are determined by physical or biological forces (pp. 17–18). Furhman (1986) wrote of the disappearance of the moral self in human nature or society. What is unclear is the sense in which humans are responsible agents or if we still have any use for the notion of persons at all.

To pose the issue in this light seems to call for a choice between science and persons or between scientism and humanism. This is a familiar and long-standing storm at the heart of Western culture that shows little signs of abating. Every generation seems to have its B. F. Skinner, heralding the end of freedom and dignity, and its C. P. Snow, defending a hegemonic role for science against the culture's superstitious deference to humanists. Yet, it is not hard to find proponents of what Holton (1993) called antiscience. For example, Roszak wrote important and influential critiques of the citadel of scientific expertise, of the impact of information technology on education and politics, of reductionism on our moral images of ourselves, and so on (e.g., Roszak, 1986). Witness the scathing repudiation of science for treating humans as garbage in Kurt Vonnegut's *Wampeters, Foma & Granfailoons* (1974).

Needless to say, not everyone is happy with the issue posed in these terms. There is a long tradition that refuses to grasp the science–person nettle and argues instead for a distinctive human science. Certainly, since the classical works of Dilthey and Weber, the idea of an interpretive social science (or human science) that utilizes some kind of hermeneutic method for dealing with human action in terms of values, meanings, and reasons has received enormous attention. According to this view, *person* represents a unique ontological kind that requires a different kind of science tailored to the distinctiveness of persons.

On the contemporary scene, this debate tends to focus around the issue of the relation between scientific psychology and so-called folk psychology (e.g., Bogdan, 1991). Common sense typically ascribes belief, desire, and reasons to people and interprets action in terms of these mental states. Just what is the status of these commonsense notions? What (and where) in the world (or brain) are reasons, desires, and beliefs and how do they relate to neural structures? In some ways, this is a replay of the old mind/brain problem. What is the relation between mental functioning and brain functioning? What is the relation between intentional idioms (meaning, intentionality, belief, etc.) and neurological idioms? Are they identical? What relations exist between meanings and brains? Is talk about persons in terms of meanings complementary to talk about persons in terms of molecules (or cells, neurons, and brains)? Are they rivals? Should (can) we eliminate intentional idioms of so-called folk psychology altogether in favor of neurophysiology?

The possible variations on these themes are too numerous to mention and even classification into broad types is difficult because there is no one issue that divides or unites the various positions, except perhaps the nearly uniform rejection of Cartesian dualism. Hardly anyone wishes to locate the person in some nonmaterial realm contingently related to the body and brain of the human animal. However, this widespread agreement conceals a host of differences. For some, anti-Cartesianism takes the form of reductive physicalism (Churchland, 1988, 1989, 1995). Others accept a materialist (token) identity thesis, but insist on the ineliminability of intentionalist idioms instrumentally interpreted (Dennett, 1987).

Yet, apart from a generalized anti-Cartesianism, the consensus rapidly breaks down. Even the anti-Cartesians have differing motivations. Most materialists reject the traditional Cartesian model because of its appeal to immaterial substance, yet some versions of functionalism and computationalism have been classified by critics as materialist dualism. Locating the self and its properties, parts, and states in some bit of brain activity seems to be a kind of dualistic materialism. Postulating modules for memory functions, thought, will, and so forth, begins to look like traditional faculty psychology in materialist dress. So, for example, Dennett (1991) claimed that seeking a central control unit or a central "meaner" in the brain is residual Cartesianism in materialist guise.

Most social constructionist versions of anti-Cartesianism emphasize, not only issues associated with mind and brain, or persons and bodies, but also the relations between persons and communities. In other words, unlike many other forms of anti-Cartesianism, one of the primary concerns of social constructionism seems to be the radical individualism in the Cartesian ontology of persons.

Our point is that there is no single issue that unites or divides the contemporary landscape in theoretical psychology. There are not only differences between naturalistic and hermeneutic approaches, but also convergences. Furthermore, there are substantive differences in each school of thought. For example, all of the champions of folk psychology and of hermeneutic or interpretive social science see some ineliminable place for interpretive methods and reject, for a host of complex reasons, the reduction of intentional categories to, or replacement by, physiological ones. To confuse the issue, Dennett, who affirmed the traditional third person, naturalistic approach, also accepted the irreducibility of intentionalist idioms. Moreover, some social constructionists seem to hold that physiological inquiry is irrelevant to understanding persons and their actions. In other words, there are, among a number of champions of folk psychology and its scientific extensions, those who would eliminate as irrelevant to psychology any reference to biological or physiological mechanisms and processes in explanatory accounts. Others, by contrast, who adopt the social constructionist label, reject this sharp separation and argue for some kind of coordination between these two types of research (e.g. Harré, 1990). Harré was committed to the claim that intentional idioms are necessary for understanding human action and irreducible to physiological categories, but he was also committed to a multileveled account of human beings who are not only rational and social animals (Harré & Gillett, 1994, p. 80) but also physical and biological beings (Bhaskar, 1990, p. 352; Harré, Clarke, & De Carlo, 1985, p. 13; Harré & Secord, 1972, p. 264).

We have been arguing that the question of a science of persons or the choice between science and persons is a tangled web of overlapping issues. We propose to look at some representative social constructionist arguments for a distinctively moral science. The emphasis on morality plays a complex role in social constructionism. Minimally, it seems to involve the following claims: (a) The practices of third-person mechanistic science are immoral in that the practices of research are themselves dehumanizing; (b) the image of persons as automata promotes immoral social and political practices; (c) as social constructs, persons are created in a morally qualified process of negotiation and dialogue and their action is intelligible only with reference to various moral orders that are created and sustained in conversation and communal practice.

In order to focus the conversation, we briefly examine an exchange between John Shotter and Rom Harré. Shotter's "moral science" approach to psychology has significant convergences with Harré's discursive psychology. Both reject most traditional approaches to psychology and both defend versions of social constructionism. Yet, there are important divergences as well. The differences become apparent in their debate about realism (Bhaskar, 1990). We want to explore the way that Shotter and Harré view the relation between the molecules and meanings or, less telescopically, between the natural and the normative order. Shotter drew a sharp contrast between the natural and the moral and a corresponding contrast between the referential and the nonreferential uses of language. His basic position was that the language of reasons, thought, evaluation, meaning, intentionality and so on, are nonreferential and to treat them in realist terms, as referring to mental entities, mental processes, or generative mechanisms, is theoretically false and morally pernicious. Harré accepted many of Shotter's criticisms of traditional realist psychology and shared many of his positive proposals. For Harré, too, mentalist idioms do not *refer* to processes; they *are* those processes. Harré defended a place for natural scientific theorizing about humans, was committed to what he called "policy realism" about theoretical entities, and tried to coordinate the various accounts of human experience and behavior in nonreductive ways.

We want to argue that antirealism about minds, generative mechanisms, and so on, is at best ill-conceived and unmotivated by any of the arguments that Shotter offered on its behalf and at worst counterproductive in terms of his own concern with a morally responsible science of persons. In our view, Harré rightly rejected the antithesis between realism and constructionism. The issue is not real versus unreal, but the mode of being of thought, conversation, experience, cognition, and so forth. Harré was also right to reject any strong antithesis between the natural powers of humans and their personal dimensions. He rightly saw the necessity of coordinating natural scientific accounts of humans and human science accounts. We argue that simple compartmentalizing is an inadequate response to the problems posed by reductionistic scientism. What is needed is a revisioning of both natural and human sciences.

In our view, part of the motivation for Shotter's strong opposition to realism and naturalism was his presumption that naturalistic science in a realist mode creates a form of life in which humans are constituted as automatons and where scientific expertise lays claim to hegemonic authority and institutional power that erodes our own moral authority and personal power. We criticize this idea by means of a discourse analysis of a case study presented by Sacks and Wasserman (1987) concerning one man's struggle to come to terms with a brain injury. We try to show that the natural scientific enterprise is not as one-dimensional or monolithic as Shotter assumed. Neurophysiologists are more than scientific experts and need not reduce their relation to their patients to that of expert management of a physical object; natural scientific explanations become important to the moral and personal challenges faced by Mr. I (a brain-injured patient). We conclude that the distinction between human and natural science does not map onto the distinction between moral and amoral discourse. A morally and politically sensitive science has to take account of the ways that descriptions of humans as physical objects or biological organisms are value-laden. Likewise, our accounts of ourselves as moral agents will have to give due place to our physical embodiment.

PERSONS AS AGENTS IN RELATION

Since *The Explanation of Social Behavior* (Harré & Secord, 1972), Harré consistently criticized what he sometimes called "chuckle headed materialism" in psychology. Harré rejected most of the forms of naturalistic social science as profoundly wrong-headed when it comes to understanding humans. He frequently alluded to the hidden political and moral presuppositions underlying the standard automata model of human beings and insisted that these models are based both on mistaken epistemologies and unhelpful ontologies.

Most standard approaches to social science labor under positivist misconceptions of the nature of science. Harré rejected the idea that science is primarily about correlations between observed phenomena. He rejected any kind of naive experimentalism that failed to take account of the social and moral context of human action. He criticized many social psychological experiments for drastically altering the social reality in the course of experimentation (Harré, 1983). He rejected the idea that the social psychological behavior is generated by some mechanism internal to the individual human person (like the brain or some more diaphanous part like a soul or mind substance).

Most forms of modern psychology are either ontologically coy (e.g., various forms of behaviorism or the innumerable covariation studies that use operationally defined variables) or vigorously materialistic and mechanistic. The most popular version of modern mechanism uses the digital computer as the principal explanatory model. The underlying assumption is that the only alternative to dualism or behaviorism is some form of mechanism. Science is thought to be naturalistic and naturalism is thought to require some form of mechanism. The assumption is that psychology faces a trilemma with respect to culture, thought, and language. Either we give up naturalism and adopt some form of dualism, we maintain a studied ignorance about mental and cultural realities in favor of behaviorism, or we explicate, by reduction, the distinctive human forms of cultural and cognitive life in mechanistic terms.

Harré rejected the problem posed in these terms; he rejected dualism.

He found various forms of behavioristically inspired approaches to psychology methodologically naive, morally and politically suspect, and scientifically barren, but found the various attempts at reductive explanation incoherent. After all, science itself is a cultural enterprise with a strong moral dimension (Harré, 1986). We must give an account of human beings that makes sense of the social, psychological, and moral character of those very accounts.

In brief, Harré criticized conventional psychology for its positivist preoccupations with correlations, for its experimental naiveté, for its individualism, and for its obsession with inner mechanisms (mental or mechanical). Because science itself is a product of the actions of cultural beings, a reasonable view of humans must make sense of human agency, of humans as social, cultural, and moral beings, if it is going to make sense of the very scientific process of theorizing about humans. So, in the end, there can be no science–persons antithesis.

Crucial to Harré's view is the idea of "powers" (Harré & Madden, 1975). One of the basic categories in Harré's ontology was that of a *powerful particular*. Particulars function in a context (In Newtonian science, the basic particulars are atoms and the framework or context of interaction is space and time. The basic form of interaction is causal. The basic properties are mass, force, etc.).

Powers are thought to be grounded in (enabled by) the inner structures of things (Harré, 1986; Harré & Madden, 1975). They are dispositions or propensities to manifest certain features or properties subject to certain kinds of relationships with, interactions with, or manipulations by other powerful particulars.

Humans are themselves powerful particulars. By means of their physical and biological endowments, they interact with their environment. Harré (1990) said:

> Human life is lived with respect to two intransigent, imperfectly knowable "realities." As embodied beings we are located in physical space-time and have such powers as our material embodiment endows us with. But as psychological and social beings we are locations in another world. (p. 352)

Our powers are derived both from our material embodiment and from our sociocultural heritage in complex intertwinement. "Reality" in the first instance is our *umwelt*—those features of the world that are manifested to us in socially shaped, culturally conditioned, biophysically enabled interaction with the environment. These two realities or realms are not separate. As physical beings we engage in social action. As social beings, we engage in material practice and embodied action.

Harré took natural science to be a means of extending the human umwelt and as a means of building explanatory models of the generative mechanisms that give rise to the experienced world. He took social science to be understanding the discursive process and relations that enable, occasion, and constrain social action.

Science is about the enabling structures, the generative mechanisms, the available dispositional powers that make up the world. In the case of the natural world, science is interested in those powers inherent in things. In one sense, these powers are thought to be independent of human beings (Harré, 1986, p. 281). In another, they are dependent on human action and experience. The phenomena about which science theorizes (building explanatory models of the generative structures) are "defined by the available experimental equipment" (Harré, 1993, p. 154) and are "brought into being through some human intervention" (Harré, 1986, p. 281). We theorize, by means of science, about a world made manifest by the actions of particular kinds of beings. Those interactions are enabled (and limited) by the nature of whatever sensorimotor faculties we inherited or enlarged by means of sense-extending instruments.

The material practice dimension of science is conditioned (and constrained) by both the embodied character of humans and the inherent powers in the world. The social practice dimension (which is always interwoven with material practices) is conditioned by the location of scientists in a network of social structures. Social, political, moral, and economic forces all play a role in shaping the discursive practices of the scientific community.

A science of persons need not (and cannot) confine itself to investigating inherited biophysical structures. The most distinctive features of human action are only explicable with reference to the social realm. In this domain, the generative structures are not primarily physical but linguistic (or "grammatical") and moral. The social realm is best thought of as a network of speech-acts in which persons are seen as nodes in the network. Humans are embodied agents whose biophysical powers are shaped and enlarged in social contexts. To understand human action is to understand the moral orders, social institutions, and communication channels. These moral orders certainly condition human action, but they do not cause speech-acts in the same way that a match causes hydrogen to explode. Speech acts are not "caused" by other speech-acts, but are occasioned by them in accordance with rules of appropriateness (Harré & Gillett, 1994).

Harré was especially critical of any confusion between these two dimensions (e.g., Harré, 1984). Moral orders are not to be understood in mechanistic terms; they are not brain or gene mechanisms. Humans act in accordance with their understanding of the moral and social context of their action. Our biophysical constitution certainly enables action, but we cannot explain human action exhaustively (or even explicate its most distinctive features) by appeal to body mechanism. On the other hand, Harré showed no inclination to turn theoretic incommensurability into some kind of ontological separation. We cannot confuse the moral and the material, and we cannot separate them (see especially Harré, Clarke, & De Carlo, 1985; Harré & Gillett, 1994).

Even this way of putting the matter might lead to misunderstanding. Harré's strong distinction between moral and mechanical types of explanation did not map onto the fact–value, description–evaluation, objective–involved distinctions. For Harré, all forms of discourse—all modes of explanation—have a moral component. Even natural science is a moral as well as material enterprise. The difference for Harré was not that natural science is morally neutral and social science is morally involved. The difference was that natural science is morally qualified discourse about natural generative mechanisms and social science is morally qualified discourse about social structure and moral orders. The focus of study is different and Harré warned against treating moral orders as mechanisms. Yet, there is no absolute distinction between description and evaluation. There is only an important distinction between morally qualified descriptions of actions being performed in accordance with social norms and equally morally conditioned accounts of mechanical events that happen in accordance with causal laws. Descriptions of all kinds are morally conditioned. Some of those descriptions refer to processes that are mechanical and some of them to processes that are themselves moral and discursive processes. In a given human being, moral and mechanical orders are, in a certain sense, united or coordinated. The causal, mechanical structures of the organism are subjected not only to physical law, but also to human intentionality and social norms.

Shotter shared many of Harré's concerns and articulated many of the concerns of the hermeneutic tradition in an exemplary fashion. Not only is it the case that a reflexive psychology that embraces theorizing psychologists themselves cannot be coherently formulated in the natural scientific tradition (Gauld & Shotter, 1977, p. 4), but it is immoral to treat humans as if they were mere bits of the mechanism of nature (Shotter, 1975, p. 13). Humans are not only natural organisms, but also crucially, cultural beings. Shotter borrowed from Renaissance humanists the idea of humans as "self-defining beings" who are not enclosed inside a deterministic causal order. Humans are agents who act in accordance with meanings, reasons, and understandings and do not just move under the impact of efficient causes (Gauld & Shotter, 1977, pp. 5–7; Shotter, 1975, pp. 12–14).

Naturalism has increasingly tried to include humans in its general mechanist picture with paradoxical theoretical and questionable moral results. The mechanistic picture of the universe that one finds clearly exemplified in Descartes allows us to relate to the world in terms of mastery and control. Yet, the inclusion of humans in that mechanical order would make us subjects rather than masters. How is scientific inquiry with its controlled experiments possible if all action is really the outcome of blind mechanical forces (Gauld & Shotter, 1977, pp. 4, 69)? Both thought and action in a mechanistic world are ultimately mysterious (Shotter, 1975, p. 30).

For human action to be intelligible in its human distinctiveness, we must relate to humans not simply as things, but as persons. Persons act by construing themselves as agents with moral accountability. To be human is to act under the guidance of some conception of oneself in relation to the rest of the universe and one's fellow humans. It is not enough to be recognizable to an outside observer as an organism whose activity is the result of a system of interacting parts; to be a person is to recognize oneself as responsibly taking action. To be a person is to make sense to ourselves and to others (Shotter, 1975, pp. 19–21). Persons cannot be understood simply by taking an outside observer stance. We need to see them as integrated embodied agents with interests and needs. This requires taking into account experiential criteria that we know about from our own action and experience (p. 68).

The results of modern psychology, with its mechanistic bias, do not serve to reveal that humans are "really" automata. It simply participates in the creation of more machine-like humans. We establish the automata image of humans along with the results of our experimental inquiry. The practices and prestige of psychological science actually serve to promote or *create* the kinds of humans implicit in the mechanistic paradigm (Shotter, 1975, pp. 27–28).

Shotter (1975) claimed that modern mechanism is the inconsistent wedding of classical Greek notions of humans as isolated contemplative minds set over against the material universe and modern materialism, which sees us as submechanisms of the great mechanism of nature (p. 30). As objective knowers, we are a mind apart; as objects known, we are automata. In Shotter's (1990) view, mechanistic psychology "suppressed genuine individuality and led to us all being treated as indistinguishable atoms" (p. 207). Appeals to mechanism were used to disclaim responsibility and avoid accountability. Academic psychology committed to mechanistic assumptions lent support for dubious political and morally obnoxious proposals.

Social constructionism was Shotter's antidote to this antihumanistic view of persons. People are first and foremost agents. They are immersed in the world and have the power to act and change their surroundings. Furthermore, they are fundamentally communal beings. They are constituted as persons by their adopting the task of giving intelligibility to the world and to their lives. For Shotter, as for Harré, persons are agents in relation (Shotter, 1975, p. 31; Shotter, 1990, p. 212).

MORAL ACTIVITIES VERSUS GENERATIVE MECHANISMS

In his earlier work, Shotter had recourse to the idea of personal powers adapted from Harré. He was particularly interested in those personal powers that Harré called "capabilities." *Capabilities* are just those powers that people acquire without changing their fundamental character (Harré, 1970, p. 93). Shotter (1990) saw this as a framework for exploring the process by means of which children learn to "appropriate their own natural powers and to bring them under their own control as personal powers" (p. 208).

However, despite his shared interests with and debts to Harré, Shotter also had reservations about Harré's approach. Shotter identified these reservations as follows:

> Harré tended to concentrate on "the already socially aware person" (Shotter, 1990, p. 208). People not only adopt roles and follow rules, but they also create, challenge, and correct them. Shotter wanted to understand the developmental process through which rules come into being and are transformed and the ways in which they are appropriated by the child from the adult. According to Shotter, Harré's work with Secord (Harré & Secord, 1972) assumed people who had already internalized a body of rules and adopted certain roles (Shotter, 1990, p. 208). Shotter was more concerned with exploring the process by which the moral order (with its roles, rules, and meanings) developed through negotiation in a social context.

> The *personal appropriation of natural powers view* was an interindividual concept of persons rather than a genuinely social one. Personal development was seen as unfolding, expressing, or revealing of natural powers somehow given with the nature of the organism. According to Shotter (1990), this omits "almost everything of historical, moral, and political importance" (p. 209). Using Vygotsky and Wittgenstein, Shotter came to emphasize that personal action is action subject to our awareness of the copresence of others and subject to evaluation by them and by us. Such judgments and evaluations are dynamic and subject to negotiation. Such negotiation takes place in a context of unequal rights and obligations, but not in a private inner space (Shotter, 1990, p. 210).

Shotter acknowledged that Harré himself shared most of these concerns and came in time to shift his emphasis on roles and rules to negotiation in a morally differentiated social sphere. Like Shotter, Harré (1983) insisted that "the primary human reality is persons in conversation" (p. 58). Despite these shifts of emphasis in Harré, Shotter remained unsatisfied with Harré's version of social constructionism because it was insufficiently radical. Shotter believed that social constructionism is fundamentally at odds with a realist philosophy of science.

As should be obvious, Shotter's earlier work assumed a fairly sharp contrast between psychology as a moral science and the realm of the natural sciences (Shotter, 1990, p. 209). In his later work, this demarcation between natural science and moral science was radicalized. In fact, he found it necessary to reject any realist interpretation of persons, minds, or selves because realism carries naturalistic baggage that is incompatible with psychology as a moral science. We find this rejection instructive because it helps pinpoint what we take to be a fundamental flaw in Shotter's whole program.

Shotter's critique of Harré, in a nutshell, is just the claim that realism is naturalistic and social constructionism is antinaturalistic, so Harré cannot consistently be both a realist and a social constructionist (Shotter, 1990, p. 207). In our view, it seems that Shotter was operating with a set of contrasts and oppositions that were alien to Harré's perspective. Although there are others, the following seem to be the most important:

- *Individualism versus Holism.* Shotter was strongly anti-individualist. Even though he showed concern about preserving a conception of the unique individuality of persons, this was coupled with an equally strong insistence that humans are not atomic, self-contained entities and that we need a different conceptual framework in order to understand beings whose identity is nonlocal and nonsubstantive (Shotter, 1990, p. 214).

  It is not clear why a social holism or a social constructionism should be at odds with realism at this point. Harré's version of realism had no special preference for substances over field notions or for intrinsic properties over relational ones. It is true that many historical forms of realism tend toward atomism, but Harré's version of "policy realism" had no such prejudices.

- *Invariant lawfulness versus variable particularity.* The defenders of *Geisteswissenshaften* usually insisted that human action is relative to context and widely variable. It may be possible to treat quasars as identical objects subject to invariant laws, but humans are variable particulars subject to a host of local conditions. Shotter emphasized that the rules, customs, and moral orders that constitute human action as meaningful are different from standard causal laws in two ways: They may not be universal or invariant for all people the world over (Gauld & Shotter, 1977, p. 94) and they are constituted by being known, produced, and reproduced by the community of moral agents. Observable regularities are the outcome of rule creation, observance, and maintenance by a community of intelligent, moral agents (Gauld & Shotter, 1977, pp. 97–98).

Harré clearly rejected the idea that the real is identical with the invariant. He argued that, given the role of language in the construction of persons, it is unlikely that many of the features of human psychology are universally shared. Although we can expect many features to be universal, we should also expect there to be differences in developmental stages, differences in emotional responses, and even differences in the perception of space and time (Harré, Clarke, & De Carlo, 1985, p. 7). Interest in the universal features of human animals can go hand in hand with indigenous psychologies of persons.

- *Reduction versus emergence.* Defenders of an autonomous social science have usually held that there are properties—aspects or features—of persons not reducible to physical states or properties. In its most extreme form the autonomy of human science is grounded in an ontological dualism. More moderate versions depend on some kind of notion of emergence, according to which nonphysical properties are said to emerge from or be supervenient on physical properties. Although Shotter was generally critical of Cartesianism in all of its aspects, he also clearly rejected reductionism: "Organisms cannot be reduced to mechanisms (though organisms may contain mechanisms), and people cannot be reduced to either organisms or mechanisms (though they may contain both)" (Shotter, 1975, p. 124). Rather than address the question of whether the mind is or is not something "over and above the functioning of the brain" (Gauld & Shotter, 1977, p. 97), he insisted that hermeneutic accounts of human action are indispensable and that such accounts cannot be incorporated into physiological accounts. He also spoke of a developmental process by means of which the natural powers of humans become transformed into personal powers (Shotter,

1990, p. 208).

Harré shared Shotter's antireductionist concerns. He also rejected the idea that in talking about minds, we are talking about some substance inside the human organism. He rejected the idea that minds and brains can be dealt with inside of a single ontological framework. Yet, the fact that minds are not real as substances within the brain does not mean that they are not real in some other fashion—as a set of functional properties that relate the human organism to its environment in a communal context, for example.

That the mind is not a piece of (material or mental) mechanism does not mean that we cannot name, describe, or explain various mental functions such as perception, memory, or thinking. That such mental functions are emergent or that they develop in social conversational contexts does not preclude the possibility that these are real functions. That talk about thinking, deciding, evaluating, and so on is not reducible to talk about neurophysiology does not entail that there is no relation between brain functions and mental functions. Just because we cannot find a mechanism that produces thought (the way a boiler produces steam) does not render inquiry into brain function irrelevant to understanding human thought and action.

It should be pointed out that Harré's interest in generative mechanisms was only one aspect of his view of how science should deal with human beings. Harré wrote of the brain as "the repository of meanings in that it serves as the physical medium in which mental content is realized and plays a part in the discursive activities of individuals" (Harré & Gillett, 1994, p. 81). Harré was interested in both how these mechanisms enable or provide the medium for discursive activities and also how the higher level social and cognitive functions shape the structure and function of the brain. Antireductionism does not require antinaturalism; it also does not require disinterest in brain mechanisms. It only requires an attention to the distinction and relations between various ontological and methodological levels.

• *Reasons versus causes.* It is sometimes claimed that even though atoms may be subject to invariant laws and blind causes, humans, by contrast, act in terms of a framework of rules and meanings, and to understand action is to grasp the reasons, not to understand the causes. Shotter did not deny that it is sometimes appropriate to offer causal explanations of human actions or aspects of human actions (Gauld & Shotter, 1977, p. 97). He did, however, deny that such accounts are adequate in themselves for a full account of human action (pp. 12, 97). A full account must address the purposes, desires, and calculations of the agent. We have at present no understanding of how such rational accounts can be coordinated with causal accounts. There may be some link between neurophysiology and intentionality, but we certainly have no good idea of what it might look like. We may revise our notion of cause in order to allow for reasons to be causes, but Shotter was not optimistic about this possibility (pp. 152–153). The rational, moral order of human meaning is a product of human agency and is irreducible to the causal order as that is conventionally understood (p. 179).

Harré showed significant sensitivity to this issue. Humans are not simple causal mechanisms. They are agents in a moral order who act in accordance with rules and plans and evaluate their performances. Even computers cannot be understood in terms of simple efficient causality. The functions of a computer are not explicable simply in terms of physical architecture (Harré, Clarke, & De Carlo, 1985, pp. 9–10). Harré talked of control hierarchies and about how the discursive functions shape and regulate brain function (Harré & Gillett, 1994, p. 81). He suggested that decisions and plans might be considered as a special category of cause (Harré, Clarke, & De Carlo, 1985, p. 10) and wrote of resurrecting "the full Aristotelian conception of a human being as a rational, social animal" (Harré & Gillett, 1994, p. 80). Thus, there is nothing about Harré's commitment to realism that is antinaturalistic or incompatible with recognizing the importance of the distinction between reasons and efficient causes.

- *Facts versus values.* Natural science discovers laws about what is the case. It describes what is, not what ought to be. Things are moved about subject to pre-established laws. People, on the other hand, act in terms of beliefs and conceptions about what they think ought to be. The moral domain and the very quality of personal action is formed through negotiation (Shotter, 1975, pp. 217–218). This comes very close to the crux of the matter for Shotter. In his view, stating facts about humans is fundamentally different from personal participation in morally conditioned action. We can state facts about mechanisms or engage in free, responsible, moral action. We can name, describe, and explain objects or evaluate, persuade, decide, or plan as personal subjects. Facts are static. Moral conversations are dynamic processes in which the reality is not fixed but created in conversation. Substances are (apparently) determined. In conversation, persons are constituted as moral agents by the very process of the conversation. Referring to substances is inappropriate in psychology because it removes the person from the process of moral negotiation and fixes them at the end of the observer's gaze or as a passive product of a generative mechanism.

Shotter (1990) argued that social constructionism requires an ontology of "diffusely distributed, non-locatable, morally structured activities that can *only* be investigated from a position of involvement within them" (p. 213, emphasis added). Harré's realism, with its talk of persons as powerful particulars, suggested a mechanistic "structure of locatable powers and competencies" (p. 213).

The issue between Harré and Shotter here is particularly obscure. Harré granted that conversation is the primary human reality. He argued that the basic "things" or basic particulars of psychology are not individual humans, but speech-acts. Individual persons are the locations among which conversations occur. Persons are derived, secondary constructions. They are to be treated as analogous to space and time in Newtonian physics. The object of psychological research "ought to be the resources, the 'grammars'...that are any individual's means for action" (Harré, 1990, p. 352).

The language of emotion and thought are not names for inner processes, they are those very processes. To speak of the mind is not to name an inner entity or mental mechanism. Speech-acts constitute *minding*—a process of communication, negotiation between people. Psychological phenomena exist as the various processes of discourse (Harré & Gillett, 1994, p. 22). Mind exists as the processes of conversation, moral appraisal, and so on. Persons can be credited with having minds to the extent that there is some longitudinal integrity to the way they adopt positions within communal discourses and fashion for themselves a unique complex of subjectivities (Harré & Gillett, 1994, p. 25). The issue for Harré was not "are minds real," but "how are minds real?" His realism about minds and persons was not a commitment to the idea that the mind is an inner mechanism and is not incompatible with social constructionism. Given all this agreement, the exact nature of Shotter's discontent was difficult to decipher.

Perhaps it had something to do with Harré's insistence not only that humans are also physical things, but that this fact is relevant to understanding human behavior. So, even though Harré denied that the ontologies of these "worlds" mesh or that a single theoretical framework can be constructed to deal with the complexity, he believed that both were important to understanding human beings. Furthermore, he was committed to exploring the ways in which brain mechanisms enable or provide the medium for the discursive processes and to the ways that discourse shapes the structure and function of the brain (Harré & Gillett, 1994, p. 81). Perhaps it is here that Shotter wanted to part company. He had no interest in these latter questions. As he put it, "as far as Psychology is concerned, humans might just as well have porridge in their heads as brains" (Shotter, in conversation, 1995).

DECONSTRUCTING CONVERSATIONAL ESSENTIALISM

In his reply to Shotter, Harré (1990) emphasized their shared commitments rather than their differences. We believe that the differences are highly instructive and represent important issues for social constructionist psychology. In our view, Harré's position was the more promising one. It seems important to maintain both the distinctiveness (autonomy) of modes of explanation that appeal to reasons and moral orders from those forms of explanation that appeal to mechanisms and at the same time, to find some kind of coordination of these differing accounts.

Shotter seemed ill-disposed to accept "realist" minds even if they are socially constructed, relational processes between people. To talk of the mind as real makes it sound like the term *mind* refers to some "thing" behind the talk. The result is the illusion of some inner entity that is already there, fixed and finished. Mind talk refers to no thing at all. What it does is specify what ought to be; it evaluates, evokes, and brings forth a self in dynamic exchanges between people. To talk as if there is something that is already there is to foreclose the process by means of which people become, by means of which they exercise moral agency (Shotter, 1990, pp. 214ff.).

There are puzzling features to this argument. There seems to be some kind of assumption that moral accountability and responsible action are not possible if we concern ourselves with what we find to be the case about the human animal or the world in general. Shotter seemed to link the domain of the moral to a local process of construction. Amoral structures that are "there" are intrinsically opposed to the morally responsible practice and process of dialogical negotiation. Fact stating and moral evaluation are just different activities and, as a moral science, psychology should not concern itself with facts about structures, mechanisms, or substances. Shotter seemed to think that realists who concern themselves with the facts in this fashion are secret moralizers (or immoralizers) who are blind to their own moral commitments. Shotter implied that there are no facts here to be found and that realists like Manicas and Secord (1983), and perhaps Harré, are substituting the finding of pseudofacts for the responsible making of social reality (Shotter, 1990, pp. 214ff.). Now, there can be no doubt that concealing one's moral and political commitments by discovering them in the facts is a common game of dubious moral and political pedigree, but in our view pitting moral construction over immoral or amoral fact finding is unnecessary and unhelpful.

Our assessments of *what there is* are no less contested, negotiated, and responsible than our specifically moral commitments. As Harré (1986) pointed out, all science takes place within a moral order. The material practices of experimentation go hand in hand with the social processes of rhetorical argument and debate within an essentially moral framework. In a sense, to claim the right to name, describe, or explain something is to claim moral authority in a community (p. 8). As he put it elsewhere, "the physical sciences...are themselves part of the Conversation" (Harré, 1990, p. 351).

In other words, we need to understand natural science in moral and political terms. Shotter (1990) wrote of "enlarging the sphere of public accountability" (p. 222). One way of achieving this end would be to take seriously the implications of postpositivist philosophy of science. There are no neutral facts. Not only is our identity an essentially contestable domain, but so is the whole fabric of our knowledge of the world. As Hesse (1980) pointed out:

> It is impossible in studying theories of evolution, ecology, or genetics, to separate a mode of knowledge relating to technical control from a mode relating to the self understanding of [humans....since] the very categories of these theories, such as functionality, selection, survival, are infected by [our] view of [our]selves. (p. 186)

This claim should be generalized. Rouse (1991) pointed out that even our understanding of causality is related to our understanding of ourselves as agents (p. 53). He argued that to see our natural scientific categories as somehow separated from our self-understanding is in effect to insulate them from critique. If we accept the idea that natural science gives us neutral categories for understanding natural reality, then these categories are somehow immune from moral and political critique, and our moral exhortations about what ought to be are thereby seriously weakened.

Shotter (1990) was concerned that realists were incapable of self-reflexivity, that to talk in realist terms is to insulate such categories from critique (p. 215). This is a valid concern (although obviously overstated) that, in our view, should be addressed not by outlawing referential talk (or theory) or every kind of realism, but precisely by insisting on moral and political accountability across the board. If we want to be sensitive to the moral dilemmas posed by the hegemony of science in our culture, then what is needed is a thoroughgoing rejection of the myth of objectivity in all areas of human life. Like Rouse (1991), we believe that "a sharp separation between the social and the natural is incapable of grasping much of our current political situation" (pp. 53–54). What is needed is a political philosophy of science, a revised sense that in both nature and society, we are responsible moral agents who negotiate with our fellow humans our sense of ourselves and our wider reality.

The contrast between the human domain, in which what humans think and agree on enters in their very constitution, and the natural world, in which we find things ready-made, is false and pernicious. In fact, the assumption that there are some natural structures or mechanisms that are irrelevant to human moral judgment perpetuates another neutrality myth. This does not enlarge the domain of human accountability; it simply perpetuates a Humean is–ought dichotomy. Then, it attempts to maintain the priority of the moral through the studied neglect of the natural.

Shotter seemed to think that a moral science, a science of human beings, should (must) refrain from referring to humans and must instead address them. We are, it is claimed, self-interested moral agents and when we engage in those practices called "social science" in our culture, we must grasp that fact in our scientific practice. In our view, this assertion confuses a number of issues. Humans are self-interpreting agents. Science, whether social or natural, is conducted by humans who inhabit a framework of practices, assumptions, moral obligations, authority, and so forth. Whether looking at emotion or energy transfer, this background is operative in some way. Yet, it is clear that this background does not simultaneously need to be the focus of our inquiry. In fact, it functions precisely as tacit background. Humans can attend to (describe, interpret, explain) trees without paying explicit attention to the process of interpretation or the nature of humans as interpreters. When directing their inquiry toward human beings they may attend to the process of interpretation or to the nature of humans as interpreters (or not). They may attend to them as point masses, biological organisms, orators, or lovers.

Here, again, Rouse's critique of a similar argument in Charles Taylor is helpful. Rouse interpreted the defenders of a distinctive interpretive human science as arguing that in the human sciences, we ourselves are at stake in a way in which we are not in the natural sciences (Rouse, 1987, p. 172). Our identity is constituted (at least in part) by our self-understanding and self-understanding is at stake in the human sciences. In contrast, although interpretation is involved in our understanding of natural objects, the being of natural objects is not altered by our changing interpretations of them. According to Rouse (1987):

Taylor begins with the point I and his critics happily acknowledge: all knowledge is interpretive, and can be intelligible only against a back-ground of meaning and practices. But he infers from this point that when we take ourselves or others as objects of interpretation, we must take account of them as interpreters working within a particular configuration of meaning. (p. 173)

Rouse (1987) argued that this conclusion of Taylor's (and we suggest that the same applies to Shotter's similar version) did not follow from the premises. All science is necessarily hermeneutic, but not all science focuses on the interpretive practices or interpretive capacities of humans. The fact that science must conduct its studies within a configuration of meaning "says nothing about how human beings will show up as objects within that configuration" (p. 173). In the context of Newtonian physics, they show up as point masses. In the context of the practice of trying to close an overfull suitcase, they appear as things (Harré, 1991, p. 13). In epistemology or brain science, they might—depending on the operative theory and methodology—appear as information processors, self-reflec-tive interpreters, or what have you (cf. MacKay, 1991).

Shotter (1990) thought that to see humans as anything but conversa-tional realities is ultimately self-defeating or that to do so is to be self-deceived (pp. 215, 221). Why this is self-deceived is not entirely clear. Presumably, it is self-defeating because to see humans as point masses is to render unintelligible the very interpretive enterprise itself, including the process whereby we make sense out of the notion of point masses. This conclusion follows only if one makes additional assumptions to the effect that the practices behind the notion of point mass are somehow incompatible with the conversational processes undergirding all inter-pretation. Yet, this only holds true if we accept the exclusive validity of a physicalistic, reductionist account.

However, there is another aspect to Shotter's claim here. We are tempted to call this his *conversational essentialism*. Nothing in Shotter's social constructionism prepares us for the kind of a priori rejection of different ways of conceiving or understanding human beings. After re-jecting ahistorical facts, reified human natures, and essences that are not the products (or processes) of conversation, there is no consistent way for Shotter to insist that the only proper interpretive context for under-standing humans is conversation. Apparently, humans are essentially self-creating meaning makers.

In our view humans are not essentially anything. We argued earlier that we cannot distinguish between the natural and human sciences in terms of their moral character because all science is a moral enterprise occurring within a framework of practices and assumptions subject to negotiation and evaluation. Likewise, we cannot (and have no need to) privilege one type of inquiry over another. There are many ways that humans are, and every true description captures one of those ways. These ways of being, including our physical, organic, emotional ways, are not mutually exclusive and no one way is more real than the others. All of our activities, including biophysical processes, are morally conditioned and discursively shaped and our discursive activities of moral evaluation are conditioned—shaped, limited, enabled—by our physical and biological constitution. If this is the case (and we cannot mount a serious argument for it here), then not only is Shotter's essentialism at odds with his constructionism, but it is also at odds (dare we say it?) with the nature of things.

In the final analysis, moral evaluation is not just about what *should* be the case; it is also about what *is* the case. A great deal of human discourse blurs the distinction between referring and evaluating. This is not the same as confusing moral and mechanical orders, however. A contract exists between two people as a moral and legal reality. Moral and legal structures exist not as mechanisms, but precisely as moral orders. The moral domain is not just about imperatives or prescriptives, it also has an indicative dimension.

One important dimension of the social constructionist brief against conventional forms of psychological theory is the complaint against false universalism. Local contexts and practices are crucial in understanding human beings. In fact, Shotter often rejected naturalistic theory on the grounds that it was at odds with the self-understanding and discursive practices of real people. Yet, the essentialist contrast between generative mechanisms and moral discursive practice itself seems to be at odds with a wider range of ordinary experience.

For example, the strong description–evaluation dichotomy seems alien to most ordinary language. Hampshire (1989) argued the Humean is–ought dichotomy does little justice to the practices of description and evaluation. He illustrated this claim with reference to the predicates that are applied to people's movements. Terms like *clumsy, stiff, delicate, tense, agitated, gentle, hesitant, stately, tentative,* and so on blur the distinction between description and evaluation. Hampshire noted that these "impressionistic" predicates apply not only to persons, but also to the whole universe, as it is experienced in relation to human needs and interests. We do not separate our responses, with their emotional colorations or self-interested directedness, from the object in itself. We operate "as if we are in dialogue with the external world" (p. 97). More generally, our grounds for evaluating some object as good or bad are inseparable from our grounds for classifying it as an object of a certain type.

The interdependence of factual and moral–political issues can also be clearly seen in any public debate about significant social developments, so too can the use of various fields of expertise and various genres of writing. For example, Van Dyck (1995), in her study of discourses shaping the public debate on in vitro fertilization (IVF), showed, quite clearly, how the same issue has multiple dimensions and that the boundaries between them are constantly subject to negotiation. Van Dyck found static contrasts between politically dominant and oppositional discourses unfruitful in her work. She instead offered a more dynamic formulation of the exercise of oppressive power. "Rather than defining discursive categories as sites of oppression, I...explicate the power relations that condition and limit dialogic possibilities in a public debate" (p. 198). Although oppositions such as medicine versus feminism or science versus journalism prove too simplistic to account for the unfolding IVF debate, they can be replaced with questions like: "Which discourses are drawn upon in the formulation of journalistic accounts and policy debates?"

This more subtle characterization emerges from the strong permeability among the discursive forms of science, journalism and fiction identified by Van Dyck (1995):

> The limits between discourses are never established once and for all; these limits are themselves the provisional outcome and the stakes in the battle for signification. Rather than policing boundaries, postmodern "reality" prompts us to develop alternative ways of thinking about the relation between the still dominant hierarchy of institutional discourses and hybrid categories of text and genre. (p. 37)

In the public debates about IVF, we see a continual interaction among the discourses of science, journalism, feminism, and fiction as well as a process of mutual appropriation among these discursive forms in news-letters, journal articles, and media reports.

The processes of negotiation shaping the discursive unfolding of the IVF debate span the full range of description and evaluation while deploying complex variations of co-optation, critique, convergence, and creative reconstruction. For example, some feminist critiques effectively encompass elements of medical discourse while resisting the naturalization of IVF as standard medical technique. Van Dyck herself creatively appropriated institutional discourses of journalism and medicine in the service of her own project, advocating an expansive, dialogic version of public debate. In this manner, she cogently embodied a local pluralist form of criticism that successfully couples evaluation with description and identification and deconstruction with advocacy.

The interdependence of description, evaluation, and criticism high-lighted by Hampshire (1989) and Van Dyck (1995) has important ramifications for the supposed contrast that Shotter (1990) insisted exists between referring and exhorting or between natural scientific theorizing and social scientific moralizing. Shotter claimed that naturalistic bio-logical inquiry is irrelevant to and incompatible with a moral science of persons. Yet, if evaluation and description are as closely related as Van Dyck and Hampshire suggested, then Shotter's claim is clearly problem-atic. In Shotter's view, irrelevance arises because the practices of realist theorizing preempt the moral negotiations that characterize responsible conversation. Following Van Dyck's lead, we want to briefly elaborate on the interdependence of evaluation and description, as well as high-light the permeability of disciplinary and institutional boundaries, by exploring discursive activities arising in the domain of health care. Thera-peutic contexts readily implicate both our embodied interests and our moral concerns. We highlight this dynamic interdependence of natural and personal domains through a case study in clinical neurology. Fur-thermore, in this clinical context, Shotter's thesis about the irrelevance of biology to psychology may become morally and therapeutically de-bilitating.

COLORFUL CONVERSATIONS

Is natural scientific discourse necessarily impersonal and amoral? Is the discourse of personal coping with health matters confined exclusively to ordinary language? Does the institutional power of medicine and science take shape solely in hegemonic, depersonalized discourses? Is personal coping with health matters completely isolated from the discourse of natural science and medicine? These are key questions sparked by Shotter's thesis about the irrelevance of description to moral action. Against this thesis, we have pressed a number of considerations about the relation between description and evaluation, the moral character of scientific research, and the interplay of various modes of discourse in real-life public debates, such as the IVF debate chronicled by Van Dyck. Now, consider in more detail a case presented by Sacks and Wasserman (1987) concerning Jonathan I's encounter with brain damage, and let us see if we can illustrate more fully the problematic character of this claim about the mutual relevance of different kinds of discourse in understanding and coping with brain damage. The point here is not that we can understand neurological function by appeal to moral norms or reduce moral norms to—or derive them from—information about neurology, but rather that we can understand the personal experience of Jonathan I and assess appropriate therapy strategies only by drawing on multiple and diverse forms of discourse.

Sacks and Wasserman (1987) wrote in a popularized genre of the clinical case study. The rhetorical resources they marshaled in their account exemplify the same kind of dynamic permeability among discourses articulated by Van Dyck. By publishing in *The New York Times Review of Books*, these authors take on the mantel of science journalists telling a good story. As clinical neurologists presenting a case study, they took on positions as medical and scientific experts. Yet, this familiar form of hybrid discourse (*popularization*) also incorporates self-qualifying elements imbued with clear moral dimensions. Jonathan I was depicted as one whose personal experience and art work contributed to and qualified the accounts provided by brain science and clinical expertise. Although conservative and dominant in its political tenor, their account did display the permeability and plurality of discourses identified by Van Dyck through an interweaving of oppositional forms. To trace these threads, we begin with a description of Jonathan I adapted from Sacks and Wasserman.

Jonathan was an accomplished visual artist who was in a car accident at age 65. He suffered minor brain damage in the accident, resulting in the complete loss of color vision. The ubiquitous black-and-white tones took on ghastly dimensions for Jonathan. Color was central in his painting, but it was also intimately intertwined with his entire life. His enjoyment of music was affected because, prior to the accident, he experienced vividly colored visual images in association with tones. These images of synesthesia lost their color as well. People, including his own reflection in the mirror, seemed like animate statues, rendering social interaction extremely aversive. Food lost its palatability to the point where, for a while, he chose to eat foods that were naturally colored black and white (e.g., coffee, olives, rice) to minimize the effect of the changed perceptions. The cerebral nature of the loss meant that, unlike someone who lost the wavelength discrimination function of the retinas, Jonathan's dreams, memories, and imagination were all equally as colorless—as "abnormally gray"—as was his perception. He could not escape the grays even when he slept.

Jonathan's painting during the months after the accident reflected emerging facets of his struggle with the transformation of his vision. In an early set of experiments he used colored paints as he perceived them, but to those with normal color vision, the products were a confusing jumble. Only when the canvases were photographed with black and white film could others perceive the order or sense of these paintings. Then, he turned to painting totally in black and white as a kind of artistic survival. This artistic turn yielded Jonathan's first solace after the loss. The early black-and-white paintings were filled with the powerful and violent feelings of his deprivation. After a couple of months, Jonathan moved into a new phase, turning from the "terrifying and alien" paintings to themes of life he had not touched on for 30 years.

This new phase displayed rich vitality, movement, and sensuousness. The transformations of his art coincided with a lessening of his depression and fears and the beginnings of renewed social and sexual interests. One year after the accident, Jonathan started "becoming a night person" (his words). He drove to other places to explore, arriving at dusk and wandering around for half the night. In the night world, Jonathan knew he was the equal or superior to normal people. Alternatively, he got up to paint at night—to relish the night.

In a couple of months after his accident, Mr. I (Jonathan) wrote to a well-known neurologist about his situation. Sacks and Wasserman did not tell their readers about their relationship with Mr. I, but it is clear that they assessed him and that they also arranged technical testing done by experts in the neurobiology of color vision. These highly specialized tests provided a definitive characterization of the nature of Mr. I's deficit as cerebral, rather than retinal.

At this point in our summary, the discourses of science journalism and clinical neurology dominate the account. The novelty of following an artist's progression through the loss of color vision could signify no more than a novel twist to a story in the service of good journalism. Yet, Sacks and Wasserman (1987) elaborated their account beyond this basic form in several directions. Drawing on a traditional distinction between clinical art and medical science, the particularity of Jonathan I's personal journey and the phenomenal experience of color are explicitly contrasted with a scientific, neurological understanding of his functioning. For example, Sacks and Wasserman wrote that:

> It is not clear that the experience, the phenomenon, of color can ever be explained (or explained away) by physiology or science: it retains a mystery, a wonder, that seems inaccessible, and that belongs in the sphere of the "given," not the sphere of questions and answers....The wonder of color vision, and the horror of its loss, are not diminished, are perhaps increased, by our scientific knowledge—and its limits. (p. 32)

Although asserting the presence of mystery and wonder beyond science, Sacks and Wasserman nonetheless wanted to maintain a relevance of science to these larger domains of significance. The categories of *individuality*, *horror*, *loss*, *wonder*, and *mystery* point to the significance of color in much the same way that *agitated*, *gentle*, and *hesitant* establish Hampshire's thesis in commonsense discourse about human movements. Scientific facts pertain, although in a loosely constrained way, to some larger accounts of human significance. Even while qualifying the exhaustiveness of their scientific institutional discourse, they still wanted to assert that science has some unexplored bearing on "mystery."

Sacks and Wasserman's (1987) account presented other facets as well. They implicitly portrayed a reconstitution of self in light of the fundamental place of color in Jonathan I's self-understanding and self-perception. The inherently social dimensions to this reconstitution come through vividly. In Jonathan's journey of artistic survival, the early painting experiments failed when he used colors merely as they appeared to him. Apparently, the failure depended, in part, on the inability of others to see his point, unless they worked through the secondary medium of black-and-white photographs of his work. Solace emerged for Jonathan when he took up painting in black and white, evidently because artistic survival required sharing the sense of his work with a viewing audience. Moreover, in Jonathan's reconstitution as a night person, an important dimension of his transformation was worked out in the context of his capacities, in relation to those around him—whose color vision was normal. Jonathan's healing took place in a dynamic new social and physical context—the night world. It seems that crucial features of this night world incorporated both physical (dimness of light) and social (visiting unfamiliar communities) dimensions. Moreover, the significance of Jonathan I's transformation into a night person is intrinsically intertwined with Sacks and Wasserman's delimitation of science discourse. The mystery, horror, and wonder alluded to by the neurologists expand the contexts of a case study beyond neuroscience and medicine to include questions of identity and existential significance.

In a third extension of the basic case study genre, Sacks and Wasserman's (1987) reliance on Jonathan's self-descriptions can also be highlighted. The respectful way in which they engaged his self report and his art work also delimits their expertise. Not only are they as scientists and clinicians dependent on Jonathan's verbal accounts and experimental responses to provide the basic data of observation, but his art work is also offered as a legitimate, even admired, source of data during Jonathan's reconstitution. Although taken for granted by most clinicians, the accounts offered by human "subjects" of scientific inquiry provide ineliminable access to important dimensions of human functioning, even as defined within the confines of neurological discourse (cf. MacKay, 1991; Wynne, 1988). In particular, Jonathan's expertise as an artist is marshaled in the Sacks and Wasserman account to sustain the references to wonder and to identity themes.

What of Shotter's stark contrast between exhorting and referring, between making morals and finding facts? By his account, moral negotiation in natural science discourse is unintelligible on its own terms and ultimately self-defeating. It seems to us that this case study illustrates the local nature of negotiation, the limited nature of expertise, the permeability of disciplinary boundaries, and effectively serves to counter Shotter's attempt to put these various modes of discourse in totally separate domains. A salient dimension for evaluating the moral coherence of the case study is the personal status of Jonathan I. Can this case study, as formulated by experts like Sacks and Wasserman, sustain a morally and personally sensitive stance toward Jonathan or does this genre inexorably diminish Jonathan's status as a moral agent, negotiating and participating in the human conversation? For our purposes, we probe two potential facets of significance for Jonathan I in his case study. Why did Jonathan cooperate with Sacks and Wasserman's assessment process? What sense might the neurological account of his injury have for Jonathan's wife?

Why did Jonathan contact the experts in the first place? Assuming that the experts were honest enough to admit that they had nothing to offer by way of treatment, why did Jonathan agree to participate in bothersome testing, share his art work, and maintain contact for 1 year? A sympathetic ear may be the answer. Furthermore, some people who have become patients find an expert account reassuring by supporting their own sense-making activities. Sometimes, the authority of a neurological account is crucial and at other times, science discourse can help make sense of specific discomforts or symptoms. Yet, it is also possible that Jonathan I submitted himself to the demands of additional neurological assessment as part of his own existential journey. Many people in our culture strive for significance in their suffering and among those who are successful, one finds those who adopt a script of "benefiting humanity" or "advancing science." Experts may tell you that your problem is rare or not well-understood, that what they learn from you can advance science, and furthermore, that such advances may well benefit others in some indeterminate future. If one successfully adopts a script of this form, one can access cultural resources available to the legitimately altruistic among us. Sacks and Wasserman (1987) provided little detail on this point for Jonathan I, but such a script comports well with Jonathan I's identity reconstitution project and with several other features of the available account. In short, it is entirely plausible in this instance, and is actual in other situations, that the fact-finding enterprise itself implies

certain moral consequences for participants even aside from any pragmatic benefits associated with health care. Moreover, any contribution
made by Jonathan (through his cooperation) is a direct function of both
the precise kind of injury—acquired cerebral colorblindness—and his
recognized talents as an artist. Each category reflects fundamental features of both exhortation and fact, description and evaluation.

Another dimension of potential human significance arises from this
case study when one asks about Jonathan I's wife (call her Jane for the
moment). Although Sacks and Wasserman were virtually silent on this
point, her role in his identity reconstitution and general coping is likely
to be substantial. Consider, for example, a conceivable significance to
the disruption of their sexual relationship following the brain damage.
Jane might well ask herself (or Jonathan or his doctor) if Jonathan's lack
of sexual interest was grounded in his colorblindness or vice versa. To
put it crudely, "Is Jonathan really colorblind or is it a symptom of something else, perhaps something deeper?" Such suspicions can certainly
engage a neurological account with interest. For example, the results of
the sophisticated testing procedures recounted by Sacks and Wasserman
(1987) made it highly implausible that Jonathan's colorblindness was an
"unconsciously motivated symptom" with no biological structure (generative mechanism) involved. The clue paralleling "glove anesthesia" is
simply absent for Jonathan. If the neurological interpretation made sense
across accounts and events, clinicians could, in response to questions
grounded in suspicion, offer legitimate, expert assurances that this particular colorblindness was real, thereby reinforcing a specific moral status for Jonathan's accounts of his motives in the conversation. Although
the significance of such assurances depends largely on factors other than
that of neuroscientific accounts, it is plausible that such assurances could
have been consequential for Jane and for Jonathan's attempts to make
human sense out of his injury and in the task of finding a valued form of
life within the limits imposed by his injury.

What is it about realist biology that carries weight in the conversation? For social constructionists, there is no absolute relevance. Since
the significance attributed to accounts of generative mechanisms varies
with local conversational contexts, it is helpful to elaborate a likely local
relevance for Jane's question as posed earlier. Jane is requesting accounts
of Jonathan's sexual motivations and performances. In our culture, many

different language games are made relevant to this kind of request. Even if we were to attribute a high degree of sophistication in the neurobiology of color vision to Jonathan, his performance in the complex perceptual tasks, recounted by Sacks and Wasserman, makes *"hysterical colorblindness"* an improbable account. Expert characterization of Jonathan as really colorblind or not depends in part on their determination of what *kind* of colorblindness it *is*: cerebral rather than retinal. For example, his visual performance did not show simple insensitivity to color, but instead displayed a complex pattern of variable sensitivities and insensitivities to different wavelengths. The complexity of the pattern of (in)sensitivities was accounted for by the neurological mechanisms posited by a realist biology in conjunction with fully functional retinal discriminations. The possibility of Jonathan simulating that pattern adequately, even if he wanted to, failed Sacks and Wasserman's standards of credibility. Ascription of the moral status of *honest* to Jonathan's accounts of his visual experience, then, fits with his performance in the testing procedures and thus, facilitates conversational developments around his incapacities. Van Dyck and Hampshire's insight into the profound interdependence of description and evaluation seems unavoidable. At least some of the exhortations that might be constructed in conversation with Jonathan depend on generative mechanisms underlying color vision and the structures that we find associated with his visual performance. In addition, the same accounts of generative mechanisms facilitate the construction of intelligible accounts of transformations in his art, his changing tastes in food, and more broadly, his reconstitution of self. None of these forms of relevance for the neurological account required Sacks and Wasserman to vitiate science discourse, constrained as contingently and locally significant.

Like Hampshire's talk about bodily movements and Van Dyck's debates about IVF, Sacks and Wasserman's account seems to easily span distinctions among description, evaluation, and critique. Despite the fact that expert assurances implicitly re-assert the power of clinicians and scientists in some sense, conversations among Sacks, Wasserman, Jane and Jonathan can still remain open to questions about the moral significance of the expert account, the place of medicine in people's lives, and even the inequities of power shaping relevant institutions. If we, with Shotter, rule out, a priori, any relevance for accounts of neural mechanisms to the moral landscape of Jonathan's care and reconstitution, the conversation becomes impoverished by an unnecessary uniformity of voice. We support Shotter's emphasis on enlarging the sphere of public accountability and on the continuous local negotiations that ground a fundamental indeterminacy to conversation. Yet, we see neuroscience, its boundaries, and its conversational status as simply more topics for local, situated negotiation, not as abstract pronouncements to be determined in advance—whether by hegemonic medicine or by an overly zealous social constructionism.

WIDENING THE HORIZONS OF CONVERSATION

Let us recapitulate what has become something of a sprawling argument. Shotter's thesis of irrelevance—between understanding and coping with brain injury as a moral agent on the one hand, and explaining and intervening with injured patients in a medical mode on the other hand—depends on a number of unexamined assumptions and hidden premises of questionable pedigree, of which the following seem to be the most important:

1. Natural science is inherently amoral and impersonal and meaningless. Science is about facts, not values. To explain neurophysiological processes is to treat humans not as moral agents for whom injury has moral and personal significance, but as mechanisms undergoing physical–causal processes, bereft of personal significance and moral meaning. The integrity of natural science and of personal agency depends on maintaining the strictest separation between these two domains. The point is not that humans do not have brains or that these are not in some sense enabling conditions for lived experience, but rather that theory about embodiment in a naturalistic mode is necessarily and uniformly at odds with our experience of ourselves as moral agents. The ontology of natural mechanisms and that of moral agents are necessarily incompatible.

2. Morally meaningful discourse about our embodied experience is legitimate, but only in a commonsense, ordinary language mode. Commonsense discourse is the mode of personal agency. By means of ordinary language, we exhibit, express, and constitute our selves

as moral agents. The language of theory is inevitably observer- (rather than participant-) centered and so on. Discourse appropriate to a person coping with bodily injury must be ordinary language discourse. The language of theory and that of lived experience are necessarily incommensurable. On this account, discourse analysis is not theory, but is a form of commonsense discourse and is therefore a form of moral meaning making.

3. What is metaphysically impossible and methodologically incoherent is nonetheless humanly possible. Reductive naturalism is a form of praxis, an illegitimate human form of life that embodies these paradoxes. Neuroscience and medicine, invariably hegemonic, participate in an incoherent denial of human subjectivity and agency as well as a set of depersonalizing practices that eventually reconstitute humans as patients who are managed by the medical establishment, thereby invalidating them as moral agents who make sense out of their injury and pain. The result is a (im)moral and political practice that acquires unique authority as neutral scientific "fact." This "factual authority" allows it to hide its own moral character from itself even while it denies moral status to patients.

4. The cure for this problem is to recognize the incommensurability of these different forms of discourse and the incompatibility of these different ontologies and to keep the two activities entirely distinct. Psychology should not try to avail itself of the methods and metaphysics of natural science. To do so is to lose the person in the quest for reductive explanation and to repressively and illegitimately foreclose the moral negotiation that makes up the realm of the personal. Whatever the interests that biologists might have in the brains of humans as animals, for psychologists interested in humans as persons, such findings are irrelevant.

In our view, only Point 3 has much merit in an overall critique of institutional discourse and that thesis is logically independent of the others. The case study shows Sacks and Wasserman coordinating, albeit in a politically conservative frame, multiple discourses. Their mixed genre revealed neuroscientists engaged in natural science discourse and simultaneously qualifying their expertise via personal reflections on the moral and personal significance of their findings (in the spirit of a "romantic science"; see Luria, 1979). We also evoked plausible possibilities surrounding the utilization of neuroscience accounts by Jonathan I and his wife as part of their personal, moral sense making. The theoretical incommensurability of these various forms of discourse (e.g., nonreducibility, nontranslatability) does not justify a radical insularity.

Obviously, we are not holding up Sacks and Wasserman as the epitome of self-reflective awareness or even a model of morally sensitive science. There are many tensions and paradoxes in their work. Yet, we believe that this case illustrates a complexity in the diverse roles of the neuroscientist, a permeability among different forms of discourse, and the mutual relevance of scientific and everyday practices.

Therapeutic contexts accentuate certain problems with Shotter's (1990) contrast between moral activities ontology and realism about generative mechanisms. His account presumed that a realist stance must be discursively uniform, exclusive, and highly stable in practice and furthermore, that that morally qualified discourse must be exclusively nonreferential. Yet, if we exclude all talk of generative mechanisms, our moral deliberations over health care might become impoverished. Moreover, in separating natural science from and insisting on its irrelevance to personal life, Shotter thereby threatened to protect natural science from critiques highlighting the inherently moral nature of all human enterprises.

We conclude then that the tension that Shotter saw between realism (or at least the version of realism defended by Harré) and social constructionism is a function of a set of oppositions derived more from classical debates than from Harré. In stronger terms, Harré rejected most of these oppositions; he rejected the notion of value-free science, the equation of science with the formulation of invariant generalizations, the opposition between the natural and the social, the constructed and the real. He rejected the equation of real with physical as well as the atomistic prejudice that holds individuals more real than communities. He considered the possibility that reasons might be a species of cause different from efficient causation. Rather than simply take one side or the other in these oppositions, he examined the assumptions about reality and science that underlie most of them and found them wanting. The result is a view of science (including natural science) as a moral and communal enterprise and a revised human science that recognizes the irreducibility of the personal and the social to the physical on the one hand and the need for some kind of coordination between our knowledge of brain function and our knowledge of human communal activity on the other hand. It is a view of science that acknowledges that there may be significant cross-cultural differences between persons and rejects any simple universalistic psychology. And it is a view of science that comports with practices available to participants in clinical contexts.

So Harré's realism was not incompatible with the recognition that we need a different ontology in order to deal with human uniqueness and in some cases, different methodologies that are sensitive to those ontological differences. Yet, Harré, rightly in our view, refused to make this the basis for some claim about the irrelevance of generative mechanisms or for the irreality or unreality of any aspect of the human being whether physiological, psychological, or social. Harré insisted on keeping the relations between the various levels clear and the various forms of inquiry and theory distinct. Yet, he did not see any necessary conflict between personal powers and moral acts ontologies (Harré, 1995).

CONCLUSION

In our view, there is no way to avoid the questions of how mechanisms and meanings are related. There are several reasons for this. One is the imperatives of scientific research itself. It seems unavoidable from within a theoretical concern to address questions concerning the possible identity or other relations between belief–desire accounts of human action and biophysical accounts. Unified science—positivist style—may well be chimera, but some kind of nonreductive coordination of such multiple accounts certainly seems desirable. How mechanisms and motives fit together in one person certainly seems to be an important theoretical issue. Harré argued for this both early (Harré, 1972) and late (Harré, 1991; Harré, Clarke, & De Carlo, 1985) in the corpus of his work.

On a more specific note, contemporary research on brain mechanisms relies on verbal reports of experimental subjects in order to pair the experiential with the experimental. That is, we know that some facet of the brain is associated (somehow) with speech, memory, or perception by eliciting such experiential reports from subjects, either as an input into some brain imagining technique or as an output following some brain stimulation. As MacKay (1991), Margolis (1987), and others pointed out, the possibility of physiological research depends crucially on the utility of experimental subjects giving accounts in essentially folk psychological terms of their experiences.

Again, the converse is true. Our understanding of the relation between the physical–causal and the rational–moral order is itself a profoundly moral issue. Maybe Sorell (1991) was a bit extreme when he suggested that deterministic science might undermine our widely accepted human practices of holding people responsible for their actions, but certainly, our practices of moral evaluation could not be, and in fact are not, unaffected by accepting certain scientific views about genetics or psychology. This concern about how scientism and mechanistic approaches to persons might have undesirable moral and political consequences is perfectly understandable and widely shared.

We have tried to show that the moral meaning and practical coping of human beings may well depend, in part and in some cases, on specifically scientific knowledge of bodily processes. This should occasion no surprise. Folk psychology is not some hermetically sealed compartment unaffected by natural scientific research. Our image of ourselves, of our capacities, moral liabilities, obligations, and so on are deeply influenced by what we know, both commonsensically and scientifically, about ourselves and the world in which we live. The moral orders or meaning frames in which humans orient themselves in the world are influenced by, challenged, and sometimes drastically altered by scientific findings. So, the questions about the possible reduction, coordination, or insulation of these differing approaches to understanding human behavior have important moral implications.

We are not claiming that there can be some grand synthetic theory that gives us a unified account of all dimensions of humanness. We are also not interested in mental physics, in the search for homunculi—diaphanous or mechanical. We are claiming, minimally, that no particular practice, no single voice, is self-sufficient. No one science is adequate and none is irrelevant in any absolute sense. Essentialism of whatever stripe is unhelpful. We are also claiming that antirealism about persons and minds is unnecessary in order to avoid mental physics, individualism, unified science, determinism, or any of the other "bugbears" that lurk in this maze. We can refer to persons, describe persons, and ask about the relationship between humans understood as persons and humans understood as point masses without assuming that the options are exhausted by: "person" referring to a ghost in a machine, "person" referring to the control module in the brain of the human machine, "person" being a misleading way of referring to a blob of protoplasm, or "person" being a nonreferring term that serves a function orthogonal to the descriptive task of science. "Person" refers to a natural and moral being with a complex set of properties and powers. Some of these properties are linked to the physical and biological composition of humans. Some are linked to their complex relationships with their physical environment; some are linked to social contexts and practices of mutual recognition and exhortation. These different contexts are neither reducible to nor independent of each other. To disregard any of them results in a loss of the person in psychology.

REFERENCES

Bhaskar, R. (1990). Introduction: Realism and human being. In R. Bhaskar (ed.), *Harré and his critics* (pp. 1–13). Oxford, England: Basil Blackwell.

Bogdan, R. J. (1991). *Mind and common sense*. Cambridge, England: Cambridge University Press.

Churchland, P. (1988). *Matter and consciousness: A contemporary introduction to the philosophy of mind* (Rev. ed.). Cambridge, MA.: MIT Press.

Churchland, P. (1989). *A neurocomputational perspective: The nature of mind and the structure of science*. Cambridge, MA: MIT Press.

Churchland, P. (1995). *The engine of reason, the seat of the soul: A philosophical journey into the brain*. Cambridge, MA: MIT Press.

Dennett, D. (1978). *Brainstorms*. Hassocks, Sussex, England: Harvester Press.

Dennett, D. (1987). *The intentional stance*. Cambridge, MA: MIT Press.

Dennett, D. (1991). *Consciousness explained*. Boston: Little, Brown.

Furhman, E. R. (1986). Morality, self and society: The loss and recapture of the moral self. In M. L. Wardell & S. P. Turner (Eds.), *Sociological theory in transition* (pp. 86–108). Boston: Allen & Unwin.

Gauld, A., & Shotter, J. (1977). *Human action and its psychological investigation*. London: Routledge & Kegan Paul.

Glover, J. (1990). *I: The philosophy and psychology of personal identity*. Harmondsworth, United Kingdom: Penguin.

Hampshire, S. (1989). *Innocence and experience*. Cambridge, MA: Harvard University Press.

Harré, R. (1970). *The method of science*. London: Wykeham.

Harré, R. (1972). *The philosophies of science*. London: Oxford University Press.

Harré, R. (1983). *Personal being*. Oxford, England: Basil Blackwell.

Harré, R. (1984). *The philosophies of science* (2nd ed.). Oxford, England: Oxford University Press.

Harré, R. (1986). *Varieties of realism*. Oxford, England: Blackwell.

Harré, R. (1990). Exploring the human Umwelt. In R. Bhaskar (Ed.), *Harré and his critics* (pp. 297–364). Oxford, England: Basil Blackwell.

Harré, R. (1991). *Physical being*. Oxford, England: Basil Blackwell.

Harré, R. (1993). *Social being* (2nd ed.). Oxford, England: Blackwell.

Harré, R. (1995). The necessity of personhood as embodied being. *Theory & Psychology, 5*, 369–373.

Harré, R., Clarke, D., & De Carlo, N. (1985). *Motives and mechanisms*. London: Methuen.

Harré, R., & Gillett, G. (1994). *The discursive mind*. London: Sage.

Harré, R., & Madden, E. H. (1975). *Causal powers*. Totowa, NJ: Rowan & Littlefield.

Harré, R., & Secord, P. (1972). *The explanation of social behavior*. Oxford, England: Blackwell.

Hesse, M. (1980). *Revolutions and reconstructions in the philosophy of science*. Bloomington: Indiana University Press.

Holton, G. J. (1993). *Science and anti-science*. Cambridge, MA: Harvard University Press.

Luria, A. R. (1979). *The making of mind: A personal account of Soviet psychology*. Cambridge, MA: Harvard University Press

MacKay, D. M. (1991). *Behind the eye* (V. MacKay, Ed.). Oxford, England: Basil Blackwell.

Manicas, P. T., & Secord, P. (1983). Implications for psychology of the new philosophy of science. *American Psychologist, 38*, 399–413.

Margolis, J. (1987). *Science without unity*. New York: Blackwell.

Postman, N. (1988). Social science as moral theology. In N. Postman (Ed.), *Conscientious objections*. New York: Knopf.

Rosenberg, A. (1988). *Philosophy of social science*. Boulder, CO: Westview Press.

Roszak, T. (1986). *The cult of information*. New York: Pantheon.

Rouse, J. (1987). *Knowledge and power*. Ithaca, NY: Cornell University Press.

Rouse, J. (1991). Interpretation in natural and human science. In D. R. Hiley, J. F. Bowman, & R. Shusterman (Eds.), *The interpretive turn* (pp. 42–56). Ithaca, NY: Cornell University Press.

Sacks, O., & Wasserman, R. (1987, November 19). The case of the colorblind painter. *The New York Times Review of Books*, pp. 25–34.

Shotter, J. (1975). *Images of man in psychological research*. London: Methuen.

Shotter, J. (1990). Rom Harré: Realism and the turn to social constructionism. In R. Bhaskar (Ed.), *Harré and his critics* (pp. 206–223). Oxford, England: Basil Blackwell.

Shotter, J. (1995, October). *Group discussion at the annual meeting of Western Canadian Psychologists*, Banff, Alberta.

Sorell, T. (1991). *Scientism*. London: Routledge & Kegan Paul.

Van Dyck, J. (1995). *Manufacturing babies and public consent*. New York: New York University Press.

Vonnegut, K. (1974). *Wampeters, foma & granfailoons*. New York: Delacorte Press.

Wynne, A. (1988). Accounting for accounts of the diagnosis of multiple sclerosis. In S. Woolgar (Ed.), *Knowledge and reflexivity* (pp. 101–123). London: Sage.

CHAPTER 9

The Dispersal of Subjectivity and the Problem of Persons in Psychology

Henderikus J. Stam
University of Calgary
Calgary, Alberta

PERSONS, BOUNDARIES, AND THE MASCULINE

As a discussion that began with the problem of "depersonalization" in psychology, this volume has become a patchwork of metaphors that seeks to redress the serious grievances inflicted on our understanding of personhood by a technical rationality. Such discussions are crucial to a reformist program in psychology, notwithstanding its institutional inflexibility, but are at one remove from considerations of practice. What follows seeks to take the discussion in another direction, partly out of a discomfort with the acceptance that our task ought to be about reconstituting the "person" by relying on the kinds of moral and depth metaphors that make up the bulk of this collection, partly out of a discomfort with the all-male discussions and writing that led to this volume, and partly out of a discomfort with the lack of acknowledgment that the group that produced this volume is geographically, if not institutionally and culturally–territorially, unique. In addition, the wide range of intellectual resources that come to play a large role in the preceding chapters are meant to constitute a notion of personhood that will, once again, attempt to provide foundations for the discipline of psychology. I submit that boundary maintenance was part of the problem in the first instance and the reification of conceptions of personhood for a future psychology will only take us back to the lacunae that are so clearly specified as problems by many of the authors in this collection. As a contribution to this section on "Critical Perspectives," I argue that the topic of persons is the wrong one, that it forces us into a disciplinarity that is at once conceptually inadequate, but also scientifically shallow and that the practice of searching for conceptual grounds is, after all, both a local as well as a moral, academic and institutional endeavor. Unlike House and McDonald, I do not believe we can solve our conundrum by liberalizing our conversations, no matter how well-intentioned or informed, because the foundations of such conversations leave the disciplinary, institutional and technological project untouched. What follows should clarify these claims.

Despite its purported subject matter, this volume is unreflexive about its own construction. Reflexivity, of course, has multiple connotations in science studies, the social sciences, and literary studies. I use reflexivity not only in its negative sense (i.e., the notion that reflexive practices are a constituent of the human sciences, intentionally or unintentionally; see Morawski, 1992), but also in its positive sense, namely that a theory of intellectual practice is an integral component and a necessary condition for any psychological work (Bourdieu & Wacquant, 1992; see also Bourdieu's *Homo Academicus*, 1988, on this matter). *Person* is a legal term and an abstract term. To speak of depersonalization, don't we have some notion of the person already available to slip in its place? Is this nostalgia? Is it a search for a philosophically secure world? If only Watson or Wundt had gotten it right, this exercise would be unnecessary or if we go back to Dilthey, Hegel, Marx, Vico, Vygotsky, Popper, or whomever, we could work out a proper understanding. I do not wish to belittle such attempts for they are crucial in recovering a tradition of practice and argument in psychology that has been thoroughly lost to us. (In addition, this chapter attempts to do some of the same.) As Hoffman (1989) remarked, however, nostalgia is both poetry and fidelity, yet it can readily become a mere antidote to shallowness. There is something of a fantasy of winners and losers in this game and our nostalgia shifts into parody. We parody our peers in their labs, searching for some truth however small that truth might be.

If the modernist quest in psychology was a search for persons in their organismic or engineered detail then the postmodern version of this is a search for bodies, for the flesh. The person, like the soul of a Cartesian, is an abstract concept, but it has also been invariably regarded as male. The idealized sexlessness of persons may be a way of privileging maleness by other means (see Bordo, 1990; Harding & Hintikka, 1983; Lloyd, 1993). Hartsock (1990) argued that "the philosophical and historical creation of a devalued 'Other' was the necessary precondition for the creation of the transcendental rational subject outside of time and space, the subject who is the speaker in Enlightenment philosophy" (p. 160). Just as the maleness of reason has been inhabited by a sexless soul in philosophy, so does the sexless person co-exist with the maleness of science in psychology. What is relegated to the body, and the feminine, is incarnated in psychology as the sex life of rats or the irrationality of children—problems to be mastered through the progress of science. Neither science nor reason are male however; this masculine–feminine dimension is part of the "contingent features of western thought, the elusive but real effects of which are still with us" (Lloyd, 1993, p. x; for developments in feminism and epistemology, see Alcoff & Potter, 1993; for recent feminist psychology that deals with similar issues, see Kaschak, 1992).

What else do we parody—the masculine dinner table conversation—as philosophy? An evening with Mr. Rorty? As a male participant in this ritual of academic discourse, I am never *exclusively* male or wholly a participant in all these contingent features of Western thought. None of us are; yet, these categories have elusive boundaries. Do we need aggressive dinner table conversations to discuss ideas at all?

To raise such issues about papers discussed at meetings with, until recently, only male academics present and published in a volume to which only men have contributed, rather quickly leads to charges that one is merely displaying degrees of political correctness. Here, I take as telling Susan Bordo's (1990) point that it is impossible to be "politically correct." All thought, no matter how emancipatory, excludes someone somewhere and is "haunted by a voice from the margins" (p. 138). This does not prevent us from discovering common ground under some purpose. Raising masculinity in this context is raising the issue of the maleness of Western thought, in general, and of psychology, in particular.

With respect to the contributions to this volume, I believe it important to recognize that we speak from male bodies whose history includes the colonization of the feminine. Gender issues (and their absence) are inextricably linked with questions of power (Radtke & Stam, 1994). In this respect, I am in full agreement with Bernie Kaplan (1990) when he reminded psychologists that:

> Feminists should, by now, have convinced us that our socially constructed genderic status in the particular society in which we spend our lives will impact on how we live in our world, see our world, describe and explain our world, and all the things and events, large and small that we take to constitute it. (p. 8).

Abstract discussions of persons are no different. They inevitably contain masculinist preconceptions of the good man, the whole man, the just man, the moral man, and the knowing man.

This chapter is an attempt to resist the relocation of persons in an abstract discourse of a "psychology of persons," as if such a task can still be performed in an unreflexive manner and in a manner exempting the gendered bodies of those persons or of those doing the theorizing. In what follows, talk of persons is construed as a moment in the reconstitution of the centrality of the subject and the logocentrism of Western thought. The metaphysics of Western thought seeks a coherent body, a docile body, and a signified body, all of which can be found in the concept of the person. I will not offer an alternative; the critique itself is an attempt to loosen the talk of persons. In doing so, I draw on Deleuze and Guattari and turn their questions into a local question. This is a ploy to avert us from the temptation to contribute to abstract dialogues in universally conceived academic forums; as if what is said about persons by a group of Western Canadian academics partakes of a desire to know that that is shared by all who think. More important, it obscures our own particular talk as persons living in a particular locale and time that is, despite global communications, fixed not in a universal conversation, but in our fragmentary appropriation of conversations determined by the peculiar institutional properties of the discipline.

Much also has been found in the common areas of nightmare to which we are all vulnerable (advertising, news, etc.).
> —Thomas Merton, *The Geography of Lograire*

PHILOSOPHY, FRIENDSHIP AND GEOGRAPHY

I want to problematize the question of persons as one that demands a confrontation with alterity and difference and with the impossibility of finding final or singular meanings in such a psychology. In order to do so, I ask, with Deleuze and Guattari, what it is to think about such topics in the first instance, how such thinking inevitably becomes transcendent, and how we might relate such thinking back to questions of territories, both real and imagined. Yet, Deleuze and Guattari's approach is paradoxical, if not difficult. From *Anti-Oedipus* (their "Introduction to the Non-Fascist Life," in Foucault's words) to *What is Philosophy* (their introduction to the thinking life), their collaborations have mapped out a continual struggle of difference against unity and transcendence.[1] Published 4 years after the events of 1968, *Anti-Oedipus* (1983) became an antitext for all manifestations of desire and its repression in capitalism. The failure of the Fourth Republic and the return of DeGaulle had galvanized various institutions and movements in France, which culminated in the general strike and so-called "events" of May 1968. By 1972, the Union of the Left (the French Communist Party [PCF] and the Socialists) made it appear inevitable that they would take office. When it finally did under Mitterrand in 1981, the reality was far different, of course, and the PCF and socialist politics went into their long decline. Like other so-called poststructuralist works of the period, one does not read *Anti-Oedipus* in order to explain the text through a simple historicism, but rather to provide it with possible boundaries.[2] Given what Deleuze and Guattari understand about the relations between thought and place, *What is Philosophy*, originally published in France in 1991, is a startling yet sober reflection on both the possibilities of thought and its limitations, written in the shadow of the earlier works and the realities of French

---

[1] *What is Philosophy* is also the last of their various joint efforts; Félix Guattari died in August 1992; Gilles Deleuze committed suicide in November 1995.

[2] Rabid antileft historicism is what frequently passes for comment on postwar French thought, including that written by French commentators themselves (see for example Khilnani, 1993). That there is a context goes without saying, but not one that requires the diminution of all intellectuals to the simple categories of left versus right (Elliott, 1994); see Pavel (1989) for an alternate—linguistic—critique of poststructuralist French thought.

academic and political life. I want to reflect on the possibilities of thought in psychology using their work as a back-drop, a stage or a setting.[3]

Deleuze and Guattari (1994) maintained that philosophy is the creation of concepts. These were not possible until the Greeks invented the *agon* or assembly "as the rule of a society of 'friends,' of the community of free men as rivals (citizens)" (p. 9). What *friend* signifies, especially among the Greeks, is difficult to say, except that it includes not only the friends of wisdom, but the friend that is an essence, a concept. With friendship comes rivalry. The friend as rival creates competitive distrust as well as being the "amorous striving toward the object of desire" (p. 4). *Philosophy*, in the Greek city, is the creation of a special kind of friendship that seeks the friend and rival as a social relation and simultaneously sets out the conditions for philosophy—"a plane of immanence."[4] These social relations have another consequence—they also cause free opinion (*doxa*) to appear. Philosophy must extract knowledge from mere opinion. In sum, a set of social relations—friendship and rivalry—is transferred to a plane and the possibility of opinion (orthodoxy) immediately confounds philosophy.

Concepts require conceptual personae, such as the one that populates Descartes's cogito—the Idiot. None other than the Idiot says "I"—wills himself to be a subject in the act of thought. Against scholasticism, Descartes posited the private thinker and opposed this persona to the public teacher who is concerned only with the abstraction of "man." "Here is a very strange type of persona who wants to think, and who thinks for himself, by the 'natural light'" (p. 62). Perhaps this is just the persona to overturn the authority of scholasticism. Yet, this Idiot is very different from Dostoevski's idiot "who wills the absurd" and in doing so recovers what Descartes's idiot lost in winning reason. Conceptual persona are

---

[3] This is not done to enter yet one more grand narrative into the fray, but rather I think of Deleuze and Guattari's work as a set of "critical tools" (Shotter, 1993) that allow me to open certain historical questions about the nature of psychology. In addition, having just raised the question of the masculinist preoccupations of psychological theory, I am aware of the complex intersection of Deleuze and Guattari's work with feminist thought, some of which is sharply critical (see Braidotti, 1994; Grosz, 1994).

[4] The plane of immanence is the condition for philosophy; it is prephilosophical—presupposed by philosophy—but cannot exist outside philosophy (see p. 41).

the actors on the stage of philosophy, neither aesthetic figures (as they are found in literature) nor psychosocial types (although they always refer back to the historical), but rather entities such as Kierkegaard's *Don Juan* or Nietszche's *Zarathustra*. They show us thought's territories.[5]

Thinking always takes place in relation to geography, territory, or geophilosophy. We are always deterritorializing, going beyond any territory, and reterritorializing, restoring territories. Because "every territory presupposes a prior deterritorialization," there is no beginning to which one might point, no anthropology that might alert us to some original territorialization (Deleuze & Guattari, 1994, p. 68). By analogy, there are psychosocial types that show us how this works, for example, in the merchant who buys a territory, "deterritorializes products into commodities, and is reterritorialized on commercial circuits" (p. 68) or in capitalism when property itself is deterritorialized and labor is abstracted from the means of production thus, becoming reterritorialized in wages.

The birth of philosophy is like this: It emerges out of the conjunction of immigrants (Ionians) in a Greek milieu and the encounter between this milieu and the deterritorialization of thought (or the reterritorialization of the plane of immanence). Philosophy survives in Greece and the West because of its relation to a relative deterritorialization. The West propagates itself, is continually displaced, and reconstituted and philosophy itself is connected to this relative social milieu—the vast deterritorialization of world capitalism (see also Guattari, 1992, on the historical process of deterritorialization). Yet, this relation between modern philosophy and capitalism is contingent. Deleuze and Guattari resisted the degradation of philosophy for a commodity with its own exchange value that reduces philosophy to opinion, to a concept fit for advertising.

The point is that philosophy is not reterritorialized on the modern democratic state and human rights because there is no universal demo-

---

[5] As in the case of science, philosophy is projected onto characters that populate its stage. These are not actors or literary or aesthetic characters, however. They remain the projections (imagination) of a particular author allowing the unfolding of possibilities in thought that could not be accomplished otherwise, lest it be entirely or only abstract.

cratic state; in capitalism the only universal is the market.[6] We are not Greeks, and friendship and its simple rivalry, as understood in antiquity, has not survived the modern world. We are all sullied by the modern state, not only in its extreme manifestations of destruction and violence, but in our experience of shame in simply being human.[7] We experience shame, according to Deleuze and Guattari (1994):

> in insignificant conditions, before the meanness and vulgarity of exist-
> ence that haunts democracies, before the propagation of these modes of
> existence and of thought-for-the-market, and before the values, ideals,
> and opinions of our time. The ignominy of the possibilities of life that
> we are offered appears from within. We do not feel ourselves outside of
> time but continue to undergo shameful compromises with it. This feeling
> of shame is one of philosophy's most powerful motifs. We are not re-
> sponsible for the victims but responsible before them (p. 108).[8]

In this manner Deleuze and Guattari echo Adorno for whom the body signals not pleasure but suffering. In his essay on Adorno, Eagleton (1990) remarked, "In the shadow of Auschwitz it is in sheer physical wretched-ness, in human shapes at the end of their tether, that the body once more obtrudes itself into the rarified world of the philosophers" (p. 41). Adorno (1973), of course, would have no truck with the body as an affirmative category because it would suffer the same reification as all other such

---

[6] Deleuze and Guattari took up the question of the national characteristics of philoso-phy in 17th century France, 18th century England, and 19th century Germany. Such national characteristics are philosophical opinions, that is to say that it is philosophy reterritorialized on a particular people and their conception of right. What is crucial here is that the friendship that made philosophy possible was made impossible by the state itself.

[7] The shame of being human is a theme that Deleuze and Guattari took from Primo Levi (see his *Survival in Auschwitz*, 1961).

[8] Wittgenstein (1980), in a discussion on religion, in 1944, remarked, "We could also say: Hate between men comes from our cutting ourselves off from each other, be-cause we don't want anyone else to look inside us, since it's not a pretty sight in there. Of course, you must continue to feel ashamed of what's inside you, but not ashamed of yourself before your fellowmen" (p. 46).

categories. Like Deleuze and Guattari, he saw in our present conditions no possibility for the philosophy that was. If there is still thought after Auschwitz, it is the thought that continually turns on itself.

Deleuze and Guattari also refused a reduction of philosophy for communication, which is for them, nothing more than what the advertiser uses to oil the wheels of the marketplace. It is not that we lack communication, but that there is already an oversupply of it. Instead, what we lack is creation: "We lack resistance to the present" (p. 108).[9] What is philosophy to do? Without calling for emancipatory knowledge or a new utopia, Deleuze and Guattari nonetheless insist that:

> The creation of concepts in itself calls for a future form, for a new earth and people that do not yet exist. Europeanization does not constitute a becoming but merely the history of capitalism, which prevents the becoming of subjected peoples. Art and philosophy converge at this point: the constitution of an earth and a people that are lacking as the correlate of creation. (p. 108)

This is not utopian, for utopia is still subject to history even when it opposes history. (See Adorno, 1973, on the irony of emancipatory or utopian thought.) Foucault's notion of the actual as something not of what we are but "what we are in the process of becoming," or our becoming other, most nearly renders this problem for Deleuze and Guattari.

Philosophy, at least in the Anglo world, lives in (if not under) the shadow of science. Deleuze and Guattari, like many of their continental colleagues, sharply distinguished between these two modes of thought (using art as a third) without deriding science in the process. I briefly recapitulate their discussion of science insofar as it allows me to talk about the science that would be psychology.

Science is not concerned with concepts, but with functions that are formalized as propositions in discursive systems. Functions and propositions are constituted as the language of science and the philosophical concept is of no consequence to it, although a concept may emerge from a scientific function even though in emerging as such, it has no scientific

---

[9] It should be abundantly clear how difficult this is as universities take on an explicit corporate and consumerist agenda, where the teaching of "uncomfortable thoughts," as Weber noted, becomes increasingly tangential (see Jacoby, 1987).

value. Deleuze and Guattari defended both philosophy and science as inherently unique enterprises on these grounds. More important, they implicitly claimed that it is impossible for science to exhaust the contents of philosophy (or for either to exhaust the contents of art). Philosophy gives consistency to chaos; science relinquishes chaos to give it a reference.[10] In philosophy, there are "inseparable variations subject to 'a contingent reason' that constitutes the concept from variations" and in science we have a set of "independent variables subject to 'a necessary reason' that constitutes the function from variables" (p. 126). Science does not have philosophy's conceptual personae, but rather "partial observers" whose role is to perceive and experience, although the perceptions and experiences belong to the thing studied. They are like golem installed in the system of reference.[11] It is not science itself that is a golem (contra Collins & Pinch, 1993), but instead these partial observers are golem that belong to the systems themselves. Rather they inhabit bodies and states of affairs like little monads or sensibilia. Deleuze and Guattari argued, against the positivist and instrumentalist, that sensory knowledge and scientific knowledge are not separate spheres. Rather, they wish to know what the sensibilia are that are unique to science and that make possible certain systems of coordinates. These sensibilia are like the sense data devoid of sensation, like parts of instruments or like the photographic plate waiting for a real observer to read them.[12]

The partial observers are "points of view in things themselves that presuppose a calibration of horizons and a succession of

---

[10] Deleuze and Guattari used the term *chaos* mindful of its Greek origins, to mean the abyss out of which the cosmos was formed. This is not to say that this is a kind of mythical state, but rather it has the characteristic of an existential state—the raw nature of the world that is unintelligible to us unless we lay out a plane of immanence. Science, philosophy, and art give form to chaos on different principles and in a different relation to time.

[11] A *golem* is a Jewish mythical creature made by human hands from clay and water with incantations and spells. It grows powerful, but it is dangerous because it has the potential to destroy its masters. Collins and Pinch (1993) argued that science itself is a like a bumbling golem, neither good nor bad, knowing neither its own strength nor the extent of its ignorance.

[12] Deleuze and Guattari used the positivist notion of sense data and turned it on itself.

framings...perception itself becomes a quantity of information" (p. 132). Scientific observation is never philosophical observation; the former always sees as part of a function, it is the eye of the function. In philosophy, conceptual personae "are the perceptions and affections of fragmentary concepts themselves" (p. 131) or it is the seeing through and in thought. Science, on the other hand, sees by way of coordinates and functions, in other words, through systems that are created by the scientist.

Science proceeds through the projection of certain forms of knowing (observation) whose object it is to provide functions and propositions. This is in contrast to the philosophic projection of conceptual personae through concepts. Psychology, however, is the history of the attempt to make scientific the philosophical concept.[13]

The adoption of the scientific (partial) observer in psychology was a slow process, resisted and refined in subsequent schools. I give one example here and I have chosen it because it is familiar. In addition, it indicates an ambiguity, a process on the edge of transformation from a broadly philosophical to a self-conscious, scientific manner of proceeding. James' "psychologist's fallacy," or rather, what James so diligently pursued as a fallacy and remains nonetheless, even in James, was what he saw as the requirement that science have a point of view in things themselves on the one hand, and the danger this posed to his ethical vision of consciousness on the other. James (1890) was concerned that the psychologist who was capable of seeing the subject's thoughts and the objects of those thoughts would confuse *"his own standpoint with that of the mental fact* about which he is making his report" (p. 196). That is, psychologists might be led to suppose that those whom they observe know their thoughts in the same way in which the psychologist knows them. Morawski (1992) saw this as a case of the psychologist

---

Rather than see sense data as entities that ensure the progress of science by their lack of subjectivity, they returned subjectivity to the notion of sense data by arguing that instruments themselves presuppose a certain view, a way of looking, obtained under a partial observer, a projection of the scientist.

[13] This is too quick in that one could argue that psychology never took the philosophical concept seriously in its science and thus, had to abandon it in favor of functions. The concepts it took from philosophy (e.g., perception, thought, self, person, mind, consciousness, etc.) were narrowed and chiseled beyond recognition.

distancing him or herself from nature, "including the processes of his or her mind" (p. 290). That is, the psychologists' own selves were managed as natural objects in as much as they too could be observed and be differentiated from the observer. At the same time, "these selves, in their varied relational forms, are constructed in the texts although they function to represent a 'real' self lying behind or beneath that text" (p. 290). Of course James (1890) made it clear that he meant something like this when he argued that "the psychologist...stands outside the mental state he speaks of. Both itself and its objects are objects for him" (p. 196). The scientific observer is inserted somewhere between the psychologist and the individual being studied.

I also think James was unsure of this. In one of his talks to students, he argued for a position more in keeping with his radical empiricism and pluralism. He remarked, "Hands off: neither the whole truth, nor the whole of good, is revealed to any single observer, although each observer gains a partial superiority of insight from the particular position in which he stands" (James, 1899/1992, p. 860). In the preface to his talks, he noted, "There is no point of view absolutely public and universal. Private and uncommunicable perceptions always remain over, and the worst of it is that those who look for them from the outside never know *where*" (p. 708). This is because it is through feelings ("interest" in the *The Principles of Psychology*, 1890) that we come to judge the "worth of things," and it is those feelings in others different from ourselves that we cannot ever know except perhaps through a certain tolerance and sympathy. In *The Principles of Psychology* (1890), James remarked, "Other minds, other worlds from the same monotonous and inexpressive chaos! My world is but one in a million alike embedded, alike real to those who may abstract them" (p. 289).

The psychologist's fallacy referred both to the subordination of consciousness to observation—James as 19th century positivist—and to the fear that it will destroy consciousness itself in the act of observation—James as radical empiricist. James rejected the position of the scientific observer in later years and appeared to have little sympathy for an experimental psychology. Others, of course, carry the torch; that is, they will confuse philosophical concepts with functions and propositions. They begin psychology proper, ignoring the serious doubt that James entertained. This does not give us science because psychology cannot be a natural science. Its projected partial observer is always projected back on us, the real observer.[14]

Instead, we have a proposition of opinion, or doxa. This much science and philosophy have in common: They both struggle against opinion as much as they struggle against chaos and the unknown. To turn the philosophical concept into a scientific proposition, namely a psychology, is to replace that philosophical concept with logical concepts, factual propositions, and a place in the domain of opinion. For Deleuze and Guattari (1994), *doxa* is strictly a matter of agreement and agreement is always a matter of being on the right side of things.

> *Doxa* is a type of proposition that arises in the following way: in a given perceptive-affective lived situation (for example, some cheese is brought to the dinner table), someone extracts a pure quality from it (for example a foul smell); but, at the same time as he abstracts the quality, he identifies himself with a generic subject experiencing a common affection (the society of those who detest cheese—competing as such with those who love it, usually on the basis of another quality). "Discussion," therefore, bears on the choice of the abstract perceptual quality and on the power of the generic subject affected. For example, is to detest cheese to manage without being a bon vivant? But is being a bon vivant a generically enviable affection? Ought we not say that it is those who love cheese, and all bons vivants, who stink? Unless it is the enemies of cheese who stink. This is like the story, told by Hegel, of the shopkeeper to whom it was said, "Your eggs are rotten old woman," and who replied, "Rot yourself, and your mother, and your grandmother": opinion is an abstract thought, and insult plays an effective role in this abstraction because opinion expresses the general functions of particular states. It extracts an abstract quality from perception and a general power from affection: in this sense all opinion is already political. (p. 145)

The philosophical concept that depends on events for consistency is never factual or a state of affairs, not a thing through which we ourselves

---

[14] One might characterize the history of psychology in this century as the problem of precisely where this partial observer is stationed; in the maze (seeking a drive), in the computer (seeking a symbol), and so on. In each case, the partial observer is not the same partial observer that the natural sciences evoke (as in, say, the search for a structure in an electron microscope). Instead, psychology invokes metaphorical partial observers whose readings only approximate (i.e., give certain collections of observations) those that the established sciences produce.

and our bodies pass, but the "event into which we plunge or return, that which starts again without ever having begun or ended" (p. 157). In a state of affairs, however, we seek to isolate variables, seek relations of dependence, or determine when new ones arise. The event, on the other hand, co-exists with the instant and is also a "dead time." In short, to make philosophical concepts into scientific propositions is to destroy the concept, to make it live in the world of opinion.

Persons are abstractions in the world of opinions. We do not need the notion of persons to know that we are agents—even if these are agents with only partial, fluid selves and identities. When psychologists speak of persons or functions of persons, they are looking for agreement on some abstract perceptual quality that, when we attain agreement, we call truth. When we have truth, we have orthodoxy; that is, an opinion will be true as long as it coincides with the opinions of the group to which one belongs. One joins the group by expressing an opinion consistent with it. With this view, we become professionals and psychologists of certain brands by expressing the appropriate opinion (e.g., "I am a cognitivist, theorist, realist, social constructionist, etc."). Persons are like smelly cheese.

Is all thought (philosophy) not based on opinion or a kind of proto-opinion—an *urdoxa*. Deleuze and Guattari rejected this as a possible precursor that would raise us to the level of the concept. Phenomenology hides the "European man whose privilege it is constantly to 'Europeanize'" (p. 149). The struggle with chaos, that is the task of science and philosophy, takes place at the same time as the struggle against opinion. Psychology is above all a large set of opinions and thus, cannot understand either thought's struggle against opinion or its degeneration into opinion. We are left with discussions of cheese, complete with the insults.

Persons posited as abstract entities in the world, even those entities of phenomenology that aspire toward a Being in the world, "through a double criticism of mechanism and dynamism, hardly gets us out of the sphere of opinions. It leads us only to an *urdoxa* posited as original opinion, or meaning of meanings" (p. 210). It is only when the body becomes a subject that we find the possibilities of science, philosophy, and art. These are not the "mental objects of an objectified brain but the three aspects under which the brain becomes subject, Thought-brain" (p. 210). To treat the brain as a constituted object of science makes it merely the organ for the formation and communication of opinion. Science, philosophy, and art become impossible. When the brain says *I*, the *I* is another; this *I* is "the 'I conceive' of the brain as philosophy" and "the 'I feel' of the brain as art" (p. 211).

It appears as if we have come back to the subject of thought, the self in the brain. Yet, this is my simplification and, in any case, Deleuze and Guattari made no mention of psychology. They appeared to be discussing philosophy, but what is at stake is nothing short of thought itself, thought outside of myth, outside of lived time. Yet, the shadows of Marx, Freud, and Nietzsche populate their work without ever coming into focus.[15] By reflecting their treatise off the tradition of Western philosophy, they give their considerations the appearance of an historical work. Neither history nor philosophy is at stake. Rather, all of philosophy is at stake, namely the incorporation of thought to a certain cadre of academic masters geopolitically focussed on the European–North American world. Yet, they deterritorialize this form of thought we call philosophy and reterritorialize it elsewhere, perhaps nowhere, or possibly everywhere. This is not the view from nowhere, the next totalizing abstract scheme. Their's is a philosophy cut loose from academic philosophy. The euphemization of terms in poststructuralist thought moves the reader into a play of words, ideas, and images. Deleuze and Guattari were ironists on this view. In their own words, this work must necessarily be territorialized on France of the late 20th century, including the (to us) unusual, competitive, and public nature of French academic life. Is their work some postwar, post-May 1968 Parisian hangover?

Their concept of philosophy, or their philosophy of the concept, using their idea of concept now, is foreign to our pragmatic academic world in which many of our philosophers sneer at their European colleagues as weird, deliberately obscure, and not worth the effort at comprehension or translation. Yet, the question remains, to engage in a theoretical enterprise (including one that seeks the person) is to find oneself again among others who seek the same (the friends), using concepts that emerge from

---

[15] This is not some attempt to find yet another reconciliation between for example, Freud and Marx, as in the work of Brown, Jacoby, Marcuse, or Reich. As in *Anti-Oedipus*, these figures provide opportunities for extensions and innovations of argument that are intelligible only in the context of the background that they impose.

within a community that is already territorialized (on some political/institutional/historical context). To become a subject, to retrieve the subjectivity dispersed in opinion, is to enunciate the concept. (A good example of reterritorialization and the enunciation of concepts that retrieve a subjugated subjectivity is feminism.)

> *...the need might seem to press upon us to try to know where we are in this new found land which is so obviously "terra incognita."*
> —George Grant, *In Defence of North America* (1969)

PRAIRIE CONCEPTS

Deleuze and Guattari did not provide a map to a local territory. They remained dispersed over the entire geophilosophical terrain and, as North American psychologists, we cannot follow in such endless play in order to arrive, finally, on a plane of immanence that carries the name psychology. Our chaos is of the Anglo Saxon variety, that is, of the empiricist and pragmatist sort. To envision the play of infinite thought on a plane of immanence is to experience a certain giddiness, but this limitless play is no thought at all unless it becomes our own—is located somewhere. To territorialize such concepts on Canadian soil, on prairie and mountain soil where a mere 100 years ago the first Europeans arrived in large numbers to displace and dispossess the native inhabitants, would be to begin again, to find the concept again, and to find the conceptual persona again. Who would that be—the aboriginal, the immigrant, the laborer, the midwife, the pioneer?

If George Grant (1969) is right, there can be no philosophy (in its ancient and broad sense) in North America. Our language of values and historicism, which were the advance guard of liberalism, finally turned on liberalism itself.[16] In the face of nihilism:

> the old individualism of capitalism, the frontier and Protestantism, becomes the demanded right to one's idiosyncratic wants taken as outside any obligation to the community which provides them....Nihilism which

---

[16] Grant defined liberalism as the belief that we are essentially free and that our ends in life are thus to shape the world as we see fit. Grant was a neo-Platonist and I do not follow him there. His critique of the Canadian university and its curriculum, however, still bears reading 25 years after it was written.

has no tradition of contemplation to beat against cannot be the occasion for the amazed reappearance of the "What for? Whither? and What then?" (p. 39).

For those in the mainstream of society the effects of nihilism are a "narrowing to an unmitigated reliance on technique" (p. 40). Grant was writing at a time when he took the end-of-ideology debate as a sign of the resignation of academics to "the closing down of willing to all content except the desire to make the future by mastery" (p. 40), not unlike the end-of-history debate of recent years. In response, we turn to the tradition we know unconsciously; seeking in European thought the questions we cannot ask in these territories or, if we ask them, we cannot formulate the concept nor the conceptual personae that are viable. We repopulate our thought with petrified concepts, "ready-made old concepts like skeletons intended to intimidate any creation" (Deleuze & Guattari, 1994, p. 83), without seeing that those from whom we borrow were doing something else and were "not happy to clean and scrape bones" like the psychologists of our own day. Otherwise, we turn our optimistic, pragmatic purposes to work on this thought, making it once again a matter of values or opinion.[17]

Can we turn from philosophy and psychology to other writing in our search for persons. Literature is littered with concepts, but these are not the concepts of philosophy. Instead, literature's "concepts" are aesthetic figures who are "ceaselessly becoming-other (while continuing to be what they are)" (Deleuze & Guattari, 1994, p. 177); literature (like all forms of art) is neither commemorating nor celebrating, but instead confiding "to the ear of the future the persistent sensations that embody the event: the constantly renewed suffering of men and women, their re-created protestations, their constantly resumed struggle" (pp. 176–177). We may have no philosophy, but we have much literature, branded always as a form of national treasure, Canadian literature, American literature, and

---

[17] Witness Carl Rogers (1972/1986), the champion of the person in psychology, on "the person of tomorrow" said, "We are going to have a new America, in my judgment, an America of change and flow, of people rather than objects. We have the know-how, the skills, to bring about this new America. And now, in an increasing number of significant persons...we have the determination and the will to bring it into being" (p. 32).

so on. In its designation as a product of a state, it is immediately limited, no longer capable of speaking to the local conditions of its creation or the universal appeal of its narrative. For example, Joy Kogawa's *Obasan* (1981) is set in Alberta and British Columbia. Obasan is "the old woman of many Japanese legends" Kogawa wrote, "alone and waiting in her ancient time for the honour that is an old person's reward" (p. 54). After the deportation and dispersion of Naomi—her aunt—Obasan, and her family from an idyllic home on Canada's West coast during World War II, the internments, and the grinding postwar years as laborers on Alberta beet farms, there was neither honor nor reward, only grief. Yet, Obasan's husband came once a year to the coulee: "the tall grasses stand without quivering. The tops flop this way and that...'Umi no yo,' Uncle says, 'It's like the sea' " (p. 1), the sea that was his home, and his boats that were forcibly taken from him. The date of the visit to the coulee (August 9, 1972) takes on a greater significance as the reader becomes aware of the fact that the story is a gradual unfolding of Naomi's recounting of the enforced diaspora from the Pacific coast and the fate of her mother who was in Nagasaki when the second atomic bomb was dropped on Japan on August 9, 1945. The visit to the coulee then, re-enacted every year, was "a ceremony of exile, and every August [they] commemorate not just the fate of Naomi's mother but the whole family's misfortune in Canada" (Davidson, 1993, p. 30). The power of this novel, set (in part) in the towns and farms of Alberta, is derived from the evocation of an unremitting and unjust suffering and a tedium that has no breaks. Yet, Kogawa said, in an epigraph that precedes the story:

> Unless the stone bursts with telling, unless the reed flowers with speech, there is in my life no living word. The sound I hear is only sound. White sound. Words, when they fall, are pock marks on the earth. They are hailstones seeking an underground stream.

The novel is indeed the story of one who finally bursts the stone with a telling, but it is not only a personal story. Instead, it recounts the story of a community and, in its concluding postscript (an excerpt of a document arguing against the postwar deportation of Japanese-Canadians to Japan), it reminds us of the very real wrongs brought on this community by Canadians. Thus, the story is not only about Naomi's ability to endure, but "the country's capacity to require such endurance" (Davidson, 1993, p. 80). The reader, especially one who is Canadian, is placed in an uncomfortable position that vacillates between a recognition of both the shame of racism and an identification with those who stood up to that racism. *Obasan* is important not just because it tells us "unpalatable truths with consummate art" (p. 13), but also because it destabilizes our image of ourselves and it does so through the voice of an ethnic writer. There are no abstract persons on these prairies; even our aesthetic figures require a more complex psychology of us.

Sometimes, Canadian literature is understood as great empty literature, that is, full of open spaces and people lost, trapped, or dazed in these spaces, regardless of their location—Toronto or Granton, Alberta, or the cold, gray alienating landscape of Edmonton that serves as a mirror for the identities of the characters in Margaret Atwood's (1978) "Polarities." In those spaces, we are not just uncertain of who we are, but uncertain of our relationship with those spaces. According to Atwood (1992):

> What we want of course is the same old story. The trees pushing out their leaves...the water thrashing around in the oceans...The zinnias and their pungent slow explosions. We want it all to go on and go on again, the same thing each year, monotonous and amazing, just as if we were still behaving ourselves, living in tents, raising sheep, slitting their throats for God's benefit, refusing to invent plastics. For unbelief and bathrooms you pay a price. If apples were the Devil's only bait we'd still be able to call our souls our own, but then the prick threw indoor plumbing into the bargain and we were doomed. Now we use up a lot of paper telling one another how to conserve paper, and the sea fills up with killer coffee cups, and we worry about the sun and its ambivalent rays. (pp. 141–142)

This is how we are reterritorialized on a prairie; perhaps it is only possible in literature that we can be hopeful about nihilist territory. Is psychology itself already prairie territory, our prairie reterritorialized on the California and Ivy League version of the discipline by those two home-grown Western Canadian products—Albert Bandura and Zenon Pylyshyn?

RESEARCH AND RECONSTRUCTION

Both Gergen and Smedslund have found traditional, neopositivist empirical research in psychology wanting for its circularity. Answers to the questions posed obviously appear long before the research is begun. There is no surprise in performing the research because that is precisely how it is designed and it is designed this way for largely institutional reasons—that is, as a methodological convention among the gatekeepers of the discipline. Several recovered and previously unpublished pieces of Adorno's *Minima Moralia* (1974) put this most strikingly. In his invective against the social sciences, Adorno (1993) reminded us that "what is wholly verified empirically, with all the checks demanded by competitors, can always be foreseen by the most modest use of reason" (p. 11). "The throttling of thought" that Adorno referred to here careens between the depreciation of thought by the demand for evidence and the obvious nature of any evidence that can be brought to bear on none but the most trivial thoughts.

> The endless collegial hunt, careering between the "hypotheses" and "proofs" of social science, is a wild-goose chase since each of the supposed hypotheses, if inhabited by theoretical meaning at all, breaks through precisely the shaky facade of mere facticity, which in the demand for proofs prolongs itself as research. (p. 12)

This was 1951. Adorno's postwar refusal of all utopias—his vision of authenticity in the rejection of all that is inauthentic—made him the pessimistic but politically responsible theorist he was (Eagleton, 1990). Yet, his vision of philosophy, of the possibility of thought, although thoroughly pessimistic, is as spartan and playful, even if expressed with great seriousness, as that of Deleuze and Guattari.[18]

These post-World War II expressions of philosophy maintain their relation to aesthetics and ethics. Thought is not the purview of academics and least of all the exclusive domain of the social sciences. Thought is not a characteristic of some abstract subject or person. It lives in the very gestures of life, is never final, cannot be final, and must always

---

[18] There are also many distinctions that separate Deleuze and Guattari from Adorno, especially with regard to their views on art and science. I merely point here to the desire of all three to salvage thought from the marketplace. For Adorno (1973) this was to continually think against oneself because all rationality is already instrumentality.

move beyond itself. For Adorno (1974), that great pessimist:

> the only philosophy which can be responsibly practised in face of despair is the attempt to contemplate all things as they would present themselves from the standpoint of redemption...all else is reconstruction, mere technique. Perspectives must be fashioned that displace and estrange the world. (p. 247)

CONCLUSION: DESTABILIZING DEPERSONALIZATION

Depersonalization in psychology is now merely the obvious result of a failure of nerve. Modern psychology could not exist other than in its thoroughly functional orientation. It is thoroughly depersonalized if what we mean by that is the alienation of ourselves from our work, the alienation of our subject matter and teaching from ourselves. Our search for persons is a reconstitution of the functional project; the term itself is already a thoroughly abused concept. As textbooks about personality often note, it is derived from the Latin *persona*, which was the mask used by a player or else a being having legal rights; in the 17th century, it could have been used as a verb meaning *to represent*. The list of meanings itself could provide us with a judicial and political history of the English language. A reconstituted notion of the person in psychology would suffer the same fate (and has suffered the same fate—witness humanistic psychology) as most other concepts have; they are reducible to abstract, functional entities. Our concepts have to be other, recovered, or both.

Should we not, like Spinoza, say that the mind is the idea of the body? Or, that "the mind does not know itself except in so far as it perceives the ideas of the modifications of the body" (Spinoza, 1949, Part II, prop. 23, p. 101).[19] Lloyd (1993) remarked that "the 'powers and pleasures', in Spinoza's phrase, open to a female body in 17th century Dutch society differ in ways from those open to a male body" (p. xii). Hence, the ideas

---

[19] Spinoza's treatment of idea was, of course, radically different from its use in ordinary discourse and referred to a kind of act, an act of thought, that has an object (*ideatum*), namely "that which is 'idea-ed'" (Shirley, 1982, p. 25; see Spinoza, 1949). Spinoza's emergence in the late 20th century, out of the shadows of his romantic and Marxist interpreters of the last century, appeared to be less of a consequence of the attraction of his complex system of metaphysics (never much accepted in any case) than it is of his attempted conception of the unity of persons and nature.

of those bodies are not uniformly constituted. "Their differences will express not only the physical and social restraints on sexed bodies but also the different significance those bodies are accorded in the symbolic structures" (p. xii). There is no schism between reason and passion here, contrasting Descartes. Bodies are not just or only endowed with metaphorical differences, but with differences that have real consequences in our daily, gendered, discursive existence. In Deleuze and Guattari's words, Spinoza refused to compromise with transcendence. Do we trade opinion for immanence? I doubt it; I am incapable of it; it cannot be thought on the prairies.

ACKNOWLEDGMENTS

I am indebted to the participants in the Western Canadian Theoretical Psychologists' meetings for their careful and critical responses to earlier versions of this chapter. I am also grateful for further extensive comments by Leo Mos, John Mills, John Shotter, and Marvin McDonald. Although none of them may agree with the final rendering, I hope the point is all the more debatable for their efforts.

REFERENCES

Adorno, T. W. (1973). *Negative dialectics.* New York: Seabury Press.
Adorno, T. W. (1974). *Minima moralia.* London: New Left Books.
Adorno, T. W. (1993). Messages in a bottle. *New Left Review, 200,* 5–14.
Alcoff, L., & Potter, E. (Eds.) (1993). *Feminist epistemologies.* New York: Routledge.
Atwood, M. (1978). Polarities. In I. Owen & M. Wolfe (Eds.), *The best modern Canadian short stories* (pp. 59–77). Edmonton, Canada: Hurtig.
Atwood, M. (1992). *Good bones.* Toronto: Coach House Press.
Bordo, S. (1990). Feminism, postmodernism, and gender-scepticism. In L. J. Nicholson (Ed.), *Feminism/Postmodernism* (pp. 133–156). New York: Routledge.
Bourdieu, P. (1988). *Homo academicus.* Cambridge, England: Polity Press.
Bourdieu, P., & Wacquant, L. J. D. (1992). *An invitation to reflexive sociology.* Chicago: University of Chicago Press.
Braidotti, R. (1994). Toward a new nomadism: Feminist Deleuzian tracks; or, metaphysics and metabolism. In C. V. Boundas & D. Olkowski (Eds.), *Gilles Deleuze and the theater of philosophy* (pp. 159–186). New York: Routledge.
Collins, H., & Pinch, T. (1993). *The golem.* Cambridge, England: Cambridge University Press.
Davidson, A. (1993). *Writing against the silence: Joy Kogawa's Obasan.* Toronto: ECW Press.

Deleuze, G., & Guattari, F. (1983). *Anti-Oedipus: Capitalism and schizophrenia.* Minneapolis: University of Minnesota Press.

Deleuze, G., & Guattari, F. (1994). *What is philosophy.* New York: Columbia University Press.

Eagleton, T. (1990). *The significance of theory.* Oxford, England: Blackwell.

Elliott, G. (1994). Contentious commitments: French intellectuals and politics. *New Left Review, 206,* 110–124.

Grant, G. (1969). *Technology and empire.* Toronto: House of Anansi.

Grosz, E. (1994). A thousand tiny sexes: Feminism and rhizomatics. In C. V. Boundas & D. Olkowski (Eds.), *Gilles Deleuze and the theater of philosophy* (pp. 187–210). New York: Routledge.

Guattari, F. (1992). Regimes, pathways, subjects. In J. Crary & S. Kwinter (Eds.), *Incorporations, Zone* (Vol. 6) (pp. 16–37). New York: Urzone.

Harding, S., & Hintikka, M. (1983). *Discovering reality: Feminist perspectives on epistemology, metaphysics, methodology, and philosophy of science.* Dordrecht, The Netherlands: Reidel.

Hartsock, N. (1990). Foucault on power: A theory for women? In L. J. Nicholson (Ed.), *Feminism/Postmodernism* (pp. 157–175). New York: Routledge.

Hoffman, E. (1989). *Lost in translation: A life in a new language.* New York: Penguin.

Jacoby, R. (1987). *The last intellectuals.* New York: Basic Books.

James, W. (1890). *The principles of psychology* (Vol. 1). New York: Henry Holt & Co.

James, W. (1992). Talks to teachers on psychology and to students on some of life's ideals. In *William James: Writings 1878–1899* (pp. 705–887). New York: Library of America. (Original work published 1899)

Kaplan, B. (1990, August). *Current literary theory/criticism/history as a paradigm for a new psychology.* Paper presented at the Annual Convention of the American Psychological Association, Boston.

Kaschak, E. (1992). *Engendered lives: A new psychology of women's experience.* New York: Basic Books.

Khilnani, S. (1993). *Arguing the revolution: The intellectual left in postwar France.* New Haven, CT: Yale University Press.

Kogawa, J. (1981). *Obasan.* Toronto: Lester & Orpen Dennys.

Levi, P. (1961). *Survival in Auschwitz.* New York: Macmillan.

Lloyd, G. (1993). *The man of reason* (2nd ed.). Minneapolis: University of Minnesota Press.

Merton, T. (1968). *The geography of lograire.* New York: New Directions.

Morawski, J. (1992). Self-regard and other-regard: Reflexive practices in American Psychology, 1890–1940. *Science in Context, 5,* 281–308.

Pavel, T. G. (1989). *The feud of language: A history of structuralist thought.* Oxford, England: Blackwell.

Radtke, H. L., & Stam, H. J. (1994). Introduction. In H. L. Radtke & H. J. Stam (Eds.), *Power/Gender: Social relations in theory and practice* (pp. 1–14). London: Sage.

Rogers, C. (1986). Some social issues which concern me. In R. May, C. Rogers, & A. Maslow (Eds.), *Politics and innocence: A humanistic debate* (pp. 23–32). Dallas: Saybrook. (Original work published 1972)

Shirley, S. (1982). Translator's forward. In B. Spinoza (Ed.), *The ethics and selected letters* (pp. 21–29). Indianapolis: Hackett.

Shotter, J. (1993). *Cultural politics of everyday life.* Buckingham, England: Open University Press.

Spinoza, B. (1949). *Ethics and on the improvement of the understanding.* (J. Gutmann, Ed.; W. H. White, A. H. Stirling, R. H. M. Elwes, & J. Ratner, Trans.). New York: Hafner.

Wittgenstein, L. (1980). *Culture and value.* Oxford, England: Basil Blackwell.

CHAPTER 10

Resurrecting People in Academic Psychology: A Celebration of the Ordinary

John Shotter
University of New Hampshire
Durham, New Hampshire

...the problems that education represses without solving. I say to those repressed doubts; you are quite correct, go on asking, demand clarification!
—Wittgenstein (1974, p. 382)

Both ontogenetically and in the history of culture, our first expressions are in public space, and are vehicles of a quite unreflective awareness. Later we both develop more refined media, in concepts and images, and become more capable of carrying out some part of our expressive activity monologically; that is, we become capable of formulating some things just for ourselves, and hence of thinking privately.
—Taylor (1985, pp. 91–92)

Actually I should like to say that...the words you utter or what you think as you utter them are not what matters, so much as the difference they make at various points in your life. Practice gives words their significance.
—Wittgenstein (1980a, p. 85)

Only in the stream of thought and life do words have meaning.
—Wittgenstein (1981, no. 173)

*...the term 'language–**game**' is meant to bring into prominence the fact that the speaking of language is part of an activity, of a form of life.*
—Wittgenstein (1953, no. 23)

We are concentrating...on the occasions on which [words] are said—on the enormously complicated situation in which [an expression] has a place, in which the expression itself has an almost negligible place.
—Wittgenstein (1966, p. 2)

An utterance is never just a reflection or an expression of something already existing outside it that is given and final. It always creates something that never existed before, something absolutely new and unrepeatable, and, moreover, it always has some relation to value (the true, the good, the beautiful, and so forth). But something created is always created out of something given (language, an observed phenomenon of reality, an experienced feeling, the speaking subject himself, something finalized in his world view, and so forth). What is given is completely transformed in what is created.
—Bakhtin (1986, pp. 119–120)

As the chapters in this volume attest, a broad movement is currently afoot (and has been so for some time now), not only in academic psychology, but in social theory at large. It has something to do with attempting, within the academy, to overcome the lifelessness of the humane and social disciplines; it has to do with resurrecting what academic psychology has, until now, treated as as-if-dead: people! The movement can be formulated in many different ways. Some might suggest that it constitutes an interpretative, linguistic, hermeneutical, or discursive turn. Others are calling it a turn to social constructionism or rhetoric. Still others call it a move to relational or dialogical formulations; or to the recognition of the importance of others, of Othernesses, and of difference and differences; or an appreciation of non-representational or expressivist notions of meaning. It constitutes a move from centering our studies in thought to a focus on people's activities, a shift from focusing on individuals to a focus on the social; a turn away from rooting claims to knowledge in abstract theory toward basing them in our social practices. It is a turning away from universal principles toward a study of the concrete details of our social exchanges, along with a growing interest in embodiment, a return to values and ethics, and to a concern with what matters to people. It entails an interest in what we might call *agent's knowledge* (Taylor, 1985, p. 80) manifested in action rather than in the knowledge available only to uninvolved, external observers, as in the classical view. These, and many other formulations, are coming to be part of the contemporary scene. We are even beginning to see a role for the disorderly, the chaotic, and the playful and to find events on the boundaries between our activities as perhaps more interesting than those occurring at their centers. The puzzle now is how to account for our lives together as a living movement of some kind.

Given all these possibilities, is there any way in which we might grasp the nature of this shift, overall? Should we see it as a shift in frameworks or perspectives, as a shift, say, from individualistic, modernist, and romantic forms of thought to more social, postmodernist forms, as a shift from the monological to the dialogical (Gergen, 1991; Kvale, 1992). Or, is it perhaps best viewed as a shift of interests, as the end, say, of the Enlightenment passion for fashioning self-contained systems and a shift to more "mobile" forms of thought (Shotter, 1993a, 1993b)—or should we view it in quite another way altogether? For reasons that I hope will become apparent as this chapter progresses, I want to suggest here that, instead of treating it as a self-contained phenomenon, it will be more useful and more interesting to see what is happening in a way that situates it in the larger context of our everyday lives together. That is, just as Rorty (1979, p. 264, following Michael Oakeshott) called *philosophy* a "voice in the conversation of [hu]mankind," so we might also see *psychology*—along with the other social disciplines—as yet other such "voices"[1] in an overall conversation of humankind. Where such conversational activity constitutes, as Wittgenstein (1980) put it, "the *background* against which we see an action, and it determines our judgment,

---

[1] To use another Bakhtinian term (Bakhtin, 1986), psychology may be seen as yet further *speech genres* in the cultural conversation of humankind.

our concepts, and our reactions" (II, no. 629, emphasis added).

If we do this, we can see the current movement in psychology, and in social theory at large, as constituting a special moment in the speaking of all these voices in the still ongoing, endless, dialogical or conversational flow of all our intermingled lives together. Following Tolman's (chap. 1) and Mos' (chap. 4) accounts in this volume, we can see emerging among these voices a *telos*, a tacit purpose of a special kind. The conversation seems to be concerned with us (slowly and gradually) coming to more adequate formulations—or perhaps better—more just and respectful, more fully voiced, understandings of ourselves than those in the disciplinary accounts of ourselves (and the discourses and practices they motivate) we have inherited from earlier times. Instead of still seeking theoretical *representations* of things intrinsically hidden from us, accepting our embedding in the ordinary bustle of everyday life, we can now begin to see the special concepts we (as professional psychologists) produce as pointing or gesturing toward something in this bustle (Wittgenstein, 1980b, II, no. 625), as bringing something to notice for all to see. It is this celebration of the uniqueness and extraordinariness of the ordinary, that I think is quite new in all of this.

OVERCOMING EMBODIED DISCIPLINARY DISCOURSES AND PRACTICES

If we turn to our inherited recent past, those of us old enough to remember Hull's *Principles of Behavior* (1943) and the dreams for the production of an *Encyclopedia of Unified Science* (that is, those of us who were undergraduates in the 1960s or earlier) also remember the denigration of ordinary language and everyday knowledge that all such texts contained. It is instructive in both indicating the current change in our general sensitivities and the difficulty we now have in resonating to their general tone to consider some pieces of Hull's writing. In the general summary and conclusions section to his 1943 book he remarked:

> The main concern of this work has been to isolate and present the primary or basic principles or laws of behavior as they appear in the current state of behavioral knowledge; at present there have been isolated sixteen such principles...It is to be hoped that as the years go by, systematic treatises on the different aspects of the behavior sciences will

appear...[And] as a culmination of the whole there would finally appear a work consisting chiefly of mathematics and mathematical logic. (pp. 398–401)

When it was written, this was presented as a merely neutral, factual style of writing, and at the time when I first read it (in 1960 or so), I did not take any exception to it. Indeed, as a novitiate into a cultural elite, I gloried in it. Yet, notice its tone of Olympian certainty: It neither brooks nor invites any challenge; it is without a *perhaps* or a *maybe*; it talks down to us, as readers; it positions us among the little people; we are allowed only to be grateful to receive the rulings it provides. For whom is he writing? With whom does he align himself and against whom? Against what kind of background? He continued:

There will be encountered vituperative opposition from those who cannot or will not think in terms of mathematics, from those who prefer to have their scientific pictures out of focus, from those who are apprehensive of the ultimate exposure of certain personally cherished superstitions and magical practices, and from those who are associated with institutions whose vested interests may be fancied as endangered...[But] hope lies, as always, in the coming youth...The present work is addressed primarily to them. (Hull, 1943, p. 401)

In other words, we can now see that Hull's "taken-for-granted, background world" was not too different from the world Galileo outlined in his great polemical work of 1629, *The Assayer*, in which he said: "this great book, the universe...is written in the language of mathematics...without which it is humanly impossible to understand a single word of it." It is also a world of experts within which those who disagree with one's claims could be silenced by insult and ridicule, in which any claims not framed in mathematical terms could be dismissed as unintelligible, laughable, or as not being up to the right standards.

How are such worlds sustained? What is the source of their standards? To grasp what is involved here, we turn briefly to Foucault (1979) for, as he reminded us, a discipline not only " 'makes' individuals" (p.170), but it also "produces subjected and practiced bodies, 'docile' bodies" (p.138)—that is, bodies that function spontaneously in certain ways, have certain wants, urges, and desires, as well as expectations and feelings. In

particular, the modern academic disciplines—in which the central technique of disciplinary power is administered through examination and
review (see Foucault, 1979, pp.187–192)—make the quintessential modern, professional academic. To pass our exams, we must come to embody (spontaneously, unthinkingly, and automatically) the background
techniques, shared sensitivities and discriminations, the desires and aversions, shared exemplars, and so on, as well as "the will to truth" (Foucault,
1972), that are all a part of what I call a discipline's *evaluative stance* or
its *evaluative sensibility*. A crucial part of that sensibility (as we can see
in Hull's text) is an irritable and petulant rejection of what will not fit in
with a discipline's way of proceeding. As Foucault remarked, "within its
own limits, every discipline recognizes true and false propositions, but it
repulses a whole teratology of learning" (p. 223).

In other words, to pass one's exams and to be "licensed" to operate as
a professional in such a discipline as modern psychology, one must come
to embody within oneself a tendency, not just to ignore, but to actively
repel and repress alternatives to the current, ordinary everyday view of
things. Indeed, one is sanctioned if one fails to do so. Thus, we feel the
pressure to conform and the fear of being branded heretics. Yet, if it is
the case that disciplines have their origins in the disorderly, the playful,
the passionate, the feelingful, the unique, and the poetic—in short, in the
novel, unrepeatable, and living activities occurring between people—
then it is these unrepeatable background events, these living human expressions, that are excluded. They are in fact rendered invisible by "rules
of *exclusion*" (Foucault, 1972, p. 216) that are internal to discourse itself "rules concerned with principles of classification, ordering and distribution" (p. 220).[2]

---

[2] Foucault (1972) claimed there is no escape from such rules, even through the device
of producing a commentary on them:

> There is no question of there being one category, fixed for all time, reserved
> for fundamental or creative discourse, and another for those which reiterate,
> expound and comment...Play...in the form of commentary...is nothing more
> than the reappearance, word for word...of the text commented on...Commentary
> averts the chance element of discourse by giving it its due: it gives us the
> opportunity to say something other than the text itself, but on condition that it
> is the text itself which is uttered and, in some ways, finalized. (pp. 220–221)

Here, clearly, I disagree. There is, as I later suggest, another move we can make—
that toward more poetic forms of talk. It is this that can move us out from under the
domination of established discourses.

The denigration of the ordinary and the everyday, visible in Hull's writing, is now beginning to carry less and less conviction. We seem to be waking up not only to the rich diversity of our everyday lives together, but also to the indispensability of that bustle and diversity. There is at present, I think, a gradual emergence of a more adequate recognition of the part we can and do play in fashioning our relations to each other in our institutions and, as a result, a recognition of how, in constructing our own way(s) of responding to and acting in the world, we can and do fashion ourselves. Foucault's work, mentioned earlier, is just a part of this. Yet, it is also reflected in different ways in all the different chapters of this book and it is the way in which the authors do this that I want to explore in the following sections.

MORE ADEQUATE FORMULATIONS: SOCIAL LIFE AT LARGE

Sensing a problem—the absence of flesh-and-blood persons in modern psychology—it is always tempting to try to solve it directly, to ask: "What is involved in creating an academic psychology adequate to the unique, living, embodied, individual human being, a person, someone who fully counts as a citizen in a modern society, a society with a vibrant civil society to it that is able to recognize him or her as such?" Here, I want to take a more indirect, diremptive approach, to further elaborate the larger social and historical processes explored in Tolman's and Mos' chapters in this volume. It is within such a larger process that we must see people as embedded and as having their being. Our primary access to reality is as agents, inextricably engaged or involved in the flow of activity in which we are embedded—not as detached, uninvolved thinkers. This cannot be emphasized enough. It is also within such a larger social process that the cultural changes influencing our being can be seen as emerging, even if only painfully and slowly. For, if we could come to an overall, panoramic grasp this process (which is not, of course, easy)—that is, if we could come to know our way around this process, not only region by region, but also moment by moment, sphere of activity by sphere of activity, dimension (of ordering) by dimension, as if constituting an immense and richly textured "landscape"[3]—then we would be able to get a

---

[3] I am showing my pupils details of an immense landscape which they cannot possibly know their way around" (Wittgenstein, 1980a, p. 56).

sense of the relation of each part to the whole. It is in this way, I hope, that we can come to assess the significance of the other chapters in this book by suggesting an appropriate place for them—-their role—within this process of emergence.

Tolman and Mos

I first turn to Tolman's chapter (chap. 1) on the ontology of self. There, like Foucault (1972, see footnote 2), he points out how easy it is for us to deceive ourselves into believing we have escaped from Cartesianism, when in fact we have done nothing of the kind. He goes on to suggest that "the key to breaking the Cartesian ontological grip lies...not (at least immediately) in challenging its substance or its causality, but in its location" (pp. 11–12). Following Hegel, he recommends that we look for the ontology of the self, not within the individual, but in "interindividual[4] space." How might we best characterize this space?

He explores some features of it in the work of Wittgenstein, Volosinov, Harré and Gillett, and Holzkamp, and some of the crucial points he makes are highlighted here.

Straightforwardly, he confronts us with one of the most puzzling issues in all of psychology. Referring to Wittgenstein's (1980, II, no. 643) discussion of our talk of the inner in people's inner lives, and to his claim that we would not know "that pain, etc., etc., was something Inner if [we] weren't told so," Tolman makes us realize that the inner is not something literally inside the individual (p. 13). Rather, it is in the person's behavior out in the world; it is in the possibility of them being able to employ certain forms of talk. People express the "shape" of their unique

---

Language sets everyone the same traps, it is an immense network of easily accessible wrong turnings. And so we watch one man after another walking down the same paths and we know in advance where he will branch off, where walk straight on without noticing the side turnings, etc. etc. What I have to do then is erect signposts at all the junctions where there are wrong turnings so as to help people past the danger points. (1980a, p. 18).

---

[4] For the moment, I want to let this term stand, but later I am critical of it. For, like other aspects of one's psychological make-up, in the emergent view that I want to advocate, one only gradually emerges as a unique and distinct individual. Furthermore, the space between people is not just interindividual; it is a societal-moral and relational-ethical space, as we see later.

inner lives in how they unfold their different language-entwined ways of acting as they body them forth out into the world, in the postures of their body, their voice tones, the words they choose, the emphases they give them, their gestures, and so on. In other words, as Tolman puts it, Wittgenstein shifted us from "a representational self in the mind to a self constituted by language in an objective, social space" (p. 13). Volosinov (1929/1973), Tolman shows, adds more detail to such a view. For what is crucial in such a linguistically constituted view of the self (as Tolman notes), is that the word becomes "the *semiotic material of inner life—of consciousness* (inner speech)...The word is available as the sign for, so to speak, inner employment: it can function as a sign in a state short of outward expression" (1929/1973, p. 14). This means though, that "what is needed is a profound and acute analysis of the word as a social sign before its function as the medium of consciousness can be understood" (1929/1973, p. 15). One thing that is crucial in such an approach to the actual bodily voicing forth of words and the uses of such utterances in social life is a more social and practical notion of *understanding*: "Understanding is," said Volosinov (1929/1973), "a response to a sign with signs" (p. 11). He went on to remark that:

> this chain of ideological creativity and understanding, moving from sign to sign and then to an new sign, is perfectly consistent and continuous: from one link of a semiotic nature (hence, also of a material nature) we proceed uninterruptedly to another link of exactly the same nature. And nowhere is there a break in the chain, nowhere does the chain plunge into inner being, nonmaterial in nature and unembodied in signs. (p. 11)

The bustling, conversational activity of humankind is ceaseless and unending, yet within it, as Wittgenstein (1953) put it, "nothing is concealed...nothing is hidden" (no. 435). Everything of interest to us that involves the nature of our inner lives is out there in world in the chain of responsive activity between us—somewhere to behold—in the space in which we have our being.

In other words, the space between us is a space in which we can think of ourselves as positioned, a space in which some ways of being positioned are better than others, in which we can move, can get lost, can learn better to know our way about, and so on. It is a space that we find, as embodied agents, affords us, or makes available to us, only certain opportunities for action and perception, while denying us others (Gibson, 1979). It is a space constituted in different ways in different media of communication, a space that both limits our opportunities to be this, that, or some other kind of person, but that at the same time, offers us (on occasion) opportunities to change its whole nature. We might imagine it as a great flow of ecologically interdependent activity, vaguely differentiated into a set of diverse but relatively well-ordered, self-reproducing, and self-stabilizing centers of accountable, institutionalized activity, with these diverse spheres of institutional activity being separated from each other by boundary zones of much more disorderly, unaccountable, chaotic and playful activity—borders that, as Foucault remarked, must be policed if monsters are to be repulsed, but within which two or more different activities can, by "rubbing up" against each other, so to speak, create new forms of order.

This space is thus a space of a very special kind. It is created and sustained in joint action between all those participating in it (Shotter, 1984, 1993a, 1993b) and as such, has a very special nature. It is almost as if it is in itself, a developing, living being—at the very least, it has living properties that cannot be located in any of the individuals inhabiting it. Tolman's critique of Harré and Gillett's (1992) account of discursive psychology is, I think, related to this point. He remarks that they simply designate this space as having to do with "arrays of people," as if it is a merely theoretical point to list its properties. In other words, although they assumed that it was a moral and political space and provided many allusions to the broader discursive context called society, they failed to elaborate in any working detail the "customary and widely endorsed practices" it contained. "Yet," says Tolman, "it is precisely in the subject–agent's relationship to this context that the problems of depersonalization are both found and explained" (p. 18). Whereas, it is just this issue that Holzkamp (1983; Tolman, 1994), as Tolman pointed out, attempted to articulate in his notion of an individual's *action potence*— becoming a fully developed person is not a matter of self-esteem and self-actualization (American fashion), but a matter of the possibilities and opportunities offered one in relation to one's position at the moment in the societal space in which we all have our being—a political economy of developmental opportunities is at work. What other features of this space might be of importance?

Mos begins his rich and extensive chapter (chap. 4) with an exploration of Fingarette's (1969) account of self-deception and the central place within it regarding what is involved in us actively becoming (or not) "explicitly conscious of something." Fingarette suggested that this is not something "passive" that merely happens to us, but is something "active" that we ourselves do; it is a skill:

> I propose...that we do not characterize consciousness as a kind of mental mirror, but as the exercise of the (learned) skill of 'spelling out' some feature of the world as we are engaged in it...Colloquially, to spell out something is to make it explicit, to say it in a clearly and fully elaborated way, to make it perfectly apparent. (pp. 38–39)

It may refer, but need not, he said, "to the actual and elaborate saying out loud, or writing down, of that which one is becoming conscious of" (p. 39), as, for instance, we do when we instruct someone in the details of a task and say to them, "Let me spell it out to you." It is this failure to spell out, in a fully elaborated way, what is involved in society's "customary and widely endorsed practices," that Tolman complains of in Harré and Gillett's (1992) account of our social lives together.

Fingarette (1969), as I have already indicated, was primarily concerned with making sense of individuals being self-deceived, whereas, as Mos puts it: "The failure to spell out one's engagements is...the most visible feature of self-deception" (p. 76). Given what we have already seen of both Foucault's (1972) and of Tolman's comments on the ease with which we can deceive ourselves into thinking we have given something up only to find ourselves reproducing it yet again in our actions, the topic is clearly of some initial importance for us.[5] Yet, more is at issue here than us as individuals wanting to give a more faithful account of what it is we think we are doing in our actions. If we are to become undeceived, we must change ourselves in some way: We must become sensitive to certain connections and relations between things that we had missed before.[6] We must come to experience the relations between ourselves, our

---

[5] Nothing is so difficult as not deceiving oneself" (Wittgenstein, 1980a, p. 34).

[6] "Only connect," Margaret tells the morally blind Henry Wilcox in E. M. Forster's *Howards End.*

actions, and our circumstances in a new way. As Fingarette (1969) put it, "rather than taking explicit consciousness for granted, we must come to take its absence for granted; we must see explicit consciousness as the further exercise of a specific skill for a special reason" (p. 42). We must come to accept that we are always embedded in our background surroundings and that we can never attempt to spell out everything we do. Yet, it is worth noting that when we do so, we never do it in an unmoving, dead-pan way. Indeed, if we are teaching someone something, we often, as Wittgenstein (1966) pointed out, elaborate on what we are saying in this way and use "exaggerated gestures and facial expressions" (p. 2). Such talk is always interwoven or orchestrated with some other larger ongoing activity of which it is merely a part, and it works to highlight or emphasize an aspect of this activity. Thus, the kind of talk involved is always a retrospective looking back or a reflective looking on that works to draw attention to aspects of currently happening or already completed events. Yet, there is more to the special nature of spelling out talk than this.

Fingarette (1969) saw it as involving a quite distinct skill of using language in a special way—indeed, his whole approach exemplifies it:

> I am trying to isolate, identify, and discuss certain features of the self-deception situation with which there is no everyday language associated. In order to do this, it will be necessary to *bend familiar usage* and develop a terminology with which we can forthrightly express certain significant, usually unexpressed features of self-deception. My aim is to develop a way of talking about self-deception which will in turn elucidate the way we usually talk about it as well as the circumstances which lead us to talk of it in that way...At present we possess a language which permits us only hints and imputations, by means of paradox...In order to develop such a language, I have avoided making out of whole cloth a new technical language (which, to a good extent, is what Freud did). I have used, instead, a family of everyday terms, metaphors and images. (p. 5, emphasis added)

Here, Fingarette's methods parallel those of Wittgenstein (1953), when he said, "we shall constantly be giving prominence to distinctions which our ordinary forms of language easily make us overlook" (no. 132). In other words, and this is of the utmost importance, both of them emphasize the importance of certain ways of talking, the character of the medium of expression in us becoming explicitly or self-conscious of ourselves and our own activities.

Given this concern with idioms (this degree of sensitivity to our forms of talk), it is worth, at this point, briefly examining Fingarette's choice of the term *spelling out* in designating that moment or phase in the process of us bringing someone to consciousness of something. For, as Mos points out, it is very easy to see spelling out simply as "making public what is inner," as if it was merely a matter of making explicit what was already actually there, in existence, as if it was an activity one could do on one's own, monologically (p. 93). Just as at other times we might also talk of ourselves simply as internalizing or interiorizing something, as if the inner space in which it is placed is already there also. What seems to be involved, again as Mos points out, is our very constitution of ourselves as individual beings with the capacities to talk both of ourselves and others as well as of our world in the way that we do—as if beings with inner lives and inner worlds in an inner mental space. Yet, we can now see that the ability to talk of ourselves and others like this, resides, not in any capacities already existing in us as individuals, but in our dialogical creation of and access to appropriate public media of expression. Rather than in our heads, (what we are pleased to call) our minds reside in our language entwined achievements.[7] It has to do with the possibility of

---

[7] We can now, perhaps, make sense of Snell's (1953/1982) claim, that it is in their linguistic inventions—for instance, the importance of the definite article in permitting the formation of "abstractions," as we call them (p. 228)—that the early Greeks discovered the human mind.

> The discovery of the intellect cannot be compared with the discovery of, let us say, a new continent. America had existed long before Columbus discovered the New World, but the European way of thinking did not come into being until it was discovered; it exists by grace of man's (sic) cognizance of himself...The intellect was not "invented," as a man would invent a tool, or a method to improve the operation of his physical functions, or a method to master a certain type of problem....In a certain sense it actually did exist before it was discovered, only not in the same form, not *qua* intellect. (pp. v–vi)

The early Greeks discovered that they could, with the aid of certain forms of words, *direct, order,* or *orchestrate* the intertwining of their basic, biological capacities into much more complex forms, which in turn, could be intertwined with those of others and the Othernesses in their surroundings. Yet, it was only their access to a public space in which such forms of talk circulated, that made their discovery of mind possible.

people expressing, manifesting, or showing something of themselves, uniquely, as they body forth their activities into the world.

In discussing this issue, Mos turns to Charles Taylor's writings. As he points out, central to Taylor's whole approach is what he called an "expressivist theory of language" (Taylor, 1985, see pp. 215–292). What does Taylor mean by *expression* here? Well, "expression makes something manifest by embodying it" (p. 219), where by "manifest" he means that it becomes directly and spontaneously available for us all to see in public space—like people's expressions of joy or anger, we do not have to spend time cognitively figuring them out.[8] Of course, in our everyday dealings with each other, besides all the other things we do with words, there is an aspect of our bodying forth of our utterances into the world— to do with their style, their tone, pacing, pausing, and emphasis—that uniquely expresses *us*, that shows or expresses how we stand in relation to the others and the Othernesses in the space around us. As I suggested earlier in considering Hull's (1943) style of writing—that he made the evaluative stance or sensibility of the discipline of psychology, as he then saw it evident in the expressive tone of his writing—so do we, now, in our styles of writing. Indeed, an aspect of this kind of expressive meaning, is that it is only manifest in one or another kind of medium, style, idiom, or genre. Clearly, in some spheres of psychology now, as in everyday life, Hull's authoritarian, exclusive, elitist style has now been replaced by a more reticent or tentative, inclusive or invitational style of writing—hence, my strong reaction to Hull's style of writing now compared with my earlier unthinking acceptance of it.

As an embodied being in a public space of expression, surrounded everywhere, as if at sea, by activity to which we cannot be unresponsive, we often feel ourselves battered and buffeted on all sides. However, there is another property of our being in such a space that I want to bring out, for we are not wholly powerless within it. As Mos also points out, "Taylor was one of those who...began with what he termed the *agent's knowledge*" (p. 81). Here, concerned to bring out yet more of what it is like to

---

[8] Soulful expression in music—this cannot be recognized by rules....If a theme, a phrase, suddenly means something to you, you don't have to be able to explain it. Just *this* gesture has been made accessible to you" (Wittgenstein, 1981, nos. 156–157).

live in such a sea, I explore the nature of our practices in such a space of movement. As we have already seen, it is in our practices that we become docile bodies (Foucault, 1979) that spontaneously function in certain ways, that have certain sensitivities and strivings. I want to know the distinctions I notice and am moved by, what are the urges and temptations, lacks or disquietudes, I feel, the uncertainties I have, and so on. One such central distinction available to us in such a space is, as Taylor (1985) put it, "a basic, not further reducible distinction between action and what just happens is indispensable and ineradicable from our self-understanding as agents" (p. 79). Indeed, if we did not have such a sense of our own functioning in such a space—an ability to distinguish what we do from what merely happens around us, irrespective of our agency—we could not conduct ourselves as experimental scientists. It is only because we can sense, when acting in accord with theories of what the world might be like, whether the results of our actions accord with or depart from the expectations engendered by those theories, that we can ever put them to empirical test (see Shotter, 1975, p. 86).

Yet, our agent's knowledge is of a much more extensive and differentiated kind than this. On the one hand, no matter how vague it is, we always have a differentiated sense of the shape, so to speak, of the circumstances in which we are involved—whether they present us with a problem, a question, or an opportunity of this, that, or some other kind, and then, whether what we say or do is an adequate or inadequate response to what our circumstances offer or demand. On the other hand, we also have a sense of what it is that we are trying (and often failing) to do in relation to them. In both cases, it is as if there is a standard in the circumstances of our acting against, by which we can always measure the adequacy of our own and other people's activities to some extent. Indeed, there is a whole moral ecology of rights and duties to do with one's involvements and engagements in the activities in which one is embedded, associated with the first-, second-, and third-person, singular and plural positions (Shotter, 1984). Thus, yet again, we find the character of our involvement in the space between us has a mobile, shifting nature, for the shape of the opportunities it offers us to be and to act, shifts as we shift from being first-person performers, to being second-person recipients, to being third-person uninvolved observers, and so on.

Viewing ourselves in this way (as only having our being as persons in terms of how we actively and directly relate ourselves to the surrounding activities in the dynamic spaces in which we are embedded and have our being) puts most of what is of interest in academic psychology in a very different light. Indeed, what has been especially screened out of our awarenesses by the emphasis, in science, on us being uninvolved, third-person, external observers is the fact that the conduct of our social lives together is, of course, based on the right we assign to first-person performers to express themselves to us and tell us of their experiences and to have what they say taken seriously and as meaning what they intend it to mean—as long as they observe the duty of being sincere in their intentions (Antaki, 1994; Goffman, 1959; Shotter, 1984). As I intimated, not only would the maintenance of our social institutions be impossible, but all our valid forms of inquiry are based on such a right; this is where all our new discoveries about ourselves begin: with people's first-person, out-of-the-blue expressions, with things we say or do when involved in activities with others.

In 1985, Taylor suggested that these "are things that I reveal in the way expression reveals. I am making them evident in public space, and in so doing, I am shaping the kind of public space there is *entre nous*" (p. 266)—as if I pre-exist the space that I am now acting in. Later, more dialogically aware, he commented: "The self neither preexists all conversation, as in the old monological view; nor does it arise from an introjection of the interlocutor; but arises within the conversation, because this kind of dialogical action by its very nature marks a place for the new interlocutor who is being inducted into it" (Taylor, 1991, p. 312). In other words, as we move to the realms of dialogical and joint action, we find that the distinction between action and what just happens irrespective of our agency blurs and events occurring in the indeterminate boundary zone between these two possibilities are what is of interest to us—here is where we need to spell out the never-ending possibilities open to us in becoming involved in our surrounding circumstances. This is what the chapters in this volume in their own different ways all begin to do for us.

Smythe and Paranjpe

Smythe (chap. 2) and Paranjpe (chap. 3) are concerned with the concept of the person that emerges when we simply talk of what we know of persons and their attributes reflectively. For, as Smythe puts it, "the folk psychological idiom embodies a rich, if tacit, set of conceptions of person that do not need to be filtered through a particular theory of folk psychology to be understood. All that is required is a close examination of the language of the folk psychological idiom itself" (pp. 40–41)—we can, he suggests, study the folk psychological grammar of the person. Yet strangely, as Smythe points out in his chapter in this volume, even when cognitivists come to a discussion of what they have thematized as folk psychology, one searches in their work in vain for any actual mention of flesh-and-blood persons. Instead, one finds only discussions of inner mental states, propositional attitudes, supposed computational relations that people bear to their own inner mental representations—all entities with only a supposed existence, that are intrinsically hidden from our direct perception and require an extensive technical apparatus for their discussion—only experts trained in Galileo's technical terms need apply. He goes on, somewhat ironically, to remark that "an oversight of this magnitude [the complete absence of persons, as such] can only be grounded on some form of deep-seated theoretical prejudice" (p. 25).

What exactly is the deep-seated prejudice he means? Smythe goes on to discuss what he calls human science perspectives on folk psychology and the person—in particular, Bruner's (1990) *Acts of Meaning* and Harré and Gillett's (1994) *Discursive Mind*—and finds them wanting also. Although they espouse notions of agency with enthusiasm, unlike cognitivists who have qualms that agency will undermine their mechanistic explanations, the version espoused by both Bruner and Harré and Gillett, Smythe claims, threatens to undermine our sense of personhood in another way: It fragments our sense of us as having a personal unity. Quite correctly, Smythe faults both Bruner's and Harré and Gillett's attempts to situate the thought and action of individuals in the collective life of a culture, for providing a too limited view of people's agency. It is a view of agency that allows a choice only of the cultural or discursive context in which to participate, so that once the choice is made "what happens seems more under the control of the [cultural, or] discursive context than of the person" (p. 38). Like Tolman, he suggests that both Bruner and Harré and Gillett fail to give any elaborate account of how people can, besides just choosing, also negotiate, shape, or even create such contexts for themselves. In other words, the true character of our freedom as individuals is still not adequately described. In the end, it is the fact that our primary access to reality is as engaged agents, inextricably engaged or involved in the flow of activity in which we are embedded that is missed—both Bruner and Harré and Gillett stand back from any actual involvement in people's activities and talk of them retrospectively, looking back on them as already completed performances.

As Smythe sees it, it is "the distorting lens of theory" that gives us these problems and "radically different construals of persons emerge, depending on the claims that a given theory makes about the nature and explanatory status of folk psychology" (p. 40). The answer, he suggests, is to turn to an analysis of the concept of the person embedded in our everyday talk. Paranjpe's concerns are similar and he also turns to the conceptual analysis of our everyday notions of personhood as an answer. He begins with an outline of how, with the rise of science and its value-neutral stance, the study of the person became in Allport's work, the study of personality—defined as "the dynamic organization within the individual...that determines the unique adjustments to his (sic) environment" (Allport, 1937, p. 48). Again, something intrinsically hidden from us that can only be grasped intellectually through a theoretical concept constructed by an expert comes to displace an everyday concept available to everyone. Paranjpe is worried that:

> Although the ethicolegal concept of personhood is not considered very important in psychology today, it is crucial in civil life ,at least in democratic societies in which most psychologists function...Indeed, a civic society without individual rights and responsibilities is unthinkable. (pp. 53–54)

Thus, he too, like Smythe, wants in some way to overcome the value-neutral tendencies in current theory and to an extent, restore our value-laden concepts of personhood to a legitimate place in psychology.

Yet, there is a problem. It seems to me, unfavorably disposed to theory as I am, that it is not so much theory itself that is the problem as what we might call the *theoretical stance*, or perhaps, simply, the uninvolved, third-person outsider's stance. In looking back on people's completed activities, we separate the activity both from the individual people whose activity it was, and from its surrounding circumstances, and in so doing, we separate it from what its point was for them. We become concerned with what can logically be said about it, that is, with the kind of form, patterning, or order that can be discovered in it. Clearly, as both Smythe and Paranjpe exhibit, quite a lot can be said about the seemingly pre-existing order(s) our everyday activities contain. We cannot just act in our social lives as we please; we must fit in any activity in which we are involved with the uninvolved others around us. Its form, when completed, must be of a recognizably legitimate kind to them—the uninvolved, third-person outsider's stance is inevitably a moralistic stance. However, to the insider—to the engaged agent—things look different: Although they cannot be ignored, the judgments of others on one's completed action are merely one influence among a whole indeterminate range of other influences that one must take into account as one bodies forth one's actions into the world. Smythe and Paranjpe are quite right to insist on the reality and the normative force of these conceptual matters. However, the way in which, moment-by-moment, as engaged agents, we orchestrate the relations between our own capacities and aspects of our surroundings (including the activities of other people) is inaccessible to the uninvolved, third-person outsider. Conceptual analysis, in itself, still doesn't cut the mustard! The worries Paranjpe shows Allport as voicing—if we are not careful we shall become moralistic, telling people what they should or ought to do—emerge again. Conceptual analysis in itself does not exhibit the way in which—in our actions as involved agents—we always create something novel and uniquely suited in an evaluative way to our current circumstances. Concepts have to do with accountability, with retrospective judgments by others as to the suitability of our activities in relation to theirs. Is there any other way in which we can turn—one less concerned with fixed concepts?

The way in which we orchestrate our activities is not inaccessible to the involved, second-person insider. Indeed, it is only from being in a joint involvement with others in a skillful activity that we can teach it to them. This is where what Fingarette called "spelling out" and the activity of conceptual analysis differ most. In conceptual analysis, one is merely codifying the knowledge implicit in an already acquired practical skill, not teaching the skill *de novo*. Thus, Smythe's and Paranjpe's work depends on us, as readers, already being in a position to recognize the adequacy of their formulations because these are the skills we already exhibit in our everyday practical dealings with other people. Yet, one cannot be taught these practical skills by being told these codifications. Thus, spelling out something to oneself or an other in the initial learning of a skill is not a matter (as in conceptual analysis) of explicitly formulating the detailed structure of a concept, but a matter of pointing out crucial features of the activity in which one is involved that would otherwise have passed one by unnoticed in the background. This is where the work of Conway, Kuiken, and Rogers is relevant: Instead of an uninvolved, monological–retrospective stance, they take more of what one might call an involved, dialogical–prospective stance. They speak (and write) from within a similar kind of involvement with the specific pictures they discuss.

Conway, Kuiken, and Rogers

"Art," says Conway, "can offer us insights about humans, about the inner life of both artists and viewers…art is the expression of emotion" (p. 120). His concern is with exploring the way(s) in which we can be emotionally moved by photographs, particularly by those of people, and how the result of being so moved is quite different from being told something theoretically. Conway (chap. 6) points out that the pictures he cites demand our attention—we cannot ignore them—and he uses such terms as *evocative* and *resonance* to describe the character of our response. It is a matter of feeling; we are touched by them. They do not impart any new knowledge to us as such, but they morally re-position us, so to speak, so that we come to see our own situation in a new way. They break the orderly flow of our mundane thoughts and interests and, by contrast to them, confront us with an occasion, perhaps, for a re-evaluation of our own lives. Indeed, although Conway is soberly circumspect in his evaluations of some of the work he exhibits, he nonetheless points toward its capacity to arouse in us intimations of the strange, the surreal, the uncanny—that which lies there as a real part of the background to our lives and can always disturb us. This is the power of these pictures: In our involvements with them as we look over them, we can constitute, in a dialogue with them, essentially, poetic images. Although such images can only come to us in our relations to an other, they can change us in our very being. They can gesture toward, or provide the seeds for, new possibilities for reconnecting with, or re-relating ourselves to, our surroundings. In doing so, in striking us in ways which, although initially vague, are immediately accessible to us, they function independently of any pre-existing systems of knowledge. Indeed, it is with such images that any new system of knowledge must begin.

Thus, a work of art, although it is often given to us by another, can give rise to images in us that can, so to speak, become our own—we can be in-formed in our own being by them. Yet, such images are not in themselves in the pictures, in the works of art; they emerge, over time, in our dialogical involvements with such works. Yet, sometimes, our access to the world of feeling that a work of art provides can be so immediate and direct, so deep and rich in complex detail to us, that there is a sense of us being there in it. Kuiken's concern in his chapter (chap. 5), is with how this is possible. Indeed, in his own writing, I think, he also gives us a sense of being there in the middle of the processes he describes. I found his to be the most moving of all the chapters in this book, and I cannot possibly do justice to its richness here. Of particular interest to me though, given my interest in involved agency, is his discussion of what he calls *experiential boundary-crossing*—the transition from experiencing the everyday world surrounding a work of art to experiencing the possible world constituted within the work. There is something in the nature of works of art such that they "provide opportunities for participating in activities that make a possible world seem actual" (p. 108).

Kuiken's account of what is involved in this, and the stages through which one moves in achieving what he calls "depth" in one's experience, would seem to be of great importance to all of us concerned with grasping what is involved—not in coming to a new theory of the person, but in us developing a new sensibility, a new set of ways, in practice, of relating ourselves to those we study. Here, I can only outline in summary form, the different moments involved in the practice of entering into a new possible world:

1. First, Kuiken emphasizes that changing the locus of experience to the world within the work is much more than a mere shift of attention. It is a matter then—once one has shifted one's attention to the work—of actively exploring, of, in a sense, laboriously "tramping over" the new "inner terrain" to examine and experience all the relations of its features to oneself in detail.

2. Then, it is possible to move on to an examination of the tensions existing not only between oneself and events or objects within the work, but also those existing between such events and objects themselves, thus to "accentuate," as Kuiken puts it, the felt meanings.

3. Specifying these meanings in words adds a further dimension of depth. Indeed, it seems to provide something more to the experience—a horizon of yet further unspecified possibilities that one might, in subsequent involvements with the work, go on to spell out.

4. However, a crucial moment comes, Kuiken suggests, when, as a result of all these involvements, there is a meeting within oneself between these new felt meanings and one's past, a deep meeting in which one's past is actively transformed. If one is properly to acknowledge these transformed meanings within oneself, one requires courage, for they "uproot superficiality." One becomes a new person.

This account by Kuiken of the moments in us becoming new people is of the utmost importance. As we turn our attention in the future to the study of the many other kinds of involvement that we might have—in, say, a craft or a profession—it is the further articulation or spelling out of the different phases or moments involved in us achieving an in-depth grasp of the inner worlds of such crafts and professions that is our primary concern.

In a sense, Rogers, in his examination of the visual rhetoric at work in sustaining the personless view of persons in modern psychology, also implicitly draws on a scheme similar to Kuiken's. No comments of mine are necessary to help us enter into the felt meanings of the inner world represented in the hierarchical grids in the Wade and Tavris (1993) book's cover that Rogers discusses: The "bleakness" of the world it makes manifest is readily apparent. When Wade and Tavris thanked Saul Bass for helping to convey "the mystery, the challenge, the risk, and the rewards in thinking critically and creatively" (p. xxii), we can only wonder about the kind of mystery and challenge they meant. A resonance with the echoes of Hull's triumphal rhetoric sounds at this point, at least for me it does.

House and McDonald and Stam

Yet, for all this sound and fury, what is to be done? How easy is it to do? With respect to the remaining two chapters, I am inclined to say very little. I have been honored as an outsider to this group, by being invited to have my say on what I think is at issue, and I hope by now that it is quite plain: It has something to do with developing a more involved practice of inquiry, with progressively spelling out both our established, and our newly, artistically invented practices to each other. Both these chapters in their different ways also forcefully state the issue as they see it. So, I limit myself to just a few comments.

In a way not unrelated to my worried comments earlier on Smythe's and Paranjpe's concern with the concept of the person or personhood, Stam (chap. 9) also raises problems with concepts, but in an even more radical way. Drawing on Deleuze and Guattari's (1983, 1994) work, he outlines how—in a Kuiken kind of way—we are drawn into philosophy's inner world. We find in it a certain territory populated by various conceptual personae. The trouble with philosophical concepts, with these personae, is that if we go to the history of their formation, we find, Stam suggests, that talk of concepts emerged in early Greek times with the invention of the *agon* or assembly: Thus, implicit in the very notion of a concept, is that also of rivalry, opinion, and distrust. With science, we "enter yet further into" an artificially constructed world, a world not of full personae, but merely of "functions that are formalized as propositions in discursive systems"(p. 229)—that is, we enter Foucault's (1979) world of disciplinary discourses. In such a scientific world, there are only partial observers, whose role is only to perceive and experience things in the ways allowed in the propositions of the discipline. Thus, it is that Stam arrives at the conclusion that: "Persons are abstractions in the world of opinions. We do not need the notion of persons to know that we are agents—even if these are agents with only partial, fluid selves and identities" (p. 234). There is no such thing as the person in psychology. Any attempt to reconstitute psychology with any such concept at its core would suffer the same fate as all concepts at the hands of science: It would also be reduced to an abstract, functional entity. A practical psychology, or a psychology of practices may depend on certain ways of talking, but it might very well be able to proceed in its *inquiries* without the need for explicit concepts as such—the ways of talking, just as in everyday life, being adequate to our purposes.

House and McDonald still want to rescue from all these ruins, a place with some honor for science and, although it may surprise them to hear it, I am not in disagreement with them. Indeed, they quite correctly quote me as saying—in opposition to Harré's account of our social world as a world of people as locatable, powerful particulars—that I want to talk of it as "a world of much more diffusely distributed, non-locatable, morally structured activities that can only be investigated from a position of involvement within them" (Shotter, 1990, p. 213). For me, in such a social ecology as this, science can be considered as just one of the realms of human activity, along with everything else that we do. However, problems arise when it is claimed that one or another sphere of activity should be seen as providing foundations for all the rest. House and McDonald still want to preserve for science, a foundational role of this kind.

Regarding Sacks' work, I must say that, like House and McDonald, I too find it most inspiring (Bayer & Shotter, in press; Shotter, 1994), not because it confronts us with the need to take our biology or neurology into account in some undeniable basic and realist (i.e., foundational) way. Rather, it is because, as Sacks (1995) himself continually emphasized, "The study of disease, for the physician [and the rest of us], demands the study of identity, the inner worlds that patients, under the spur of illness, create" (p. xviii; see Katz & Shotter, in press, for just such a study). It has been the continual search for a way to study people's creation of their own unique inner worlds as the individuals they are—and the rejection of all the other activities that claim one's attention but stand in the way of this project—that leads me to say what House and McDonald misquote me as saying, "as far as Psychology is concerned, humans might just as well have porridge in their heads" (p. 197). It was an expression of *my* lack of interest in any kind of biological or neurological study of a foundational kind, not a moralistic expression of what should be everyone else's attitude.

CONCLUSION

There is a movement afoot that has to do with an increasing acceptance of talk about persons in relation, engaged or involved agency, and what this implies for new ways to understand ourselves. We seem to be searching for a form of understanding, not just rooted in a *"theory of practice"* like Bourdieu's (1977, emphasis added) but also in the local demands of a practice itself, whatever that practice may be. Instead of the classical kind of knowledge, seemingly got from the position of the disengaged spectator, we are beginning to wake up to the character of our own involvements in our own ways of knowing; and to what is involved in knowing from a position of involvement with the activities we are studying. As Heisenberg (1958) remarked some time ago:

> The objective reality of the elementary particles has been strangely dispersed, not into the fog of some new ill-defined or still unexplained conception of reality, but into the transparent clarity of a mathematics that no longer describes the behavior of the elementary particles *but only our knowledge of this behavior."* (p.15, emphasis added)

He continued by reminding us, as I have been trying to do in this chapter so far, that "science always presupposes the existence of man (sic) and we...must remember that we are not merely observers but also actors on the stage of life" (p. 15). The depth of what this means for us in our living it, however, is still not entirely clear to us. Only by us laboriously exploring the terrain of our inner lives together—in detail, step by step, on foot, rather than merely being content with an overview of it from on high—will we gradually, to use a Wittgensteinian term, come to "know our way around" it, but there is an enormous amount of spelling out to be done. The work in this book is just a very small beginning.

> *We shall not cease from exploration*
> *And the end of all our exploring*
> *Will be to arrive where we started*
> *And to know the place for the first time*
> —T.S. Eliot, *Little Gidding*

REFERENCES

Allport, G. (1937). *Personality: A psychological interpretation*. New York: Henry Holt.

Antaki, C. (1994). *Explaining and arguing*. London: Sage.

Bakhtin, M. M. (1986). *Speech genres and other late essays* (V. W. McGee, Trans.). Austin, TX: University of Texas Press.

Bayer, B., & Shotter, J. (Eds.) (in press). *Reconstructing the psychological subject: Bodies, practices and technologies*. London: Sage.

Bourdieu, P. (1977). *Outline of a theory of practice*. London: Cambridge University Press.

Bruner, J. (1990). *Acts of meaning*. Cambridge, MA: Harvard University Press.

Deleuze, G., & Guattari, F. (1983). *Anti-Oedipus: Capitalism and schizophrenia*. Minneapolis: University of Minnesota Press.

Deleuze, G., & Guattari, F. (1994). *What is Philosophy?* New York: Columbia University Press.

Eliot, T. S. (1944). *Four quartets*. London: Faber & Faber.

Fingarette, H. (1969). *Self-deception*. London: Routledge & Kegan Paul.

Foucault, M. (1972). Appendix: The discourse on language. In M. Foucault (Ed.), *Archeology of knowledge* (A. M. Sheridan, Trans.). New York: Pantheon Books.

Foucault, M. (1979). *Discipline and punish: The birth of the prison* (A.M. Sheridan, Trans.). Harmondsworth, England: Penguin Books.

Gergen, K. J. (1991). *The saturated self: Dilemmas of identity in contemporary life*. New York: Basic Books.

Gibson, J. J. (1979). *The ecological approach to visual perception*. London: Houghton-Mifflin.

Goffman, E. (1959). The presentation of self. In E. Goffman (Ed.), *The presentation of self in everyday life*. New York: Doubleday.

Harré, R., & Gillett, G. (1994). *Discursive psychology*. London: Sage.

Heisenberg, W. (1958). *The physicist's conception of nature*. London: Hutchinson.

Holzkamp, K. (1983). *Grundlagen der psychologie* [Foundations of Psychology]. Frankfurt/Main: Campus Verlag.

Hull, C. L. (1943). *Principles of behaviour*. New York: Appleton-Century-Crofts.

Katz, A., & Shotter, J. (1996). Hearing the patient's voice: Toward a 'social poetics' in diagnostic interviews. *Social Science and Medicine, 46*, 919–931.

Kvale, S. (1992). *Psychology and postmodernism*. London: Sage.

Rorty, R. (1979). *Philosophy and the mirror of nature*. Oxford, England: Blackwell.

Sacks, O. (1995). *An anthropologist on Mars: Seven paradoxical tales*. New York: Alfred Knopf.

Shotter, J. (1975). *Images of man in psychological research*. London: Methuen.

Shotter, J. (1984). *Social accountability and selfhood*. Oxford, England: Blackwell.

Shotter, J. (1990). Rom Harré: Realism and the turn to social constructionism. In R. Bhaskar (Ed.), *Harré and his Critics: Essays in Honour of Rom Harré with his Commentary on them*. Oxford: Blackwell.

Shotter, J. (1993). *Cultural politics of everyday life: Social constructionism, rhetoric, and knowing of the third kind*. Milton Keynes, England: Open University Press.

Shotter, J. (1993). *Conversational realities: Constructing life through language*. London: Sage.

Shotter, J. (1994). Making sense on the boundaries: On moving between philosophy and psychotherapy. In A. P. Griffiths (Ed.), *Philosophy, psychology, and psychiatry*. London: Cambridge University Press.

Shotter, J. (in press). Social construction as social poetics: Oliver Sacks and the case of Dr. P. In B. Bayer & J. Shotter (Eds.), *Reconstructing the psychological subject: Bodies, practices and technologies*. London: Sage.

Snell, B. (1982). *The Discovery of the mind in Greek philosophy and literature.* New York: Dover Publications. (Original work published 1953).

Taylor, C. (1991). The dialogical self. In D. R. Hiley, J. F. Bohman, & R. Shusterman (Eds.), *The interpretative turn* (pp.304–314). Ithaca: Cornell University Press.

Taylor, C. (1985). *Human agency and language: Philosophical papers I.* London: Cambridge University Press.

Tolman, C. *Psychology, society, and subjectivity.* London: Routledge.

Volosinov, V. N. (1973). *Marxism and the philosophy of language* (L. Matejka & I. R. Titunik, Trans.). Cambridge, MA: Harvard University Press. (Original work published 1929).

Wade, C., & Tavris, C. (1993). *Psychology* (3rd. ed.). New York: Random House.

Wittgenstein, L. (1953). *Philosophical investigations.* Oxford, England: Blackwell.

Wittgenstein, L. (1966). *Lectures and conversations on aesthetics, psychology and religious belief* (Ed. Cyril Barrett). Oxford, England: Blackwell.

Wittgenstein, L. (1974). *Philosophical grammar.* Oxford: Blackwell.

Wittgenstein, L. (1980a). *Culture and value* (P. Winch, Trans.). Oxford, England: Blackwell.

Wittgenstein, L. (1980b). *Remarks on the philosophy of psychology* (Vols. 1 & 2). Oxford, England: Blackwell.

Wittgenstein, L. (1981). *Zettel* (2nd ed.) (Eds. G. E. M. Anscombe & G. H. V. Wright). Oxford, England: Blackwell.

Author Index

Subject Index

For Product Safety Concerns and Information please contact our EU representative GPSR@taylorandfrancis.com Taylor & Francis Verlag GmbH, Kaufingerstraße 24, 80331 München, Germany

Batch number: 08159237

Printed by Printforce, the Netherlands